Network Architecture and Design
A Field Guide for IT Consultants

J. F. DiMarzio

SAMS

201 West 103rd St., Indianapolis, Indiana 46290 USA

Network Architecture and Design: A Field Guide for IT Consultants

Copyright © 2001 by Sams Publishing

International Standard Book Number: 0-672-32082-7

Library of Congress Catalog Card Number: 2001087591

Printed in the United States of America

First Printing: May 2001

03 02 01 00   4 3 2 1

Trademarks

Warning and Disclaimer

ASSOCIATE PUBLISHER
Jeff Koch

ACQUISITIONS EDITOR
William E. Brown

DEVELOPMENT EDITOR
Mark Renfrow

MANAGING EDITOR
Matt Purcell

PROJECT EDITOR
Andy Beaster

COPY EDITOR
Kim Cofer

INDEXER
Larry Sweazy

PROOFREADERS
Candice Hightower
Matt Wynalda

TECHNICAL EDITOR
Mark Hall

TEAM COORDINATOR
Vicki Harding

INTERIOR DESIGNER
Anne Jones

COVER DESIGNER
Aren Howell

PAGE LAYOUT
Lizbeth Patterson

Overview

Contents

About the Author

J. F. DiMarzio is a network engineer with 10 years of experience in system design and administration. He has worked as a consultant since 1991 for organizations such as the Walt Disney Company and the United States Department of Defense. Currently, J. F. DiMarzio is a Technical Support Consultant for Allmerica Financial in Worcester, Massachusetts.

Dedication

For Christian and Sophia, may you find a path in life that intrigues you and brings you joy.

Acknowledgments

I would first like to thank William E. Brown, Vicki Harding, Mark Renfrow, Katie Robinson, Cynthia Fields, Gene Redding, Kim Cofer, Andrew Beaster, Mandie Frank, and the team at Sams Publishing. I would especially like to thank Mark Hall for helping me through this book.

I would also like to thank, in no particular order, Joe Carchedi, Paul Desmond, Don Parkhurst, and Steven Brown.

On a personal note, I thank my parents Jerome and Agnes, my amazing wife Suzannah (for being more patient with me than I ever hoped), and finally my wonderful children Christian and Sophia.

I thank everyone who helped to make this book happen and my sincere apologies go to anybody I forgot or left out.

Tell Us What You Think!

As the reader of this book, *you* are our most important critic and commentator. We value your opinion and want to know what we're doing right, what we could do better, what areas you'd like to see us publish in, and any other words of wisdom you're willing to pass our way.

As an Associate Publisher for Sams, I welcome your comments. You can fax, e-mail, or write me directly to let me know what you did or didn't like about this book—as well as what we can do to make our books stronger.

Please note that I cannot help you with technical problems related to the topic of this book, and that due to the high volume of mail I receive, I might not be able to reply to every message.

When you write, please be sure to include this book's title and author as well as your name and phone or fax number. I will carefully review your comments and share them with the author and editors who worked on the book.

Fax:	317-581-4770
E-mail:	feedback@samspublishing.com
Mail:	Jeff Koch, Associate Publisher
	Sams
	201 West 103rd Street
	Indianapolis, IN 46290 USA

Introduction: The Fundamentals of Network Architecture (Designing Global Networks)

The Global Network

Today's network architect is faced with many issues and is expected to have a larger knowledge base than ever before. Technology has made enormous strides in the past five to ten years, adding to the amount of work an average designer must endure. Before 1990 the term "network architect" didn't exist in the mainstream vocabulary. Networks consisted of a basic client/server relationship, one protocol (possibly two), and a few shared applications. An office of 15 accountants sharing information on a server would have been a state-of-the-art network. Most companies at that time did not have external e-mail, if any at all. (Most of those who had e-mail paid per message for it.)

Now networks span geographic locations, multiple protocols, and more applications than ever before. A network designer needs to be an architect, security officer, tech support analyst, technical writer, and financial analyst. In many situations one person needs to implement security, recognize and head off potential problems, and document all of the work being done. He or she must also work within given budget guidelines while building the most efficient network possible. With the salaries commanded by technical professionals rising exponentially, most companies want more out of their networks and the staff who design them.

Gone are the days when a network encompassed a single building or campus. LANs as we have come to know them are a thing of the past. The local area network may be alive and well, but are our networks really as secluded as they used to be? Chances are, even if your company is physically located in one suite or area, you are connected to the Internet. In some cases you may have employees who require access to resources and applications from outside the confines of your physical infrastructure. These remote employees are a growing segment of the modern-day workforce. The network engineers of today must be prepared to accommodate an environment in which the LAN may not be as local as it once was. Thus, we are all doing our part to make the planet one global network.

All networks need to be designed as "global networks" to work in a global economy. Whether you have field offices down the street or home offices around the country, every network has the potential to be global. E-mail and the Internet have become such a key part of business that what affects one company's network can affect us all. The "Melissa" and "Love Bug" viruses demonstrated this fact. They showed that we are all connected to each other, for better or worse.

The key to understanding the rest of this book is to think in this context. We, as network designers, need to think about and confront network issues that no other generation of engineers has faced. A network needs to convey and extrapolate information from all corners of the Earth. All new innovations in technology are built around a "global access of knowledge." "Anything, anywhere, anytime," has become the mantra of today's businesses; and systems designers need to deliver it. More businesses are implementing networks capable of supporting users and information that may very well span the globe. Whether a company uses the Internet simply as a research tool or allows its employees to work via remote connections, the company has become a new type of worldwide organization. Keep in mind, however, that being a worldwide organization has good and bad points.

On one side you can have access to all of your corporate information from anywhere at any time. You can check your e-mail from a hotel room in Tokyo at 5:00 p.m. or prepare a stockholder presentation from home at midnight. Sales staff and field technicians can travel to any client location without the fear of losing access to company resources. VPN technology has enabled users to stay connected to vital resources anywhere. More and more people are bringing the office on the road with them, quite literally. It is hard to find a job function that cannot be performed via remote access.

Not all innovations affecting network architects revolve around remote access. Servers can hold more information than ever, transition media is faster, and the cost of connecting them is at an all-time low. In the early '90s, a server's storage capacity was measured in the hundreds of megabytes. Today it is not uncommon to see servers with a total storage limit in terabytes, some in petabytes. To prove the saying "The more you have, the more you spend (use)," businesses use up more storage media for day-to-day operations than would have been available in dedicated servers just a few years ago. Hard drive capacities keep rising, yet most businesses still struggle with disk space issues. Applications (being more server based than ever before) coupled with the data stored by users, turn typical servers into massive informational warehouses. However, now that there is more information on your servers, you need a way to carry it (reliably) from one computer to another.

Line speeds of 10Mbit are starting to be replaced to help accommodate the bandwidth requirements of today's business applications. Consultants are seeing more networks with 100Mbit line speeds. Is 100Mbit enough speed for the rising tide of bandwidth-intensive programs? Some companies are now exploring the possibilities of 1Gbit Ethernet (though the technology is cost prohibitive for smaller businesses). Finally, as the year 2001 begins, I have started work with a large service provider implementing a 10Gbit backbone. So what do we do with all of this power? Use it. The thriving "e-business" revolution has fueled an almost unending consumption of information. Network architects are giving business the keys to a wealth of data and power.

However, now that the informational floodgates are open it may be hard to control the flow of data. Data flows (for the most part) freely into and out of most companies. Those tools that make our lives worth living (larger servers, faster media, and global access) can be turned on us in an instant. Granting access to one set of people leaves the potential for others to follow. This is the dark side of every large network—keeping it secure.

How do you distinguish between friend and foe in the electronic age? To a remote computer we are all bits, and every bit looks like the next. Are VPNs exactly that, Virtually Private? Designing secure networks is one of the biggest challenges facing architects. Usernames and passwords only go so far, and for some companies, not far enough. A user checking his e-mail from home at 2 in the morning could be a cracker gaining access to your resources. The rising popularity of "anything, anytime" networking has been a godsend to crackers. They can now exploit the same lines and ports vital for business. VPNs aren't the only security risk on your infrastructure. Connections to the Internet, branch offices, and e-mail services all pose potential hazards. A network architect must be aware of all of these issues and plan accordingly. Not every hole can be patched, not every network can be "bulletproof," but we are getting close. How do architects design networks to meet the stringent demands of a changing environment? Can an engineer rely on the knowledge and skills that he or she used in the past?

The old method of network design was to divide a company into manageable pieces. The thought was that users in one part of a company (for example, Accounting or Legal) would have different network needs than the other parts of the company. The pieces would then fit together like a puzzle, creating a complete corporate infrastructure. (The software available at the time helped this mentality along. Most business applications were still very "client heavy," meaning that a large part of the application resided on the client PC. Therefore, businesses segregated PCs by business function as a way of controlling who had access to what data.) The process would begin with an understanding of each department's needs and priorities. For example, the HR department would need access to the personnel database (or at that time the personnel folders). The Accounting department would need access to the financials. (See Figure I.1.) However, in most cases, nobody from one department should have access to the others' databases. Each department would be designed as a separate network, complete with user accounts, rights, and privileges. In some extreme cases, the multiple internal networks had very little contact with each other. This method of design may seem crude by today's standards, but it worked.

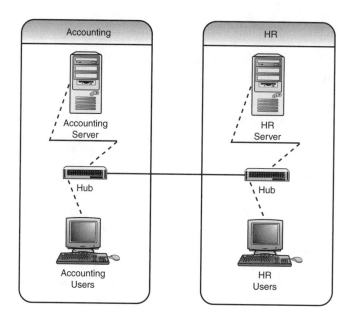

FIGURE I.1

In this example, the accounting users would log on to the accounting server. The HR users would log on to the HR server. The two sets of users would then share resources from their own hard drives.

This scenario will not necessarily work now. We no longer need to micro-design a network (as a collection of small entities); rather, we need to engage in a bit of macro-design (a small portion of a larger entity). Where we once thought of internal business functions as parts of a whole company, we should now think of companies as parts of a whole global economy. Thinking with the larger picture in mind will help you build networks that take advantage of the changing technology.

This book walks you through the design process from gathering information to implementing the final product. Included is a reference guide for product uses and quirks, a glossary of terms, and a lot of diagrams from actual projects. The most popular products (at publication) are covered in great detail (Microsoft solutions for OS, e-mail and inventory tools, and many others). Some other technologies, such as Novell OS and NetBEUI, are included but not in such detail. The book follows a logical process:

1. Gathering the Information
2. Designing the Network
3. Assembling the Components

4. Building the Network

5. Monitoring the Network

Feel free to navigate through the sections as your projects dictate (not all projects will flow the same way). However, if you are building from the ground up and have not yet started your project, please follow the sections in order; you will get more out of the book, and you may head off some nasty issues. Another point that is hammered in throughout this book is DOCUMEN-TATION. I can't stress enough the need for good documentation. The next few pages discuss laying the groundwork for good documentation and give some tips on how to organize what you have.

Finally, because the amount of information covered in each chapter is so vast, a summary is included at the end of each chapter. The summary contains all the major pieces of information covered in the chapter. It also can be helpful in reviewing the contents and product descriptions from previous chapters.

Why Document?

If you are not familiar with the ISO 9000 standards, don't worry; this is not a discourse on how to rearrange your life around documentation. I could fill an entire book on the ISO standard alone (some people already have). What I will do is offer some advice loosely based on their guidelines to help you document your work. The tips offered in this book will bring you no closer to ISO certification than you are right now, but they will make your job easier.

Most people view documentation as an extra step, a hindrance. You have to take time out from what you are doing, write it all down, and pick up where you left off. If you think like this, then documentation *will* be a hassle. Documentation needs to be thought of as a proof (a form of checks and balances). Documenting your progress helps you prove that you are doing the work agreed to. Because most if not all of the project details are agreed to beforehand, you need material to help you chart your progress. Creating a well-documented network also provides a form of reference for the client to use in training, troubleshooting, and upgrading the network after you move on. Therefore, if you are contracted to implement a network for a large company, and all of your documentation is in order, the transition will be extremely simple when you leave. Just hand over all of your papers, and away you go.

What should be documented? Everything! Included in the back of this book is a sample documentation pack from a typical design project. Look through it to get an idea of the kind of documentation you should produce. (I used Visio 2000 and Microsoft Office 2000 for most of the work.) Network maps, server names and functions, and flow charts are some of the most valuable information you can have. An easy illustration of this is shown in Table I.1.

TABLE I.1 Documentation Used in Troubleshooting

Problem	Needed Documentation	Purpose
A user in one building cannot see a resource in another branch location.	A network map, address scheme, and resource list would be very useful in diagnosing the problem.	By viewing the network map, you could see what ports and other hardware resources the workstation is trying to use.
		An address scheme may alert you to some possible conflicts or overlapping security policies.
		Finally, a resource list would quickly show you if the workstation is trying to access files in the right locations.

Not every document needs to come out of a word processor. Some of your papers may be best left as handwritten notes (just write legibly). For instance, meeting notes are a perfect example of an acceptable handwritten document.

Following is a partial list of items your documentation packet may include. (It is only a partial list because every project is different and you may need documents for one project that you may not need for another.)

- **Client Needs**—In your initial meetings discussing your network, take many notes. These will be the building blocks of your project. Ask as many questions as it takes to fully understand the needs and expectations of everyone involved and write them down. This may seem like a no-brainer, but many times expectations are set in these meetings (sometimes they are only implied) and you need a way to go back and find out exactly what was conveyed.

- **Initial Proposal**—This may not be just one document, but a series of documents. Using a professional tool such as Visio will save you a lot of work here. The content of the proposal will range from a high-level topology to a diagram of a wiring closet. Chances are the document will change many times, so keep all versions for your packet.

- **Cost/Function Analysis**—After a "final" design is agreed upon, it may be necessary to explain different options such as "100Mbit switches versus 100Mbit hubs (cost versus performance)." Because many network proposals (at the first stages) are not very granular, some details will need to be factored in. This is only one example; others might include the cost of adding an extra PDC or which UPS to buy.

- **Timeline**—Microsoft Project is a great tool for producing timelines. Your timeline should include everything needed to complete your project plus some. A good buffer amount is 50%. Remember, it is always better to finish ahead of schedule than ask for an extension (even if the schedule has been padded). You should also be very clear about who will be doing what. Project has a good task assignment feature; use it to keep track of who is pulling their weight.

- **Initial Design**—The initial design is produced just before you start working on the project. This is what the client will initially agree to as the "scope" of the project. This document may be subject to many revisions as the project continues. *It's important that you do not scrap old versions of this document.* You may need to refer back to them if any details are in dispute.

- **Final Diagram**—Produced after all work has finished and the network is functional, a final diagram may include several drawings. Wiring maps, workflow, and topology diagrams all make your final diagram. Because things can be changed after installation, hold off on producing this document until everything is settled.

All of your documentation should be kept in an easily accessible place because you are creating all of these documents for a reason: others need to see them. Keeping all of this beautiful paperwork in a three-ring binder on the back seat of your car kind of defeats the purpose. It should be kept in a place that everyone has access to and everyone knows about (again, doing all of this work is useless if nobody knows you're doing it). Inform people when a document has changed or a new one has been added. All of this work will take time but it is well worth it in the end. Having your documentation in order will also give your client a warm and fuzzy feeling knowing that you are organized and articulate. No one wants to pay top dollar for a network designer who is disorganized and sloppy.

The only documents that you will create that do not fall under these guidelines (ease of accessibility) will be all those pertaining to security. You may need to produce documents detailing security procedures, passwords, and other proprietary network information. Consult with the client to find out who should be given all security-related documents. The client may have a security officer or department head who is charged with handling the information. For obvious reasons, these documents should be secured in a safe or locked cabinet. However, some companies may be lax enough to have you include the security papers with all of your other documentation. Ultimately it is the client's decision.

Gathering Information

IN THIS PART

Preparation and Analysis

IN THIS CHAPTER

This chapter covers one of the most basic parts of any network job: gathering the information needed to start. By the end of the chapter you should have a firm grasp of what information you need to begin and more importantly, why you need it. Saving all of the technical explanations for later in the book, a discussion on how to ask questions may seem low-level and out of place. However, it is one of the most overlooked parts of any design job. Many problems with network implementations can be traced to miscommunication. A chapter about asking the right questions and obtaining all the pertinent information helps you avoid some of these issues. This chapter does not have an overwhelming amount of technical material, but we will delve in the depths of technology after discussing what you need to start the job off right.

Before beginning work on any project, all the parameters must be set. Imagine that you take your car to a mechanic. Without asking what the problem is, he starts working on your vehicle and not knowing that you only want the oil changed, he proceeds to give the car a full tune-up (changing the oil in the process). He also rotates and balances the tires and replaces the brakes.

Without setting the proper parameters for a job, anything can happen and anything can be expected from you. Each party must be sure that the correct work is being done; an insurance policy that covers both sides is needed. It can seem like a simple thing, but much can be assumed (sometimes incorrectly) throughout a job. One common assumption in network design is that a finished product will be Ethernet. This can be from habit or possibly ease of installation. (Ethernet is easier to install than Token Ring). However, not everybody has jumped onto the Ethernet bandwagon. Three of the largest companies in the southeastern United States run Token-Ring networks.

Gathering this vital information is the most important step in beginning your project. The easiest way to get this information is to meet with the client. Have a set plan and know what information you want before you start.

Defining the Project

Most network architecture projects will fall into two categories: expansion or replacement. An example of an expansion project is the addition of a second office. Many companies, through the natural process of growth, expand beyond the boundaries of their current facilities. If a business needs to expand its network to an adjoining area, the project can be considered an expansion. The main location will incur minimal upgrades, while the new location will bear the brunt of the work.

In some cases, such as expansion through acquisition (where one company purchases or assumes another), the new office space could have an existing network. This could make life interesting for a consultant. In this case the existing network in the new location must be tweaked to fit the network in the main location.

A replacement project is exactly that, the current client network being either partially or entirely replaced. In this case there is no real expansion or company growth anticipated; it might have happened months ago. However, the client has been living with the results until they became unworkable.

> **NOTE**
>
> I refer to *the client* frequently; it's an easy word to use. The client can be an outside client or people within your own company.

> Nothing is revolutionary about meeting with and talking to the client. However, like documentation, many people do not realize the importance of this step. The entire outcome of the project, successful or otherwise, depends on the information provided before the job starts.

A series of meetings might be necessary to determine all the network requirements. If you are a contractor rather than an employee, more meetings can be required. An employee will understand some of the needs of the company already (or at least know what questions to ask), whereas an outsider will need to ask many probing questions to get a clear image of what the client wants and expects. Asking the right questions is a vital part of getting the needed information. You should look for three basic types of information. (Although you will certainly need to ask more questions before the project gets off the ground, these will give you a good base of data from which to work.)

1. What is the company looking for in a network?
2. How does that differ from what they have?
3. What is the implementation deadline? (Addressed in Chapter 12, "The Final Proposal.")

The answers to these questions will provide most of the information you need to start the project.

Meeting with the Client

The first piece of information you need—what the company is looking for in a network—is a very broad area, and it is meant to be so. Do not make assumptions, but let the client give you the details. You might need to ask several questions to get all this information. Open-ended questions will help to get as much information as possible. Try not to ask questions that are pointed or guided toward a specific answer. For example, when trying to ascertain the type of network the client wants (for example, Ethernet or Token Ring) ask "What network type will you use?" not "Ethernet offers great speed and an easier installation. Do you want an Ethernet network?"

This allows the client to answer you as completely as possible and can help avoid some confusion. This doesn't mean that you should not offer any guidance at all. The client is not always going to know what they want. (That's why you're there.) Just try not to lean heavily toward something the business might not need or want.

State your questions as directly as possible. Your first question should be along the lines of "What do you need from this network?"

> This is where you start your first piece of documentation. Try to record all of the questions and answers from these meetings. Keeping these in a hand-written format is fine. Many times the first meetings are informal and your documentation can reflect that.

Now That You've Asked the Question, Listen to the Answer

Asking for the company's needs will generate different answers from different people. This can get confusing, especially when drawn out over several meetings. Make sure to clarify what people from one meeting say and compare it to what people from other meetings provide. Watch for all of the consistencies that can arise in what the clients are telling you. Think of it as asking two people what they think of the same abstract painting. Chances are you will get two different answers, but the underlying emotions will generally be the same. Networks can be abstract to many people, depending on their level of technical experience. Listen for the underlying themes in what they are saying. More often than not, they will all be saying the same thing even if it doesn't appear so.

For example, the president of the company might say, "We are growing quicker than we had expected and need a network that can handle the growth," whereas the accounting manager might say, "The accounting programs we use don't work. They are so slow nobody can get anything done." These two people can be saying the same thing. Network latency might be a problem. From these two responses you can already extrapolate some key pieces of information.

NOTE

Most (if not all) clients will have an existing network, but not all of them will have problems. Some projects will be the result of preventative maintenance. A client might just want you to rework some parts of the network that are functioning perfectly well but have been identified as areas that need extra attention. Be careful not to make problems where there aren't any. If during your informational meetings the client conveys their needs and does not mention any existing issues on the current network, don't go digging for any.

There is, however, one notable exception to this rule. Say a client wants you to revamp their network, and to save resources they insist you reuse as much of the current network as you can. To ensure a conflict-free environment, you should spend extra time analyzing the current network for problems. Anything you find that could interfere with the successful completion of the project should be brought to the client's attention. In a best-case scenario, this kind of network probing should be done before the scope of the project has been defined.

Dissect the Answers to Find More Questions

From the first statement, "We are growing quicker than we had expected and need a network that can handle the growth," you can gather that there is an existing network. Find out what will become of it. Do they want to salvage it or scrap it, or are they looking for you to make that decision? In many instances the old network will be morphed into the new one. Some pieces of equipment such as cabling might be in perfectly fine working order. In some cases they may want you to do nothing at all to the existing network but add to it. You want to know all of the tolerances of the current network.

Tailor your questions to find out what they plan on saving, what it is currently used for, and what it will be used for. Almost everything can be reused. Obvious things such as cabling and connectivity devices can be often reused successfully. However, some projects may dictate that you not use existing hardware. Take the case of a company, ABCcorp. We will use it as an example in all of our cases. ABCcorp owns XYZcorp. XYZ is breaking from its parent company and hires you to build its network. However, ABCcorp owns all of the equipment at XYZcorp and wants it back. This is a classic example of when you would not be able to use existing materials. Plan on needing a lot of equipment if this is your situation.

> **NOTE**
>
> Don't be afraid to bombard people with questions. It is better to be 100% clear on an objective than make an incorrect assumption, even for simple things such as cabling. Issues can exist with the integrity of the existing cable, and the client might want to replace it all.

The first statement by the president also tells you something about the company's size. More specifically, it indicates that there may be some network latency because of growth. Learn what symptoms make the users feel that their current network cannot handle growth. Chances are the president of the company is right; however, all of this information can help. Knowing the speed of any connectivity devices on the current network can also help determine whether latency is a problem on the current network. Two reasons can explain why you would want to make notes on the speed and type of connectivity devices in use.

If you find that the current network is in relatively sound condition, and slow connectivity devices are causing the network latency, you would just want to replace those devices. This would make a quicker, more cost-effective project. For example, XYZcorp has 20 employees on an Ethernet network. Business starts taking off and before long the company doubles its staff. Now network resources that once took seconds to open are starting to take minutes. The specifications for Ethernet definitely allow for more than 40 people on standard CAT 5 cabling. However, all the users are connected to 10Mb hubs running large warehouse inventory databases. Changing the 10Mb hubs for 100Mb hubs would improve performance a little. (Most Ethernet NICs are auto sensing for speeds of 10–100Mb. Any older computers should be checked for cards that work at a rate of 10Mb only.) The performance increase gained by moving from lower- to higher-speed hubs might not be what the client was expecting. A greater gain in speed would be accomplished by moving to 100Mb switches. Why not change to 10Mb switches? Changing from 10Mb hubs to 10Mb switches would make a noticeable change, but one thing you want to do is plan for growth. From the previous description, this company has the potential of quick and unexpected growth spurts, and you'll want to give them a little breathing room.

The second (more obvious) reason you would want to note the speed of any current connectivity devices is that you might design the greatest network in the world, order the equipment, and begin implementation before you notice that the client has 10Mb hubs. Without going into too much detail this early, hubs share bandwidth. Depending on the types of applications involved, this could slow any network to a halt.

> **NOTE**
>
> It might seem like I'm doing a lot of 10Mb hub bashing. I'm really not. Hubs in general (both 10Mb and 100Mb) do have their place in networks of all sizes. The decision to use hubs over switches used to be a purely financial one. A company might not have been able to afford the speed of a switched network, so they went with a hub-based solution. That is no longer the case. The prices of switches and hubs have become comparable. Now the decision is more of a performance/security issue. (Chapter 7, "Connectivity Devices," contains descriptions and capabilities of hubs and switches.)

All this information can be obtained from the statement, "We are growing quicker than we had expected and need a network that can handle the growth."

From the second statement, "The accounting programs we use don't work. They are so slow nobody can get anything done," you can gather a few more tidbits of information. There seems to be more than one program in use by the accounting department, and the programs are used over a network.

Are they part of relational databases? Are they currently segregated onto their own server? Many accounting packages store their information in relational databases such as Microsoft SQL Server or Oracle. This enables the users to run queries based on multiple criteria against the data stored in the database. Some older accounting programs store information in proprietary files or Microsoft Access databases. Knowing this information can be crucial to the performance of the network.

Don't Overlook Any Piece of Information—No Matter How Insignificant It Might Seem

Larger network-based database programs such as Microsoft SQL Server perform all of the processing for queries and other data manipulation on the server. The client software sends queries and receives snapshots of data. For instance, in an accounting program, if the user of a Microsoft SQL Server database wants to know how many invoices were paid this week, he or she would run a query. The client would send the query (in string form) to the server. The server would then run this query against its data and send the client a snapshot of the results. This results in less network traffic. Some programs (mainly Microsoft Access–based programs) send and receive the entire database whenever a change is made or a query is run. Even in relatively small networks, this can drain resources fairly quickly. A good way to make sure these things don't get too out of hand is to find out how many users are accessing these accounting applications. One or two people using a networked Access database might not be too bad, and probably would not justify the expense of switching to SQL. Conversely, a department of 10 or more accountants would definitely need to consider all possibilities. Ten or more people all utilizing one Microsoft Access database could bring down an average network.

Now you can get the second major piece of information you need: "How does that differ from what they have?" The answers to this question might be a little more defined. In fact, you can already have an idea of this from the responses to your other questions, but ask anyway. In most cases you shouldn't expect very technical responses. Everyone knows when something doesn't work the way they want it to, but not everyone knows why. Try asking the following questions:

- *How many users do you have now?*

  Use this information to determine the capacities of the current network. Knowing the current number of users will help you understand any issues the client is having with the existing network.

- *What kind of hardware and software is currently running?*

  Aside from looking for bandwidth-intensive applications, you are also trying to scope the boundaries of the network. "Microsoft Exchange Server" or "cc:Mail" would indicate e-mail services, whereas "Apache" or "IIS" would indicate Web-hosting services. On the hardware side, you are looking for numbers of servers and capacities along with connectivity devices.

Software Is Only Half of the Picture

Hardware is one item many people misinterpret. It is almost always assumed that hardware is a reusable item that time has no effect on (whereas software can be outgrown and outdated year after year). In many cases the opposite is true. Most hardware is composed of moving parts. Basic logic dictates that the more something moves against something else, the greater the chance of failure. Some older servers are time bombs, held together by the dust that has collected inside of them. Servers, no matter the age, are not inexpensive; they are one of the most expensive items on a network. It is for this purpose that many companies want to reuse them whenever possible, even at the expense of network performance. Before determining the fate of any existing servers, you should know five basic pieces of information:

1. Processor speed
2. RAM capacity
3. Bus speed
4. Hard drive configuration(s)
5. Age of equipment

At this point you should have a decent amount of documentation. If discussions are proceeding well, you should start to look at any existing hardware, making notes like those previously discussed. When the company is comfortable with you, discussions will probably shift to onsite inspections. Sometimes the client will ask you to perform a site survey. If not, ask for permission to evaluate the existing network. Take a look at the examples in the following section. Table 1.1 demonstrates the type of information that should be obtained about different types of hardware. The decision-makers at the company will often want to see the site analysis when you are finished. Therefore, this should be a piece of formal documentation, not a handwritten note.

Performing the Site Survey

Because of differing configurations and designs of networks, it is hard to say exactly where to start when performing a site survey. However, to ensure that you do not miss any equipment you may need to get a little creative.

First, ask the client for any existing documentation they may have pertaining to the physical network. However, don't get discouraged if the existing documentation is less than par (if it exists at all). This documentation will give you a general idea of where to begin your map and what you might encounter while creating it.

In the event the client does not have any existing documentation, you will need to physically trace the network.

NOTE

I want to suggest making a network map from scratch only as a last resort. Total network maps can be time-consuming. A resourceful designer will exhaust all other options before creating a physical network diagram. However, in some case, it can't be avoided.

To start making a physical network map, find a client (PC) machine. Starting there, try to picture the logical flow of information. Don't be afraid to grab a cable and physically trace it to the end. This is one of the best ways to ensure that you do not miss anything. When you think about it logically, for a signal to travel from one device to another, a connection must exist. Hence, if you can follow these connections you should find most pieces of equipment. You really need to understand the path of information to do this well. If you don't feel you're at the point where you can mentally trace a frame from beginning to end, the rest of this book should help you.

Chart Your Course

The part of the site survey that will be the most time-consuming is the network map. As you walk through the network, draw out a network diagram. A basic diagram is fine as long as it shows every piece of network equipment and how that equipment is connected. This might sound like a lot of work, but it will save you from second-guessing yourself later. Scribbling the diagram on a piece of paper is perfectly fine (assuming you can read it well enough to copy it into Visio). The site survey is not something you will want to do more than once because it takes a lot of time from both your schedule and the client's schedule. The network map will keep you from having to go back and trace the network a second or third time. Pay careful attention to details such as topology (Ethernet, Token Ring, and so forth), bandwidth, and protocols (is the client using TCP/IP, IPX/SPX, both, and so forth).

During this site survey you should also make sure to document equipment model numbers for all PCs, servers, and networking devices such as hubs, routers, and switches. It is also wise to have a good inventory of NIC types and inspections of existing wiring closets.

NOTE

Don't waste time trying to make your first network diagram look nice. As long as you can read the pertinent information, that's all that counts.

What Should You Encounter?

Starting with the end-user machinery, make notes of the PC hardware and operating system specs (processors, RAM, NIC, OS, and hard drives). When compiling your PC documentation you will also need a rough estimate of the number of computers related to the different specs. See Table 1.1 for an example of hardware specs.

TABLE 1.1 Hardware Specs

Processor	RAM	NIC	OS	Hard Drive
25 Pentium III 400s	64MB	10/100 Auto Sensing	Windows 2000	6GB
5 Pentium II 233s	32MB	10Mbit	Windows 95	1.2GB

> **NOTE**
>
> You may want to look at obtaining a good hardware inventory tool to help you gather this information. Products such as CheckIt by Touchstone Software can make the task of gathering hardware and software information easier.

There is a strong chance that you will need to integrate many of these machines into your designs. Obviously it helps to know what you are working with. The client may want to implement a grand "automated office" utilizing the best network equipment on the market, but you might find 486s hiding on a couple of desks. It is better to find this now than to approach the client after completion and say, "Oh, by the way, these people can't use the network we just installed because of their PCs."

You can encounter many different terminals while you are surveying the desktop situation. The presence of a terminal can be a marker for a server platform such as Unix, IBM, Tandem, or Windows Terminal Server. That's not to say these particular server products cannot exist without terminals. They can, but terminals cannot exist without a server to connect to.

How to Identify a Dumb Terminal

The terminal itself should be easy to identify. A dumb terminal will lack one obvious device: a CPU. Terminals have changed very little over the years. They are basically a monochrome monitor and keyboard that communicate over serial lines to a server.

Figure 1.1 illustrates an average terminal.

Don't concern yourself with what type of emulation the terminal provides (Unix, IBM, and so on); you usually cannot tell just by looking at a powered-off terminal. Look for the terminal server itself. The BSD, AIX, Solaris, and HP flavors of Unix will all fit on a desktop computer. A user can have both a terminal and a Unix machine in the same area. The easiest way to do this is to follow the cable on the back of the terminal. It should lead you right to the server. If the user does not have a terminal server in his or her area, but does have a terminal, look for specialized connectivity devices when you reach the wiring closets.

One type of terminal that does not follow the major terminal rules (serial connections and no CPU) is a thin client. A *thin client* is a specialized piece of hardware designed to connect to

Windows-based servers in much the same way a terminal does. Most of these thin clients connect by Ethernet connections and have small CPUs for running Windows CE. The server they connect to can be running Windows Terminal server, Windows 2000 with Terminal Services, or other third-party Windows terminal products such as Citrix.

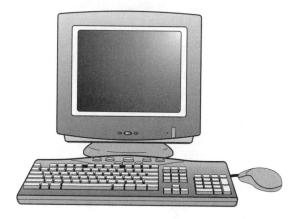

FIGURE 1.1

An average terminal.

Moving from the Desktop to the Connectivity Devices

Look at the cabling type. You will find CAT 5 in most places, but you can run into 10BASE-2 or 10BASE-5.

NOTE

I suggest the expertise of a third-party cable vendor when dealing with cable-related issues. One thing you probably don't want to get into is running and terminating cables. The physical network media is going to be the backbone of your network, and you should let a professional install and test it for you.

NOTE

If you have to trace the cabling into a crawl space, notice how the cable is labeled. You should never encounter this, but if the cable in a crawl space is not labeled "Plenum Grade" you should bring this up to the client as an informational item.

When most cabling is burned it releases a toxic gas. For this reason most ordinances state that only non-toxic cabling (plenum grade cabling) be used in crawl spaces or plenums. To compound the issue, not all cable is labeled one way or another. Some manufacturers only produce plenum cable, so they don't label it as such. The main reason a company would go with non-plenum grade cable in a normal workspace is cost. Plenum cable can be up to 50% more expensive than regular grade cabling.

If you need to call a cable vendor, be sure to inquire about what specific kind of cable is being used. The vendor may use only plenum grade cable, even where it is not necessarily needed. If the client is interested in cutting costs, ask the vendor about using non-plenum cable in all common areas.

Identifying CAT 5

CAT 5 cabling is best described as telephone wire on steroids. The other types of cable will look like cable TV cable (also called coax or coaxial). Figure 1.2 illustrates CAT 5 cabling. Figure 1.3 shows coaxial cable.

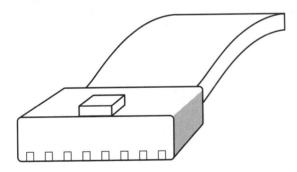

FIGURE 1.2
CAT 5 cabling.

FIGURE 1.3
Coaxial cable.

From the client (PC) over the cables, you should locate the connectivity devices. These can range from routers and switches to hubs or MAUs (Multiple Access Units). Routers, switches, and bridges tend to be out in the open and easier to identify. Note the manufacturer and model of all devices, especially if you are not sure about the type of role it provides. (Visit the Web site of any products that you are unfamiliar with.) Even if you know the role of a product—for instance, a router—get the spec sheet. The product might be capable of things that you didn't know about.

Hubs, MAUs, and repeaters have a tendency to be in less conspicuous places. Given the nature of these devices (generally inexpensive, easy to obtain, and easy to implement), they almost grow on networks like weeds.

> **NOTE**
>
> This is a perfect example of connectivity devices popping up in the most unexpected places. While troubleshooting the network of a large company known for theme parks and family vacations, we decided to get to the bottom of a lingering problem. Why, in one hotel's meeting room, was there a very sporadic Token-Ring connection? It was the kind of sporadic connection that only went out when important people were using it. Tracing the line, we were led into the ceiling of the meeting room. There we found four sections of cable loosely joined by MAUs just lying about the floor of the ceiling. It was an obvious attempt to overextend the capabilities of IBM Type I cable.
>
> A local cable vendor was called in and suggested replacing the Type I cable in the meeting room with fiber (at great expense to the company). Fiber to the desktop was not a new idea here; it had already been implemented in two other areas. Eventually it was decided to disconnect the room from the network altogether (an executive decision).
>
> These situations unfortunately are not uncommon and should be taken into consideration when planning your designs. If you need to re-run existing cable to bring it up to code, or replace existing devices with ones better suited for the job, do so. You will save yourself many headaches later.

From the Connectivity Devices to the Servers

Moving past the connectivity devices, you should reach the server equipment. Again, consult Table 1.1 for the desired information (pertaining to servers). One key point to note about servers is their current role. This is helpful if you need to re-use them. The functions of servers could range from e-mail and Web hosting to file and print services (depending on the age and OS). Going back to the example at the beginning of the chapter, the users are getting slow response from their programs after adding more users. After the site survey, you might find that the server running the accounting programs is a Pentium II 233 with 64MB of RAM. You might also find that a new print server down the hall is a Pentium III 600 with 128MB of RAM. For a client without a sizable budget, reversing the roles of these two machines might help them.

> **NOTE**
>
> If you are dealing in a Novell (or mixed) environment, you will run into other issues that a pure NT or Windows 2000 architect would not. When noting the OS type, get the Novell version number. You should also find out the role of the server (file server, bindery, and so on). Novell changed from a bindery to a tree structure in the 4.1 releases of the OS. See Chapter 3, "Network Operating Systems."

You should now have enough information to begin your design. However, if you are like most people, the bulk of the information you have is random notes scribbled across nonsequential pages. The meetings are over, the site survey is completed, and it's time to organize your information.

Organizing Your Information

This section discusses organizing your notes into documents. These documents will be your foundation for the remainder of the project. The documents you will create include Hardware and Software Specifications that will act as a reference for you to start the design process.

Getting Your Thoughts Straight

At this point you have more information than you know what to do with. If your schedule permits, I suggest you take a break. This is where you are going to want to let your mind rest for a day or so before organizing what you have. Organizing your information will help you weed out what you don't need, figure out what you still need, and establish a goal. My main tools for organizing information are Microsoft Word, Visio (now Microsoft Visio), and Microsoft Project.

> **NOTE**
>
> I am by no means a Microsoft preacher, but there is something to be said for compatibility. When I prepare documentation, it is reassuring to know that I have a greater chance of people successfully viewing my electronic documents in a Microsoft format. I also know that output from one Microsoft program can easily become input for another. Network design can be hard enough; anything that makes the job easier is welcome.

Formatting Your Notes

When approaching the stack of notes and papers that has accumulated on your desk, the first task is to get as much of it into a common format as possible. Obviously your main goal is to have most of the information in an electronic format. This will make data manipulation a breeze.

If you took your original notes on a PDA such as a Palm Pilot, this will be quite easy. Simply sync your desktops and you're ready to manipulate. I use a Cross Pad when taking meeting notes and gathering information. The process I use is similar to that used by someone with a scanner. I upload the handwritten notes to my desktop. Then using IBM ink manager, I use OCR (Optical Character Recognition) on the notes and import them to Microsoft Word.

If you didn't use a PDA and using a scanner is not a possibility, typing the notes by hand into Word is about your only option. You can weed out the information you don't need as you type it.

When formatting the information it is best to divide it into groups or categories. Like any other type of data, make sure you are comparing the correct items. It would be very hard to compare the athletic abilities of Wayne Gretzky and Larry Bird just by looking at their scoring records. In fact, a basketball player can score more in one season than some hockey players score in a career. So you need to find a common category by which they can both be compared. The same holds true for network data. You can have a more complete idea of the project if you know what you are looking at.

I try to organize my information into four categories: client concerns, hardware specs, software specs, and client needs. (Later I will add a fifth: proposed network.) By separating all the data into these four groups, I can get a better view of the overall picture.

This section takes a look at what kind of information should be included in the Hardware Specification and Software Specification documents.

Hardware Specs

This is the easiest of the four categories to organize. You will be drawing on all of the material gathered during the site survey. Divide the hardware lists into server, clients, and connectivity devices. List the brand, model, and specs for each of these categories.

Software Specs

Use the same groups that you used for hardware specs: server, client, and connectivity devices. The connectivity devices software spec will only apply to intelligent devices, more specifically routers, switches, and bridges.

An intelligent connectivity device is one that can process data and make routing decisions based on that data. Routers, switches, and bridges generally have a proprietary operating system. Consult the client or the manufacturer's documentation for instructions on obtaining the software revision. Some devices that otherwise would not fit into your designs might do so with the correct software revision.

Non-Intelligent Devices

Hubs and MAUs are not referred to as intelligent devices. Even though some hubs do have software, they do not utilize it for the same purposes as intelligent devices. The software included on some hubs is to enhance or exploit the functionality of the hardware, not add new features.

The subgroups for your software specs should consist of the following:

- Platform
- Name
- Manufacturer
- Version
- Number of users

The platform should indicate whether the software is client or server (and which operating system it runs on). The name of the software is obviously inserted under Name. The rest of the subgroups should be self-explanatory.

Client Concerns

This category, again, should come straight from your notes, even if you have to search a little. Using previous examples, your main concerns would be as follows:

1. Network cannot handle growth
2. Accounting software too slow

List the concerns of the client as facts. Try not to read into them or interpret what they might mean. If things do not go as planned you should be able to go back to this sheet. The majority of this chapter discussed what these two statements could mean. This is where you want to step back a little and list the original concerns of the client. Hopefully you will have a longer list than these two items. The concerns sheet will become the main point of reference for the project. Therefore, try not to leave anything out. Add as many details as you deem necessary under each point. For example:

1. Network cannot handle growth

    a. 40 users (growing to 80)

2. Accounting software too slow

    a. 10 users

    b. Networked Microsoft Access Database

The network map you drew up during the site survey should be included with this document grouping. Use a professional diagramming tool such as Visio to create a representation of the current network. Of all the documents you produce, the network map should look the best. Take your time with it. This is one document that the client will be looking at. Before beginning the actual project (and at the project's completion) you will be presenting the current network map to the client. The network map gives you a starting point for interpreting all the information you collected.

Client Needs

This will be the hardest of the four categories to put concrete data to. You might not be able to rely on notes for this. If you have data for the client stating implicitly "We want 'x'," then this is the place for it. However, there is more to it than that. Even if the client does know what they want, chances are they don't know what it will take to get there. The client may have an end goal in mind, but it is up to you to get them there. Don't mistake the Client Needs document for a network design. It is simply a list of items the client will need to achieve their desired result.

To create this list of client needs, you will need to interpret the data you have just organized.

Interpreting What You Have

At this point you should have a lot of great documentation, and now it's neatly ordered. Your next step is to interpret the data you have compiled. Remember the end goal: to design a network that meets the needs of the client. Interpreting the gathered data to find out what you need is the most important part of the pre-project activities. You might need to meet with the client again to clarify some issues after looking deeper into the needs of the company.

Table 1.2 represents the hardware at ABCcorp. Looking over the notes, try to determine the actual needs of ABCcorp.

TABLE 1.2   Hardware Notes from ABCcorp

Type of Device	Connectivity Devices	PC	Server
Number of Devices	3	20	1
Specs	10Mb Hubs	Pentium II 300s with 64MB of RAM running Windows 98	Pentium III 500 with 128MB of RAM running Windows NT 4.0

The client is running TCP/IP and NetBEUI over 10Mb Ethernet. Five accountants are sharing a Microsoft Access database on the one server. The receptionist has a dial-in account to the Internet.

The client complains of general network latency, and needs a way for all users to access their own e-mail accounts. On the wish list for the company is granting access to a few employees from home.

This is the information gathered from ABCcorp over a series of meetings.

To cure the network latency you need to look at the topology of the network. Twenty clients accessing one server over a relatively slow connection will cause some congestion. Figure 1.4 shows my diagram for a proposed solution.

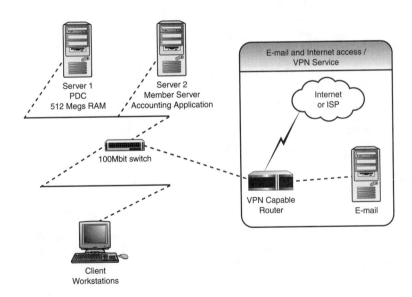

FIGURE 1.4

Author's solution.

The 10Mb hubs have been replaced with 10/100Mb switches. This will dramatically improve the performance of the network. Moving from 10Mb hubs to 10/100Mb switches may seem like a big step.

> **NOTE**
>
> A switch can improve network traffic by offering dedicated bandwidth to each port. Each port on a 100Mb switch is guaranteed 100Mb of bandwidth regardless of the number of ports in use. As a contrast, the per-port bandwidth on a hub degrades with each new user. A full description of how switches work is provided in Chapter 7.

I could have gone with 100Mb hubs, but I want to plan for growth. It will take a lot of traffic for the client to outgrow these switches.

A second server has been added to house the accounting application. The first server will have its RAM boosted and serve as an authentication server. The addition of the second server will help alleviate the processing burden on the original server. Aside from tweaking services like DNS and WINS (explained in Chapter 2, "LAN Specifics"), this should accomplish the first goal.

The second goal, allowing each employee to access his or her own e-mail, can be approached two ways. One solution would be to mock what employees already have: dial-up connections. This is not a very practical, secure, or cost-effective solution. Each employee would need a modem and an analog telephone line. This can be very costly and not too easy to set up. From a security standpoint, even though "home use" products for securing a telephone line exist, they are not as secure as enterprise products and they cannot be centrally administered.

How to Implement an Internet/E-mail Solution

Looking back at my proposed solution, I laid the initial groundwork for an Internet-based e-mail product. I included a server, one router, and T1 line.

> **NOTE**
>
> Because this chapter is about gathering the information needed to start a project, it does not discuss why you need the previously listed items, or what else you need to implement them. That will be covered in Chapter 10, "Internet Connectivity." For now, focus on interpreting the client's needs and how you can help obtain them.

Remote Access

To obtain the second goal of allowing e-mail access to employees from home, I suggested VPN. I could have gone with Windows NT RAS. However, because the client will need to purchase equipment to implement the dedicated Internet connection (required for most e-mail solutions), I can make sure the devices they get have VPN capability. VPN-ready connectivity devices can be expensive. Therefore, if the client already has a dedicated connection to the Internet, I would suggest Windows NT RAS. RAS requires no specialized hardware (other than a modem) to be implemented and can accommodate a fair amount of users. However, with RAS you are at the mercy of a dial-up connection on both the client and server side. Both solutions have their good and bad points.

> VPN (Virtual Private Network) allows outside users secure access to your network through your unsecured connection to the Internet. The client and the server pieces of the software link up to create a secure tunnel for data to pass through.

After determining the client's actual needs, draw up another network diagram that you feel represents a path to reach their goal. Go back to the client to confirm with them that these needs and goals are mutually agreeable. Then you're ready to start designing a network.

Summary

- When starting a project, ask the client every possible question you can think of. Try not to assume anything. The easiest way to ensure the integrity of your information is to ask open-ended questions. Don't lead the client into giving certain answers.

- When the client has answered your questions, listen closely. What is the client really saying? You will be able to base most of your future questions on the answers from your first. Be careful and try to look past the emotion in their answers. The best way to extract the facts from the answers is to compare the answers from one person to those of another. By spotting the similarities in what two different people say about the same thing, you'll find a clearer piece of data. Above all, do not overlook any details, no matter how small.

- After you have met with the client and have gathered enough information, it is time to make a site survey. The site survey will help you understand exactly what is going on in the network. Remember to make a map of the network. The survey itself is great if you have a photographic memory, but if you're like the rest of us you will need to draw a network diagram.

  Start your map by physically tracing the network cables from the PCs to the servers. This will give you the best results.

- Organize all the information you collect. Weed out the data that does not relate to your current project. All the information you collect can be put into these four categories:

  - Client concerns
  - Hardware specs
  - Software specs
  - Client needs

  In the process of organizing data, the objective for the project will become clearer.

  You will also want to copy your hand-drawn network maps from the site survey into a professional diagramming tool such as Visio.

- The final step in preparing for a project is to interpret your data. All the wonderful information you collected is useless if you don't know what it means. You primary goal in this is to understand the needs of your client.

  After you feel you have successfully uncovered the client's needs, produce your preliminary design.

Designing a Network

IN THIS PART

LAN Specifics

IN THIS CHAPTER

By now you should have all the information you need to begin your design. You should have an understanding of what is happening at the client's site and a good idea of what they need. The project is now at a point where you must take these client needs and produce results.

The rest of this book examines a network's key parts. Imagine a network as being like a hotel tower. The hotel consists of a ground floor or lobby, a few floors of rooms, and maybe some penthouses at the top. Elevators and stairs connect the various floors to each other. To access the hotel, you walk in the front door, check in at the lobby, and take the elevator to your floor. Once at the correct floor, you find your room by locating its number on the door. The hotel itself operates within its own set of rules and guidelines, plus those set forth by the laws of the states.

State laws governing elevators might say that an elevator must be able to carry at least 2,500 pounds, but hotel management can configure its elevators any way they want. They can have one elevator that goes between the first and fifth floors and another that goes directly to the penthouses.

This scheme relates directly to networks. The front door to the hotel is your port to the outside world, or the Internet. Information, like people, travels (sometimes freely) through the front door to gain access to the network. However, once the people are in the lobby, they don't know where to check in, where the elevators are, or where their rooms are. This information must be easy to find to have a successful hotel. The design of the hotel ensures that people walking into the hotel can find what they need without getting lost. The combination of network type and network topology ensures that packets travel efficiently (without getting lost) across a network.

A network type dictates how information is passed (from the lobby to the correct room) on the network. By checking in at the front desk, the guest has an idea as to the layout of the hotel. He is given a room number and told which elevator will take him there. The elevators are the protocols that carry information across the network. They carry a certain number of people (or packets) per run, letting them off at the floors they choose. Finally, the individual rooms can be thought of as nodes or clients on the network.

Building a successful network will be the result of following a logical chain of events. First you need to know how the hotel will operate. That is, you need to understand the topology before you can begin construction.

This chapter deals strictly with choosing the right network type for the job. We will look at the pros and cons of Ethernet and Token Ring. Not only will we cover these network types separately, but we will also look into running several types together in a mixed environment. Many companies, for various reasons, run Ethernet and Token Ring together. Again, we will cover the pros and cons of this and look at how it is accomplished.

The Hypothetical Company

Throughout this book I will use examples from a hypothetical company, ABCcorp. Different scenarios (featuring various real-life network problems) will be presented throughout the book. I encourage you to think about how you would approach these scenarios as they are presented. At the end of each scenario, I will offer and explain my solution(s) to the problems being faced by ABCcorp.

What Is a Network Type?

This section discusses network types. There are many network types to choose from, but they all have one thing in common; they can all be described as "network blueprints."

The Blueprint of a Network

A *network* describes the logical and physical connection between a server and a client whereby information passes from one to the other through a medium. This definition of a network is what I base my designs on and what I refer to when I work on projects.

Before the owner of a hotel looks for architects to design a building, he must have an idea of how the hotel will operate, how many guests he wants to accommodate, what hours the lobby will operate, how many people he plans to employ, and so on.

When considering what type of network to choose, you must look at several different factors. One of the worst mistakes you can make is to decide on one network type, implement it, and then figure out it is not the right one. (Because a network type consists of hardware that is specific to the type you choose, it can be expensive to change your mind.) Do your research before choosing your network. This book will provide you with most of what you need to make an informed decision. Some of these factors are

- Desired network bandwidth
- Number of users on the network
- Inclusion (or exclusion) of legacy equipment

The network type you choose will dictate much about how your network can function. It is most important to pay attention to the limitations of each network type. You are most likely planning for growth; therefore, choose a network topology that will not constrict you.

The type of network chosen is the basis for how you complete the project. The network type determines everything from the number of computers on your network to the speed at which they can transmit information. But what *is* a network type?

Let's look back at how this all began. The origins of intercomputer communications can be traced to ARPAnet.

> **Note**
>
> *ARPAnet* stands for the Advanced Research Projects Agency Network. ARPA (later to become DARPA) was charged by the United States Department of Defense to investigate the plausibility of reliable computer communications.

In the mid-1960s, the government began to realize that computers were not meant to work autonomously. The movement toward intercomputer communication began at the United States Department of Defense (because the complexity and expense of computer research limited the number of companies that could pull off a project like this). The Department of Defense recognized that finding a way for computers to communicate with each other was a key to the next level of mass computing. Mass computing, as it existed in the early 1960s, consisted of multiple terminals tethered to bulky mainframes. However, each mainframe (if a company had enough money, it might have multiple mainframes) worked independently of all other mainframes. If a reliable form of computer communication could be achieved, users would be able to share documents and processing power with each other. But more importantly, users at remote sites could securely access information anywhere.

> **Note**
>
> I use the word *securely* loosely here. This process was secure only because nobody really had the means to threaten it. The PC wouldn't be around for another 15 years (eons in the computer industry), and the Internet wouldn't exist (in its current form) for another 20 years.

The Department of Defense contracted various private sector firms to find a way of supporting intercomputer communications. In the late 1960s, TCP/IP (in its earliest form) was born. The creation of this protocol opened the door to computer networks and to the Internet. The first use of this new protocol was at the University of California, Berkeley.

It didn't take long for the word (and technology) to spread. Xerox PARC (Palo Alto Research Center) picked up the torch in 1972. The product to come out of PARC would revolutionize the computer industry. In 1973, Ethernet was introduced and has remained relatively unchanged.

Aloha Net

The first network type developed at PARC was known as Aloha Net (later to become Ethernet). First implemented at the University of Hawaii, Aloha Net was capable of transfer rates just under 3Mbps. The establishment of Aloha Net marked the first commercial use of a computer network. The advent of computer networking opened the door for a technology that would make possible everything from the Internet to computer gaming (not to mention the personal computer).

To understand how revolutionary a network of computers was, imagine what computing was like before. Think of the pre–Aloha Net computers as being typewriters with built-in calculators. Each computer worked autonomously. There was little in the form of sharing information, and the notion of sharing processor power (*a la* client/server computing) was almost unheard of.

Because Aloha Net was developed at Xerox, the potential was there to connect more than computers. Xerox, the leading producer of printers at the time, was setting its sites on networking printers as well as computers. Ethernet would make that a reality. The Ethernet standards that Xerox created would allow for the intercommunication of computers and printers. When the success of Aloha Net was publicized, people wanted it, and they wanted it fast.

Even though the 3Mbps transfer rate (introduced with the original Ethernet network in 1973) could have held out for a little while longer, Xerox PARC immediately began researching ways of improving it. One year later, in 1974, Xerox developed a 10Mbps transfer rate and named the product Ethernet.

> The Institute of Electrical and Electronics Engineers (IEEE) approves all standards pertaining to computer networking (among a vast array of other technologies). For example, IEEE standard 802.3 defines Ethernet, 802.3ae defines Gig Ethernet, and 802.11 (once fully approved) will define wireless Ethernet. For more information on IEEE, visit its Web site at www.ieee.org.

NOTE

> The quicker transfer rates associated with Ethernet today did not appear until 1994, when 100Mbps was introduced.

IBM Steps into the Ring

As you now know, Ethernet is not the only game in town. IBM introduced Token Ring in 1985.

IBM wanted a proprietary network type by which its mainframes would communicate with its PCs, but there was more to it. Token Ring wasn't faster (when released, Token Ring ran at a transfer rate of around 4Mbps), and Ethernet could network printers (this point can be disputed; some accounts bill Token Ring as the first network type to include printers without their PC counterparts).

NOTE

Remember that for the longest time there was only one name in computing—IBM. This company set many of the early networking standards.

So when PARC introduced Ethernet, IBM immediately noticed the potential of computer networking and began developing Token Ring. By most accounts Token Ring and Ethernet were in production at the same time, but Ethernet got to the shelf first. Even if you create the best networking type in the world, you still need hardware manufacturers to build it into their systems. IBM wasn't about to support a third-party network suite when it had one of its own in the works. Hence, we have the introduction of Token Ring.

Token Ring was (and still is) the geek's Ethernet. IBM had built into Token Ring a slew of tools for tweaking and monitoring networks, and it worked. Token-Ring architecture has changed very little since its inception because it hasn't had to.

NOTE

A consultant will be more apt to work with Token Ring as part of an integration project rather than a new network. He should pay attention to how Token Ring works, but more importantly how it works with and differs from Ethernet.

Token Ring and Ethernet grew from totally different circumstances and needs. Therefore, totally different companies will use them. The companies that use Ethernet will not be the same companies that use Token Ring.

Generally, companies that use Token Ring will not need to transfer large amounts of data across the media. Token Ring supports transfer rates of 4–16Mbps, which is quite slow when compared to Ethernet. The slow transfer rates and high equipment cost associated with this network type definitely limit its use in the business world. However, some companies use it successfully. An example of a company that works well on Token Ring is Walt Disney World. It is a geographically large company, but it needs to transmit only flat data files. (We'll delve further into the Disney network in the next section.)

Ethernet Fundamentals

Most, if not all, of the projects you work on will be Ethernet. However, Ethernet is not the Incredible Hulk of networks; it's more like the Achilles. Ethernet is strong when it's done right, but it has weaknesses. Before you start sketching out your shiny new Ethernet network, read and take note of those limitations.

After explaining the technical garble behind Ethernet, we will create a few practical designs or implementations.

The Technical Side of Ethernet

Ethernet comes in four speeds: 10Mbps, 100Mbps, 1Gbps, and most recently, 10Gbps. Depending on the installation, you can achieve transfer rates ranging from 10Mbps–10Gbps.

The network cards and the hubs and switches determine the transfer rate in an Ethernet network. An Ethernet network card is rated for four speeds. The NIC can be 10Mbit, 10/100Mbit, 100Mbit, or 1Gb. The majority of cards on the market today are either 10Mbit or 10/100Mbit. The network card transmits at its rated speed, but the NIC is not the only player in the game.

A network is only as fast as its slowest link. Look at the example in Figure 2.1 and think logically about the speed of the network.

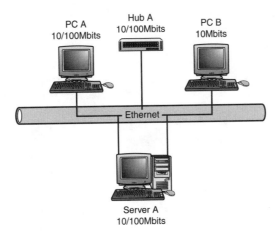

FIGURE **2.1**

The numbers by the computers represent the speed of the NIC installed. The device in the center is a hub; its speed is 10/100Mbits.

In Figure 2.1, PC A will communicate with Server A at a rate of 100Mbps. The speed of the network is partially determined by the NIC in each PC. Both PC A and Server A have 10/100 cards. Most 10/100 cards are auto-sensing. (You might need to check the setting on your card to ensure that auto-sensing is turned on.)

Determining the Speed on Ethernet

One misunderstood factor in determining the speed of an Ethernet network is the question of *half duplex* versus *full duplex*. These terms refer to the communication capability of a device over an Ethernet network. If a pair of devices are communicating at half duplex, each device is either sending or receiving information, but not simultaneously. In full-duplex communication, two devices can both send and receive (with each other) at the same time.

This affects the speed of the network in two ways. If two devices send data to each other in half duplex on a 10Mb network, they are each sending data (one at a time) at 10Mbps. Therefore, a pair of devices sending information at full duplex is (for all intents and purposes) communicating at twice the speed of the network. (The same amount of information is passed between the devices in half the time.)

The second way is more abstract. Every time a device begins transmitting, it obtains a virtual circuit for its information to travel across. The *circuit* is simply the physical path data takes when traveling from one place to another. These virtual circuits consist of the physical cabling and connectivity devices that make up a network. Using these elements in varying combinations can yield varying results. When the device has ended its transmission, it releases the circuit. The next time this device starts communicating, it could use an entirely different circuit. Devices communicating at half duplex could use hundreds of virtual circuits per session. The device sending data uses one circuit, and when it is finished the circuit is released. The receiving device then begins transmitting back on a different circuit. The actual transfer speeds obtained by devices communicating at half duplex can vary widely per session. A device could begin sending on a fast circuit, and the response could come in over a slower circuit.

On the other hand, two devices communicating at full duplex will use the same virtual circuit for the duration of the transaction, because communication between the two doesn't end until both devices have finished sending and receiving. Therefore, assuming the two devices obtain an acceptable circuit to begin with, the communication between the two will be fairly consistent.

NOTE

An auto-sensing NIC will detect the speed of the device directly connected to it and adjust its own speed accordingly. If the network card is not auto-sensing, you will need to set it manually. Usually this is done through software.

PC A will communicate with PC B at a rate of 10Mbps. Even though PC A has a 10/100 card, PC B has only a 10Mbps card; thus, the fastest speed between the two is 10Mbps.

Now, change one piece of hardware and the whole picture is different. Figure 2.2 shows the same network with a slower hub.

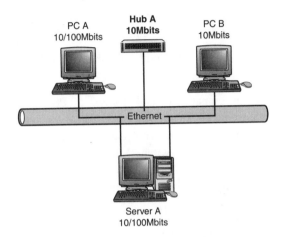

FIGURE 2.2
Network with 10Mbit hub.

In the second example we changed the speed of the hub to 10Mbps. This changes the results dramatically. Every device on the network can now communicate with every other device on the network at a speed of only 10Mbps.

Why did the hub make that much difference? This Ethernet is wired in a star topology.

In a star topology, every PC, printer, and server is attached to one central device. Tracing the cable out of any PC will lead to a connectivity device where many other PCs are connected. This hub or switch will dictate the collective speed of the network. By this logic, no matter what speed your NIC is, if your hub is only 10Mbps, your network is only transmitting at 10Mbps.

If I have a 10/100 card in my PC and a 10Mbps hub, will my PC transmit at 100Mbps and receive at only 10Mbps? No. As soon as that card boots (assuming auto-detect is enabled), it will detect that the hub is 10Mbps and set itself to transmit at 10Mbps.

Why Is This Part of Ethernet So Important?

Choosing the transfer rate is the most important part of designing an Ethernet network. At my last design job, all the PCs had 10/100 NICs, but they were connected to two linked 10Mbps hubs. Therefore, the speed of the network was 10Mbps. This was fine for a small 20-person

LAN, but the company was expanding. This particular company wanted to connect to the Internet, double its employee base, and run a large helpdesk database. The old 10Mbps LAN would buckle under the pressure.

Because this company's Ethernet network was a star topology, there was an easy solution: Replace the 10Mbps hubs with something faster. The only real advantage to using slower connectivity devices is the cost. The slower the device, generally, the less expensive it is. (However, in most cases the cost difference is minimal.)

Without taking into account software, what guidelines should you use when designing your Ethernet network?

First, determine the size of the company. A small office, 2–50 PCs, can fare well on a 10Mbps Ethernet network, even with some applications of modest size. A network speed of 10Mpbs can be achieved by implementing a 10Mbit switch (see Chapter 7, "Connectivity Devices," for a description of the functions and uses of switches). Implementing a switch here will give you room to expand. With anything over 50 PCs, you should consider using 100Mbps. Ethernet itself, unlike Token Ring, has very little network overhead; that is, Ethernet itself uses very little bandwidth without anything running on it.

Some network types have a fairly high network overhead. That is, there is information being transmitted across the network even when it is not in use (just because of the type of network employed). Networks need to employ *access methods*. These are used to ensure that everybody on the network doesn't talk at once. Every PC needs to wait its turn to ensure that the data it is transmitting reaches the intended recipient clean and ungarbled. Is a network's access method going to cause enough traffic to make a difference? No, not by any means, but you should know that they exist and how they work.

Imagine a classroom full of kids. The teacher is the lone recipient of their data. If they all speak at once, the teacher can't understand anything being said. Therefore, the teacher utilizes an access method when the students have something to say. If a student wants to say something, he waits until no one else is speaking and raises his hand to signal his intention to speak.

Ethernet uses a similar access method, referred to as CSMA/CD. CSMA/CD stands for *Carrier Sense Multiple Access with Collision Detection*. Here's how it works.

When a PC needs to send information across an Ethernet network, it first "listens" to the line. By listening to the network, the NIC can detect whether any other PCs are transmitting. Even on the largest network, only one PC can transmit at any given time.

A PC on a network is referred to as a *node*. An Ethernet network can have 1,024 nodes on a single segment. Only one of those nodes can transmit at any given time. Think of a node as an interconnected part of a network.

Figure 2.3 illustrates a network with five nodes.

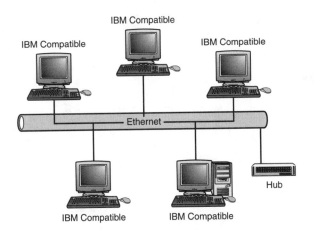

FIGURE 2.3

A network with five nodes.

Breaking your network into segments has advantages. If you find that your network has an abundance of collisions, you should consider segmenting.

The best way to divide an Ethernet network into nodes is by geography. However, you might not have any say in the matter. The protocol you use can dictate how you segment your network. We will cover IP segmenting in Chapter 6, "Choosing a Protocol," but here is a quick overview to help you work segments into your design if necessary.

At the last design job I did, I needed to connect offices in three cities via Frame Relay (I cover this later). Anyway, because of the requirements of our provider, we segmented the three locations. Figure 2.4 illustrates this.

Notice that I took a natural obstacle and used it to my advantage. By segmenting along geographic borders, network traffic is reduced and information flows more efficiently. In most situations you will want to segment your network along geographic lines. The guideline I use is the WAN Guideline. If each office in a location has 50 connections or less, and can be directly connected with fiber, I generally will not segment them. Conversely, if each location has more than 50 connections or cannot be linked by fiber (that is, a connection such as a Frame Relay or a T1 is needed) I will almost always segment them. However, if the network is large enough (in one geographic location) you might need to find another basis for your segmentation. Some large corporations (inhabiting equally large office buildings) can have hundreds of people per floor. In this case you can find yourself segmenting network traffic every couple of floors.

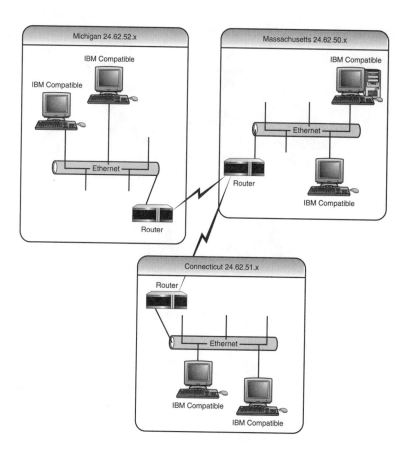

FIGURE 2.4

Network segmentation.

Returning to CSMA/CD, if the PC waiting to send information hears traffic on the network, it will not transmit. This is the *collision detection* part of CSMA/CD. The NIC then waits a random amount of time before listening again for traffic. As soon as the NIC detects no traffic on the line, it transmits the data it needs to send.

However, at some point a network gets so large that CSMA/CD begins to affect performance. The more devices you have on a network, the longer each one must wait before transmitting. The access method will need to wait longer with each new device added to the network. Unfortunately there is no magic number here. I can't tell you *x* amount of devices is too many for CSMA/CD to keep up with. The easiest way to learn this is by watching your network performance and looking out for collisions.

Most connectivity devices have a collision light, or a software-based collision monitor. If your device has a collision light you should see it flicker every now and then. (Collisions are pretty unavoidable in large networks, so expect to see some collision activity.) When the light starts to flicker constantly or even to turn solid for a period of time, you have an issue.

Software-based collision monitors can offer you more information (number of packets lost, number of collisions, and so forth), but it can be harder to interpret the meaning of all the numbers. The best way to approach this is to baseline your network. By running the software during peak and non-peak times on your network, you can establish a baseline by which to gauge future activity. If future scans by the software start to show large spikes in the collision activity, you might have a problem.

The unfortunate piece of this equation is that if you have a large unsegmented network, chances are it is going to be a pain to fix. The key here is prevention. You don't want to leave a job only to have the client call someone else in to fix it.

> **NOTE**
>
> Here is a quick note on software-based collision monitors. As a rule of thumb, I sub-tract 3%–5% from the total I get from these. I find that many software-based colli-sion monitors cause collisions themselves. Keep that in mind. Again, prevention is the key. Designing a network correctly (segmenting when necessary) will save you headaches later. You don't want to spend your time hunting down collisions if it's not necessary.

Preventing Collisions in Your Designs

Following are some simple design tips that can save you many headaches. As almost any net-work designer will attest to, segmenting existing networks is difficult.

For a network of fewer than 50 PCs, 10Mbps should suffice. I assume (for this example) that you have CAT 5 to the desktop. If you have more then 50 PCs, then 100Mbps is your best bet. If the network is going to transmit massive amounts of information such as Web-based com-merce or fully rendered animation, then that's when you consider 1Gbps Ethernet.

> **NOTE**
>
> Remember, right now we are finding out whether Ethernet is right for you. These cri-teria will not be the only ones you need to consider in all situations.

When designing an Ethernet network from the ground up, you should also keep in mind the fact that someone else will administer this network when you leave.

2

LAN SPECIFICS

Designing with the Administrator in Mind

You can use three design techniques to plan an Ethernet network that will help the new administrator. The first and most important is to design for growth.

Find out in the beginning whether the company plans to expand in the near future. This information can be vital to the final shape of your design. For example, suppose you have a start-up Web company of 25 people in New Mexico. Next year they plan to finalize a buyout of an ISP in Denver (for the purpose of utilizing the servers in Denver). As for the Ethernet LAN in New Mexico, how would you design it? Figure 2.5 illustrates the new network in New Mexico.

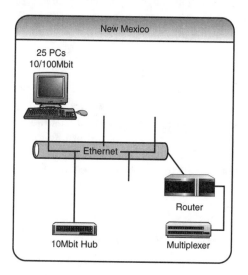

FIGURE 2.5

The new network in New Mexico.

It would have been perfectly all right to design this network as a 10Mbps Ethernet based on what we know and the guidelines we have. However, one year from now the client would be scrambling to upgrade the network. A better solution might be 100Mbps Ethernet. This way we have designed for growth, and the client now has enough Ethernet breathing room for the impending acquisition. Here is a second solution for the same problem.

In this example I have chosen to go with fiber to the desktop, a pretty bold move, even by my standards. My justifications are twofold. First, the client really isn't sure what kind of business they will be doing a couple of years from now. If they will need to transmit large animations (or other graphic and data-intensive designs) from the desktops to Denver, they will require a big pipe to do it through. Fiber will help the transition to 1Gbps Ethernet. Secondly, with only 25 PCs to link, the cost at the desktop is not as great now (as opposed to waiting until after the merger). Fiber as a desktop solution is still very cost prohibitive, but don't overlook it if the conditions are right.

Working with Fiber

When you are working with fiber there are several things you need to consider.

Although fiber is more flexible than coax, it is not nearly as flexible as twisted pair. Fiber can be brittle, so be careful how you run it. When running fiber, kinks in the cable can be a problem.

Keep track of the running length of your fiber. Depending on the type of the fiber you are using, you can achieve runs between 2–14km. Multi-mode fiber (using a standard light-emitting diode) is accurate up to 2km, whereas single-mode fiber (using a laser emitting diode) has been tested up to 14km. (Single-mode fiber and equipment is more expensive than its multi-mode counterparts.)

Make sure the types of fiber, transceivers, and equipment all match up. If you are using single-mode equipment you need single-mode cable and transceivers. That may sound logical, but it can be easy to get them mixed up.

This design does have its Achilles heel. The connectivity devices cost the same whether you connect 20 or 120 devices to them. That, by itself, can be a great expense. If this company does not buy the Denver ISP, they have the glorious distinction of owning the fastest 25-person network in the country. Figure 2.6 illustrates a better design option for the New Mexico office.

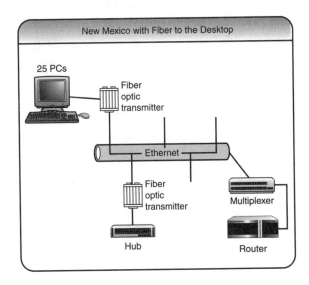

FIGURE 2.6

Another design for the New Mexico office.

Another thing to consider when designing for the new administrator is to centrally locate all of your equipment. A clean, neat data center is essential. You can start by using professional rack equipment. This equipment can include computer racks, patch panels, and cable management ties. (You will get more referrals from a well-managed data center than you will from having chosen the fastest speed for the network.)

You should also (if you haven't already) invest in a label gun, and label, label, label. The new administrator (or team) should not have to hunt for equipment in your data center. If you clearly label every piece of equipment, everyone will be happier. I tend to label equipment with the following information.

Server (PC)	Connectivity Device	Patch Panel
Computer Name	Device's Name	Label each port with a number or letter corresponding to the and office the port runs to.
Protocol Address	Role (router, switch, so on.)	
Number corresponding to the computer's port on a KVM (Keyboard, Video, Mouse) switch if applicable	Protocol Address	I also color-code the cables. I use blue cables for servers, gray for PCs, yellow for terminals, and so on.

The purpose here is to make the transition between you and the client as seamless as possible.

The final key is to document everything. You would be surprised at how many networks I have walked into and had to figure out what was going on without the aid of documentation. If you document everything on the network the client won't have any guesswork to do. Your referrals will go through the roof.

Upgrading Ethernet

It is very easy to upgrade an existing Ethernet network (as opposed to a Token-Ring network). Most network cards on the market today are 10/100, so you might just need to upgrade the connectivity device. Swapping out a 10Mb hub for a 100Mb switch will do wonders for a slow network (10Mb NICs are still widely in use, especially in older networks—the kind of networks you would probably be upgrading). Therefore, always check the NIC speed before making assumptions.

In this chapter I wanted to give you what you need to figure out whether Ethernet is right for the network you're designing. If you're just as confused now as you were when you started the chapter, don't worry. After we cover a few more topics you'll be designing networks with the best of them.

Token Ring Explained

Token-Ring networks were prevalent 5–10 years ago. However, today you don't see as many as you used to. The majority of the Token-Ring networks you will see will be part of integration jobs. For this reason you need to know how they work.

You need to know how Token Ring works for most jobs involving an older company, especially if mainframes are involved. When IBM developed Token Ring they built it into all of their mainframe products. Many older companies that run mainframes such as the AS/400 will most likely run Token Ring. Walt Disney World is an example of this. The main reservations system is housed on multiple AS/400s. Therefore, the majority of the resort was Token Ring until about 1996, when the company started working Ethernet into the newer designs.

One feature of Token Ring that lends itself to making Walt Disney World's network successful is its management toolset. Walt Disney World spans multiple geographic locations, which can make it hard to manage. For this reason, Token Ring has features such as the Active Monitor (discussed later in the chapter) that aid in the troubleshooting of a large network. These tools can prove invaluable to a network administrator working on a large network.

For a company such as Walt Disney World, Token Ring works and it works well. To communicate with a mainframe, clients need to transmit flat text files. These files are not bandwidth intensive (usually consisting of a few kilobytes). When you're transmitting nothing but reservations data (dinner, hotel, or entertainment), your files tend to be fewer than a hundred lines of text. These small transfers are perfect for Token Ring (anything larger and Token Ring might not be able to keep up with it).

Should you not design Token-Ring networks for clients wanting new networks? In some cases I would say leave that decision up to the client. However, it is your responsibility to design the best network possible for the client's needs. This may mean advising the client of other (more economic) choices to fulfill the client's expectations. Token-Ring networks do have their place, even as a new network. Your job is to be able to recognize it.

Token-Ring Cabling

If you actually run across a Token-Ring network you will find it cabled in one of two fashions. The first (and older) method is using coaxial cabling. Coax cabling looks like cable TV wire. The coaxial cabling is attached to the PC using a T connector (see Figure 2.7).

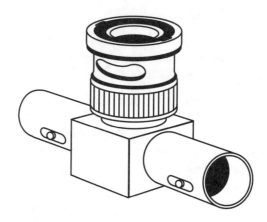

FIGURE 2.7
A coaxial T connector.

One side of the T attaches to the PC to the right, and the other side attaches to the PC to the left. In this manner the PCs actually do form a physical ring. The other method looks similar to Ethernet. CAT 5 or IBM Type 1 cables run to the desktop, thus forming a physical star. However, the connectivity device is a MAU, or Multiple Access Unit. The job of the MAU is to form a ring. (See Chapter 7 for further explanation of how a MAU functions.)

How Is Token Ring Different from Ethernet?

One difference that will jump right out at anyone setting up a Token-Ring network is the transfer rates. Token Ring can only transfer data at 4Mbps or 16Mbps. Compare this to Ethernet, which is capable of transferring data at up to 10Gbps, and the difference is clear—Token Ring is just plain slow.

This might seem extremely slow, but if Token Ring is implemented at companies with certain kinds of traffic needs, the slowness does not become a factor. In terms of network speed, in Token Ring the network connectivity device does not determine the overall speed of the network. In Ethernet, the hub or switch on the network determines what speed data flowing over the network can travel. In Token Ring, the connectivity device is usually an unintelligent MAU. This means that the speed of the NIC determines the speed of the network. A Token-Ring network card is 4, 16, or 4/16Mbps. However, unlike Ethernet, most 4/16 cards are not auto-sensing. In fact, most dual-speed Token-Ring cards are hardware configurable. This makes upgrading Token Ring from one speed to another very difficult. Why? Every device on a Token-Ring network needs to be the same speed or the entire network could grind to a halt.

This also means that all Token-Ring NICs on the same network need to be the same speed or you will get a beacon. A beacon is an alert sent (in essence) to all clients on a Token-Ring network. If left alone, beacons can bring a Token-Ring network to its knees.

Another difference between Ethernet and Token Ring is the topology of the two.

One very crucial difference between Token Ring and Ethernet is that Token Ring is exactly that, a ring. Every computer on a Token-Ring network is connected to every other computer on the network in order. Figure 2.8 illustrates this logically.

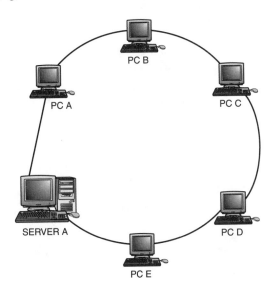

FIGURE 2.8
A Token-Ring "logical ring" design.

If PC A wanted to send information to Server A, the data would hit every PC along the way. The information from PC A would stop at PC B. PC B would realize it was not meant for that device and send it along to PC C. This would happen until the information finally reached Server A. This process has one big drawback (see Figure 2.9).

Take out PC B, for example, and the information leaving PC A stops. The ring is broken and the entire network goes down. Some designers implement what is known as self-repairing or redundant rings (see Figure 2.10).

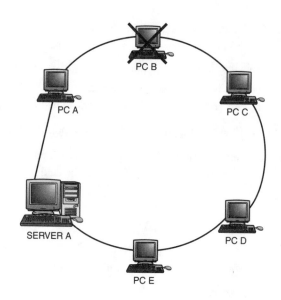

FIGURE 2.9

A broken ring.

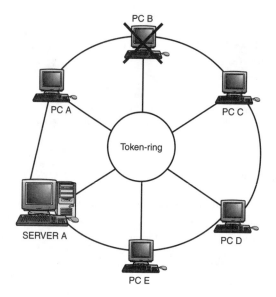

FIGURE 2.10

A self-repairing or redundant ring.

When a second ring is in place, it picks up the slack when a failure occurs in the primary ring. In the previous example the data traveling from PC A would jump to the second ring and head back to Server A. The second ring always travels in the opposite direction of the first.

If you have a failure on the second ring, you are out of luck. However, as far as redundancy goes, it works pretty well.

How Does Information Travel Around the Ring(s)?

Token Ring, like Ethernet, implements an access method to control which PCs talk on the network and when. The access method employed by Token Ring is aptly called *token passing*.

The big toe when it comes to token passing is the Active Monitor.

> The Active Monitor is established randomly through an election. The Active Monitor is one of those geek tools that I mentioned earlier. Active Monitor is one of those things that make working with Token Ring almost fun. When an Active Monitor is selected, it is the king of the network until users turn their PCs off. (That's the other fun thing about Active Monitor—you never know if your PC is it.) Once the current Active Monitor is offline, a new one is randomly chosen.
>
> The job of the Active Monitor is to send out tokens, repair tokens, monitor the ring for breaks, and keep track of upstream and downstream neighbors.

The Active Monitor can be any PC on the Token-Ring network. When a user's PC is chosen as the Active Monitor, it remains so until it is taken off the network. The Active Monitor sends out the first token.

The token is simply a few bits of information that continually travel around the ring. When the token hits a PC, the PC determines whether it has any data to send out. If the PC does have data to transmit, it attaches that data to the end of the token and sends it back onto the ring. The token is then processed by every PC on the ring until it reaches the intended recipient of the information. When the recipient PC releases the token, the process starts over again.

NOTE

One quick note on Active Monitors. The Active Monitor is chosen by network address. This means that it is not uncommon to have a printer chosen as Active Monitor. Most of the time this is not an issue. However, if the printer has a sleep mode that kicks in fairly regularly, that could create havoc on the ring.

What Else Does the Active Monitor Do?

The other major job of the Active Monitor is to watch the ring for breaks. The Active Monitor does this by sending out a status token every seven seconds. This status token tells every device on the ring the address of the Active Monitor. The next PC to receive this token is known as the upstream neighbor. The *upstream neighbor* records in its cache the information about the Active Monitor and who its upstream and downstream neighbors are.

If a PC does not receive a status token in a seven-second time frame, it assumes that its downstream neighbor is off the network (in effect breaking the ring). When this happens, the PC beacons.

Beaconing in Token Ring

When a PC does not receive a status token from its downstream neighbor, it sends out a beacon. A beacon contains three pieces of information: the address of the machine sending the beacon, the address of its downstream neighbor (the machine suspected of breaking the ring), and the type of beacon (in this case, a ring break). The beacon circles the ring until the issue is resolved.

To see beacons and Active Monitor information you need a third-party tool such as a LAN sniffer. These tools are an absolute requirement for larger Token Rings or mixed networks. The sniffers will display all of the information in the tokens and usually other helpful information.

Token Ring might not have caught on because of its complexity, but it has the tools to make it manageable. If you have ever worked with Token Ring this was probably enough to scare you off. However, don't be intimidated by it, because Token Ring is a good topology when it is taken care of. The information in this section should be enough for you to effectively design and manage a mixed network, but I would read an entire Token-Ring book before trying to set up a Token-Ring network from scratch.

Designing Mixed Networks

Designing a mixed network can be tricky at best. A mixed network occurs when a client integrates two or more network topologies. The most common mixed network is an Ethernet/Token-Ring network. Usually the client will have an existing Token-Ring network and an Ethernet network will be integrated with it.

Mixed networks can function very effectively when done correctly. When designing a mixed network, keep in mind the places where each network topology excels and where each fails. Careful planning will mean the difference between one good mixed network and two failures.

Companies are becoming more diversified. Larger companies are constantly acquiring smaller ones without thought as to their network infrastructure. Situations such as these are the breeding ground for mixed networks.

When Can Mixed Networks Work?

A mixed network can function extremely well when each topology stays within its functional guidelines. This means that the Token-Ring network is used where Token Ring is most effective and Ethernet is used where Ethernet is most effective. One common mistake made when designing mixed networks is leaving the older (usually Token-Ring) network alone and designing a new (Ethernet network) to coincide with it.

> **NOTE**
>
> This might seem to contradict the statements I made in the introduction of the book. I realize that networks should be designed with a greater picture in mind. Global networking is key to the survival of any business. Don't let a mixed network diminish that. Think of the two topologies as parts of a greater whole.
>
> This is one of the only areas where I will advocate micro-network design. To have a mixed network that functions well, each part must work with the other, not against it. If one topology handles a part of the network that would be better served by the other, the two are not working together.

Making Sure Each Topology Does Its Part

For the rest of this chapter, I will assume two things (safely). The first is that your mixed network will be composed of Ethernet and Token Ring. The second is that the Token-Ring network is the older, existing network. The reason for the assumptions is that 99.9% of mixed networks you will need to design will follow that pattern. All but one of the mixed networks I have designed has fit into this mold. The other .1% will most likely be a client with an existing Ethernet network who is setting up an AppleTalk network and wants the two to be happy together. Because so few companies are rushing to design AppleTalk (or AirTalk) networks, I won't discuss them specifically, but the same rules apply. The network diagrams for the one Mac-to-PC mixed network that I designed are included in the book.

Many mixed networks are the result of corporate takeovers. When one company buys another, there is usually a part of that company that they want. Here's where you need to look at the network roles. Imagine a band of venture capitalists with their eyes on a small Midwestern chain of travel agencies. There are only three of them in two towns (encompassing about 5 miles). The small company has a tiny, informational Web site where it does some advertising and order requests. The Web site is created and hosted internally by a team of three people. They run a small but effective Token-Ring network. The venture capitalists have an idea. They are going to create BUY-YOUR-TICKETS-HERE.COM, the world's largest Internet travel agency. Finally, to give the Web site an edge, they are going to complement it with a small chain of Midwestern brick-and-mortar agencies. The three-person team in the Midwest will continue to work on the Web site.

You are called in to design the new network for BUY-YOUR-TICKETS-HERE.COM. How do you do it? What stays and what goes? The surefire way to fail would be to design the network as shown in Figure 2.11.

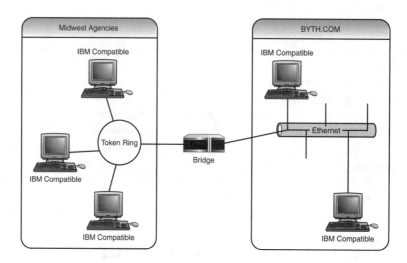

FIGURE 2.11

An incorrect mixed network design.

This network will function (for a short while) if put in place. However, it is definitely not the best network for the job. What this diagram illustrates is the existing Token-Ring network (unchanged) attached to the new Ethernet network. The two networks are simply connected with a bridge (many routers can be used to serve this same purpose). Functionally, this proposal will combine the two networks into one working mixed network.

This network fails in one key area. The three designers who stay in the Midwest will grind the network to a halt. If they continue to work on the Web site (the new and improved biggest Web site in the world), their needs will exceed that of Token Ring. Remember, Token Ring is optimal when network traffic is minimal. Therefore, when these designers start pushing graphics and such back and forth (at a rate needed to support a large Web site), the network will begin to crawl.

To remedy the problem, first look at the existing Token-Ring network. The Ethernet network from the new company must extend into the area where the designers are located. Figure 2.12 shows a new diagram for the Midwest agency; notice the changes.

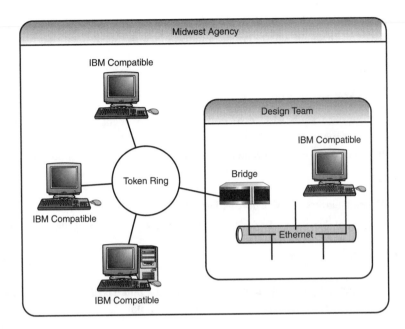

FIGURE 2.12
The Midwest agency's network.

One small change adds years of functionality to the network. In this example, a small Ethernet network was put in place at the Midwest site. Even though this Ethernet network would only support three people, it should be 100Mbps switched. (See Chapter 7 for a explanation of switching.)

The theory behind making the small Ethernet network 100Mbps switched is to allow for a seamless transition to the larger Ethernet network. Now the parts of the network that are adapted to Token Ring (the less trafficked reservations lines) can stay on Token Ring, and the parts that might see growth (the designers) are migrated off. Doing this one small step before tackling the larger job is essential.

Don't be afraid to migrate as much or as little of the old network as you see fit. This is the key to mixed networks.

Specialized Hardware Required to Run a Mixed Network

Because Ethernet and Token Ring use different access methods, they cannot exist together. An intermediary that can distinguish and translate between the two is needed. In the previous diagram I used a bridge to symbolize this piece of hardware. In most cases you will use a specialized router to perform this role.

This chapter introduced you to designing three different networks: Ethernet, Token Ring, and a mix of the two. Although we did not go into too much technical detail, you are well prepared to move on.

Scenarios

Remember our old friends ABCcorp? Following are two scenarios. Start planning networks fitting their requirements and we'll compare notes as we go along. Obviously right now you only know a little bit about what is needed in a network, but we will fill in the gaps as we go.

Scenario 1

Corporate headquarters for ABCcorp, a large online Data Warehouse, are in a new building in Boston. ABCcorp has 100 employees and will occupy two floors of the office building. The sales staff will work exclusively from the road.

Scenario 2

ABCcorp (fitting the preceding requirements) has just purchased XYZ Inc, a small database developer group located in Orlando. They have 20 employees and occupy a small office suite. Their existing network is 16Mbps Token Ring.

Summary

- A network type is the blueprint for how a network will function. The type will dictate how information gets from point A to point B and will also dictate what the rest of your design looks like.

- The two major network types in use today are Ethernet and Token Ring.

- Ethernet began in 1972 as Aloha Net. Developed by XEROX PARC, it was the first practical computer network standard.

- IBM developed Token Ring several years later.

- Ethernet is capable of four transfer rates: 10Mbps, 100Mbps, 1Gbps, and 10Gbps. The most common transfer rate is 100Mbps. The speed of the connectivity devices determines the overall speed of the network. Ethernet utilizes a media access method known as CSMA/CD. CMSA/CD monitors the network for traffic. When no traffic is on the line, the PC is permitted to transmit.

- Token Ring is capable of two speeds: 4Mbps and 16Mbps. Token Ring is considerably slower than Ethernet and is best suited for networks with less traffic.

- In Token Ring the NIC determines the speed of the network, not the connectivity device. If one PC on a Token-Ring network has a NIC of a different speed than the others, a beacon will be generated.

- Beacons are warnings sent out by PCs on a Token-Ring network. They can clog the network with unnecessary traffic.

- The most common kind of mixed network is Ethernet/Token Ring. The most common kind of Ethernet/Token-Ring network occurs when a company has an existing Token-Ring network and adds an Ethernet segment.

- When designing mixed networks, do not ignore the existing network. More often than not, the existing network will need some overhauling.

Network Operating Systems

IN THIS CHAPTER

The network operating system (NOS) is to a network what the CEO is to a business. The main job of a network operating system is securing access to the network. To perform this function the NOS either allows or denies access to a user based on any number of credentials. This form of network security can range from the simplistic to the elaborate. Windows 9x, for example, when used in a workgroup setting can allow access to network resources based on the address of the machine. In other words, if a machine has the correct network address, it can access all of the resources on a network. (This is not extremely secure.) Novell NetWare, on the other hand, can allow, deny, or restrict access to one, some, or all resources on a network according to user traits.

Of course, the NOS is not concerned only with security. As network technology has grown, the roles of network servers have become more and more expanded. In the earliest days of networking, the server was the only computer on a network. Mainframes were connected to vast webs of terminals. Thus, users were manipulating data that never left one location.

When PC networking was introduced, the world changed forever. Suddenly everybody could have massive computing power right on his or her own desk. The new breed of server became sentries of information flow. Servers were initially receptacles for miscellaneous files and gateways to centrally located printers. The idea that a desktop computer could replace the power and functionality of a mainframe was ridiculous. However, as the PC revolution gained ground, the line between front office and back office became more defined. Suddenly the prospect of an entire corporation being run on Intel-based machines was actually feasible. Desktop-style servers were no longer the redheaded stepchildren of client/server networking.

As the power of the servers grew, so did the power of the clients. Since server and client computers are based on the same technology, great strides in one equals great strides in the other. There was a need for network operating systems that could not only handle a more powerful server, but also adapt to the growing demands of the clients.

During this time, many developers offered systems capable of meeting these demands. Memorable yet not-so-popular entries into the operating system wars included IBM (OS/2) and Apple. Unfortunately, the OS/2 server and the Apple server never really took off the way they could have.

The products that emerged victorious were Windows NT (with Windows 3.11 through ME) and Novell NetWare. However, some diehards won't consider NetWare a true NOS because of the lack of a client OS. Novell's Client32 is an application, not an operating system.

The big winner in the Intel-based client/server battle seems to be Microsoft. Love it or hate it, there is no denying that Windows NT is the premier NOS available. Does it have its shortcomings? Of course, and we'll cover them later in this chapter.

This chapter introduces you to Windows NT/2000 as an operating system for a newly designed Ethernet network. This chapter also covers operating in a mixed environment with Novell NetWare. (These are not necessarily the same mixed environments discussed in the previous chapter.)

Why are we focusing on Windows as the operating system for a newly designed network? When designing networks, you need to plan for the most stability possible. Microsoft (for better or worse) has a large offering of products that are designed to work together. That's not to say they do not work with anything else, but in most cases this is not your money you're playing with. You need to build a product that you know will integrate with every other product on the network (without experimentation).

Planning for Windows NT and 2000

Now that you have a rough idea of the network type ABCcorp (refer to the scenario outlined in Chapter 1) needs to run, you need to decide what OS will govern the actions of the clients. The operating system itself will dictate the overall layout of the network type you choose, just as much as any other factor.

What you have right now should be a sketch of a network. Obviously you can't get into much detail because you have only a fraction of the information you need. What you do have should look like what you see in Figure 3.1.

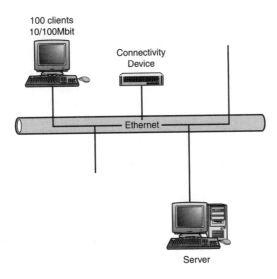

FIGURE 3.1

Preliminary network design.

You know that you need an Ethernet network with 100 clients, a server, and a connectivity device. Based on the information given to you in the previous chapter, this is a fair representation of the network you need.

NOTE

The sample scenarios I gave you did not specifically say the client needs a server or a connectivity device, but you should have been able to figure that part out.

You've decided that you will go with a Microsoft operating system for the server, but which one do you pick (Windows NT 4.0 or Windows 2000)? Then you need client software; do you pick Windows NT, 98, ME, or 2000?

Choosing Your Server

When choosing your Microsoft server, you really have only two choices: Windows NT 4.0 and Windows 2000. Everyone likes to have the biggest, newest technology, but you need to look at the established history of a product as well. Windows NT has been on the market for a while now; it has a proven record. This is important with regard to stability. You don't know who will be administering your network when you're gone. Seasoned NT administrators are easier to locate than seasoned 2000 administrators, if there is such a thing.

Most peripheral software products available for networks by Microsoft were updated for Windows NT most recently. This means that these particular products (Exchange 5.5, SQL Server 7.0, and SMS 2.0, to name a few) were made to work with Windows NT 4.0. Until more products are updated to work with Windows 2000 (and until the operating system has some history behind it), I will continue to design for Windows NT.

Novell also has more than one offering on the server operating system table. The newest operating system released from Novell is NetWare 5.1, a very strong, robust server environment. However, you may come across a couple of different versions of NetWare if you are dealing with pre-existing networks. NetWare 3.12 and 4.1 are two very popular and very different versions of the Novell operating system. I have run across more 3.12 servers in production environments than any other release of NetWare. (Novell discontinued support of NetWare 3.12 in May of 2000.)

The last of the more popular operating systems are Unix (the workhorse of operating systems) and Linux. Many die-hard Unix techs are going to scoff at the way I used Unix and Linux in the same sentence. However, they are extremely similar. Most of the differences between the two operating systems are in the packaging or the non-kernel stuff.

Unix comes in four main flavors: BSD, HP, AIX, and SCO. Each has its own set of tools and devices that set it apart from the others, but at the core of each is a kernel that is relatively similar. As one of the oldest operating systems available, Unix has developed many traits that make it desirable in a server environment. One thing that almost every network administrator will point to as the single strongest attribute of Unix is its stability.

For a long time, Linux was the redheaded stepchild of Unix. However, Linux has come into its own within the last few years. Like Unix, Linux is based on a kernel. The major difference between Unix and Linux is that Linus Torvalds released the kernel for Linux free to anyone who wants it. Numerous manufacturers have created different flavors of Linux. Some of the standouts include Corel, Red Hat, Mandrake, and Caldera, but there are many more.

Windows NT Domains

The basic structure of a Windows NT network is the domain model. A domain is a logical grouping of network devices. All users within this logical grouping or domain share certain things such as resources and privileges. Each domain on your network needs a name, in our case ABCcorp. All PCs on the network will be given the domain name ABCcorp. This will identify them as being part of the ABCcorp domain.

> **NOTE**
>
> This will become more evident as we move along, but the domain name is not the same as the computer name. Every PC on each domain needs a name that is unique in that domain. For example, Joe's PC may be called JoePC. If you have more than one domain on your network, you can use JoePC again on the other domains, but not in ABCcorp.

> The domain name you choose helps to determine the Fully Qualified Domain Name (FQDN) of the network. The FQDN is used to identify PCs and networks. In the example in the preceding note, Joe's FQDN would be joepc.abccorp.com. Anyone who has navigated around the Internet is familiar with FQDN. The address www.marzdesign.com simply points the browser to the computer www on the domain marzdesign.

A domain generally consists of a PDC (primary domain controller), possibly one or more BDCs (backup domain controllers), and the client PCs. The domain controllers are Windows NT servers that were assigned the role of PDC or BDC at the time Windows was installed. This is why you need to plan out your network ahead of time.

The job of the PDC is to be the receptacle for the master Security Account Manager (SAM) database. This is a glorified way of saying the PDC keeps track of who has rights for what. The PDC also authenticates users and is the main administration point on the network.

A BDC also has a copy of the SAM, but it uses it only in case the PDC fails. If the PDC becomes unavailable, the BDC is promoted, in essence becoming the PDC. The BDC will remain as the PDC until it detects that the original PDC is back online. The BDC also authenticates users to take some of the load off the PDC. For example, if you have a large domain with a PDC and multiple BDCs, a user would be authenticated by the machine that is physically closest to him. Before installing PDCs and BDCs, you need to determine which domain model is right for your job.

NT Domain Models

Windows NT provides the capability for three domain models: the single domain, the master domain, and the multiple master domain. Microsoft doesn't mention it in its literature on domains, but there is a fourth domain model, a complete trust domain. Each model serves a different purpose and a different configuration of computers. Which domain is right for you? The following sections go over the technical specifications.

Single Domain Model

A single domain model is exactly what the name implies: a single domain. Usually consisting of one PDC and a few clients, the single domain model is best suited for small networks. Figure 3.2 illustrates the Microsoft single domain model.

> **NOTE**
>
> We both know that you need to plan what to do if the PDC should crash. However, a client will think that you don't have enough faith in your work to leave it alone. Be as diplomatic as possible when stating your needs as a designer. Some companies may cringe when you tell them you want to add the cost of another server to the line and some may not, but the least you can do is deliver the information as harmlessly as possible.

Microsoft's rules on a single domain model are as follows. Windows NT can accommodate a SAM database size of 40Mb. This translates to 26,000 users and 250 groups (thus the 40/26000/250 rule). This is more than most companies will ever need. However, it may not be the most practical solution.

Just because a single PDC theoretically can handle up to 26,000 users does not necessarily mean that it should. In almost every case, I would suggest introducing a BDC to a single domain for fault tolerance. If anything happens to the PDC, you need to have a backup in place. Microsoft's specification on BDCs is one for every 2,000 users. I find that this estimate provides for an unnecessarily low number of BDCs. I like to plan for one BDC regardless of the number of employees. This provides fault tolerance if the PDC should need to be brought offline for maintenance.

I also like to add one BDC for each separate geographic location. If the company is large and is spread out on more than one floor of an office building, I consider each floor another geographic location. I do this to adjust the design, saving on network traffic and possible delays. Also, I add one BDC (in addition to the first BDC on the network) per 500 users in one location. This should give plenty of guidelines to design by.

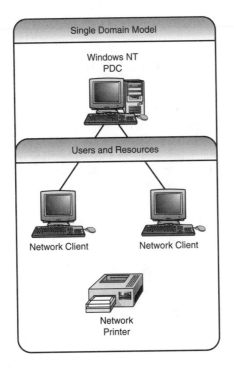

FIGURE 3.2

Microsoft single domain model.

Here is the calculation used by Microsoft to arrive at the 40/26,000/250 rule:

Object	Space Used
Users Account	1.0k
Computer Account	.5k
Group Account (up to 300 members)	4.0k

The maximum number of users you can have on a PDC before you hit the 40Mb SAM size limit is 26,000 (with 250 groups). You should make a note of this if you are planning a large network.

Master Domain Model

A master domain is geared more toward large-scale enterprises with multiple geographic locations serving different purposes. In a master domain model, one domain serves as the master. This domain is charged with authenticating users and is the holder of the SAM database. The PDC serves the same purpose in a master domain as in a single domain.

The difference in a master domain is the presence of secondary or resource domains. A resource domain will have a PDC and a unique domain name. However, in the resource domain the users will be authenticated by the PDC of the master domain. The resource domains will contain local resources for the users of the particular domain. This means that the users in the resource domains will use files and printers in their own domains, not the master domain.

This is accomplished through the use of trusts. The smaller resource domains have one-way trusts with the master domain.

Trusts in Windows NT allow one domain to have particular rights or access to resources or users in another domain. There are two different kinds of trusts: one-way and two-way.

The master domain model (because it is similar in function to the single domain model) has the same technical limitations as the single domain model. Figure 3.3 illustrates the master domain model.

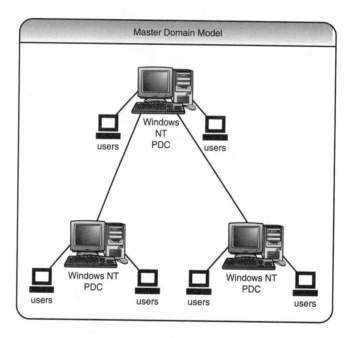

FIGURE 3.3

Microsoft master domain model.

A master domain model is good for companies that span large geographic distances. If you have a main office in New York and equally large offices in Los Angeles and Miami, a master domain model will work best. The New York office will be the master domain, with Los Angeles and Miami as the resource domains.

Multiple Master Domain

A multiple master domain consists of two or more master domains linked at the top by trusts. In this case the master domains function as separate domains. However, the two master PDCs are linked by a two-way trust. The resource domains have a one-way trust with each master domain. This enables users in one master domain to access the resources in the other. A domain model such as this would be used when two large companies with existing master domains merge. Another use of the multiple master domain model would be between a large manufacturing company and its equally large warehouse.

If the warehouse has small offices around the state (or other geographic areas), each with its own internal departments, then the multiple master domain model would be successful. In the multiple master domain model, each master domain is capable of accommodating 26,000 users per master domain. Therefore, a multiple master domain consisting of three master domains would provide for as many as 78,000 users. Figure 3.4 illustrates the multiple master domain model.

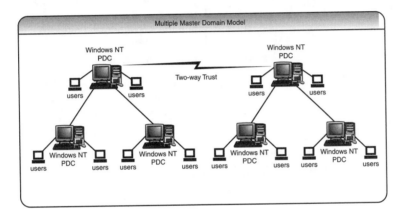

FIGURE 3.4
Microsoft multiple master domain model.

Trusts

A trust in Windows NT is a unique privilege reserved for servers. A trust simply states that one domain has the right to the users and groups from another domain. It is universally recognized that there are two kinds of trusts: one-way trusts and two-way trusts. A one-way trust allows users in one domain to access the resources in another, but the users in the second domain have no rights in the first domain.

A two-way trust, theoretically, goes in both directions. However, this is not entirely true. A two-way trust is actually two one-way trusts. This may seem like nitpicking, but there is a big difference. A two-way trust implies that one person sets up a rule allowing two domains to communicate. In fact, a one-way trust needs to be set up on each domain to create a two-way trust. This assumes a certain level of administrative expertise in running both domains.

Let's look at design for ABCcorp. It has 100 employees occupying two floors of an office building. Which domain model would be the best fit for the company's needs, based on the information you have?

Figure 3.5 shows the network diagram I came up with.

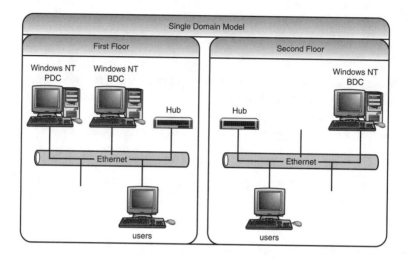

FIGURE 3.5
Sample network for ABCcorp.

The PDC is located on the first floor with one BDC, which will provide fault tolerance and take some of the load off the PDC. With the small number of users and the relatively small geographic area, the single domain model works best, although the other domain models could be made to work.

Installing Windows NT with Domain Models in Mind

We won't cover the entire process of installing Windows NT Server. Rather, we will look at how to create the domain model you design. You might be asked not only to design the network but also to have some role in its implementation. Even if you have experience installing Windows NT Server, you don't want to skip this.

First, you need a set of Windows NT installation disks. If you don't have a set, make one. I never go on a job without a set of Windows NT startup disks.

Making a set of startup disks is easy. First, make sure you have three preformatted disks on hand. Insert the Windows NT 4.0 Server CD and run `winnt.exe` (or `winnt32.exe`, depending upon your situation). Then follow the prompts to create the system disks.

NOTE

We haven't covered server hardware yet (that's the next chapter), but for this installation we will assume that there is a RAID 5 controller in the server.

Once you have a set of setup disks, insert the first one into the server and boot. (Windows NT can be installed with the use of setup disks, and that's why I am so adamant about using them.) Most servers use a third-party hard disk controller or RAID controller (by a different manufacturer than the server itself). When you use the setup disks, you will be prompted to insert the driver disk for the controller between disks two and three. An installation started by booting directly from the CD often bypasses this part of the setup. The section of the installation that I am referring to here is known as Mass Storage Detection. If you do not supply Windows NT with the driver disk for the controller, the installation will fail because the kernel is unable to see the hard drives.

The next phase of installation that we are concerned with is drive partitioning. Here Windows NT asks you to partition the hard drive and format it with the file system of your choice. Use your best judgment here. Generally if I am installing to a PDC that has 30GB of space, I will create a 2GB C: drive. I will then leave the rest unpartitioned. This enables me to use Windows NT Disk Administrator to play around with the remaining 28GB. After you choose the size of the C: drive, the installer will ask you to pick a file system. I suggest you pick FAT.

During Windows NT installation, you have two choices for file systems: FAT and NT File System (NTFS). FAT has been around since the days of DOS, and it offers nothing in the way of file security. Windows NT was built to run on NTFS, which supports file security. Using NTFS is how you implement user access security.

A FAT partition cannot see into an NTFS partition; they are two different animals. If you format the C: drive as NTFS and for some reason you need to boot the server off a boot disk, you will be looking at an empty machine. You won't even be able to see a C: drive. This is because the boot disk you are using is FAT. That is why I format the C: drive as FAT. If I need to, I can boot the server with a standard boot disk. This gives me the ability to edit suspect files in DOS and fix problems. I then use Windows NT Disk Administrator to format the remaining space as one large NTFS drive.

If you format C: as FAT and E: as NTFS, how can you do anything?

Once again there is an exception to everything. In this case the exception is Windows NT itself. Windows NT can view and manipulate both FAT and NTFS. The problem is that when you boot off a boot disk, the machine is no longer using Windows NT, it is using the operating system that made the boot disk (such as Windows 95 or Windows 98). There is no such thing as an NTFS boot disk; the formatting information is just too large.

Finally, after the kernel has installed, the server will reboot itself, and you will begin configuring Windows.

3

NETWORK
OPERATING
SYSTEMS

NOTE

The Windows NT kernel is the brain of Windows NT. The kernel is the interface between the programs (including the operating system itself) and the processor.

There are two things you want to pay close attention to during configuration. After you pick a name for the server, Windows NT will ask you to designate the server type. This is the most important option in the setup. This is irreversible, and if you mess up this step, the only way out is to reinstall the server.

The three choices for server type are primary domain controller (PDC), backup domain controller (BDC), and member (or standalone) server. Looking back at our design, we need one PDC and one BDC. (In the next chapter I will discuss what hardware is best to use for which type of controller.) Therefore, we will choose PDC for the server type.

You need to install your PDC first. When you choose BDC as a server type, Windows NT will prompt you for the name of the PDC and try to contact it. If Windows is unsuccessful in contacting the PDC, you will not be allowed to continue setting up as a BDC. You will be forced to pick PDC or member server.

What Is a Member Server?

Member servers are very valuable to a network. Chances are the network you are designing will need more than two servers (the PDC and the BDC). You may need a server to house a large application of some sort, for example. You don't want to set up another BDC for that purpose, so you use a member server. Member servers do not authenticate users, nor do they have a copy of the SAM database. They simply serve as resources, with no responsibility to the domain. Member servers can be moved between domains at will, whereas a PDC or a BDC is bound to the domain on which it is installed.

This is convenient, especially in master or multiple master domains where you have several domains in one company.

How Does This Differ from Windows 2000?

Many books have already been written on Windows 2000 and many more on Active Directory and Windows 2000 domains. If you plan to design a network using only Windows 2000, I suggest you pick up one of those other titles or get a subscription to *Microsoft TechNet*.

If you just want to add one or two Windows 2000 servers to a Windows NT network, they can be added just as any other Windows NT server would be. However, if you want to upgrade your PDC to Windows 2000, you must run your domain in "mixed mode." Your network will need to continue running in mixed mode until all of the domain controllers have been upgraded.

Introduction to Novell

This section covers Novell so as to give you enough information to design a mixed network successfully. In most mixed networks, you will likely encounter NetWare as an existing operating system on a network. Novell NetWare has gone through many changes over the years. This section compares and contrasts the major points of releases 3.12, 4.0, 4.11, and 5.0.

What's the Difference?

The default protocol supported in all versions of NetWare (excluding version 5) is IPX/SPX. IPX/SPX is a proprietary protocol developed by Novell specifically for NetWare. TCP/IP was an add-in product. (Microsoft implements a protocol called NWLink IPX for compatibility with Novell servers.) This made it very hard to design a mixed network. Most of the time you were required to use a protocol gateway to span mixed networks. However, with Microsoft's implementation of NWLink and Novell's use of the IP add-in, the task became a little easier.

Novell noticed that most network designers were choosing to implement TCP/IP as a routed protocol, so they made some changes to NetWare. Novell now uses TCP/IP as the default protocol for NetWare versions 5 and higher.

While we are on the subject of protocols, another major change to NetWare with version 5 is in the client. All versions of NetWare prior to version 5 came bundled with a client application called Client32. Client32 was installed on the desktop PC and acted as an authentication agent for the Novell network. The problem was that Client32 used Novell's TCP/IP stack. (That's Novell's implementation of the protocol. Not all implementations of the same protocol are the same under the hood.) When Client32 was installed on a desktop running a Microsoft operating system (using the Microsoft TCP/IP stack), the two IP stacks would often conflict. This made administration a very tough job. Administrators would often find that programs written specifically for the Microsoft IP stack would no longer work as designed.

From an administrative standpoint, it's the little things that matter. For instance, the user setup screen is similar to that of Microsoft Exchange. The NetWare user screen holds a myriad of information tidbits such as phone number and location. Another minor but no less important administrative difference is the messenger. Did you ever use the Send User a Message option in Windows NT Server? In nine and a half years I have never gotten it to work. The messenger in NetWare really works. Why is that so important? If you need everybody to log off the system for any reason (usually a system shutdown), the easiest way is to send a message right to their screens.

What's Different Under the Hood?

As we now know, the Windows NT directory structure is based on domains. Your rights as a user depend on the domain you belong to. The directory employed by Novell in versions of NetWare prior to 4.11 was called bindery. Bindery rights work similarly to domain rights in that the bindery the user is in determines his or her user privileges.

This changed in NetWare 4.11. Novell revolutionized the directory structure market with the tree structure. Now NetWare domains are broken down into units, each one a little larger than the one below it. Each unit has its own body of rights that cascades down to the units below but does not flow up. This means that the uppermost unit may have a rule that says "users in the staff group can access anything," but three units down there may be a rule that says "Joe

3

NETWORK
OPERATING
SYSTEMS

(who just happens to be in the staff group) can't access the accounting volume." Sound familiar? It's the predecessor to Microsoft's Active Directory.

Designing Mixed (OS) Networks

Now that you have a good base to work from, let's look at what it takes to design a mixed network. As you have learned, Novell and Windows are two different operating systems, each with its own strengths and weaknesses.

Networks made up of mixed Microsoft and Novell platforms can work well. Before implementation, you need a strong plan for how the network will operate—that is, what servers the users will be authenticated by and what servers will control resources. While NetWare does have a strong user security scheme, I tend to prefer mixed networks in which the primary authentication server is Windows NT/2000 based.

The Windows NT server acts as the master PDC, authenticating all network users. The NetWare servers, on the other hand, act as the resource controllers. They will govern access to user files and printers.

> **NOTE**
>
> Novell is known for its handling of file and print services. Therefore, let all the files and printers be stored on the NetWare servers. Here the version of NetWare is irrelevant, but for the best results and the easiest installation, use version 5.

In all versions of NetWare before version 5, the default protocol was Novell's IPX/SPX. This is Novell's proprietary protocol. It works well, but IP works a lot better. If you wanted IP, chances are you had to buy an add-on that included IP support. This was rectified in version 5. Novell's NetWare 5 has default support for TCP/IP.

This model works a lot better if installed from scratch. This is the one time I suggest installing NetWare from scratch on a new network. Both operating systems will work a lot better together if they know about each other from the beginning. Install the operating systems from scratch together, and you should have a far better outcome.

There is a preferred order to installing a mixed network. I would start with the Windows NT PDC. This allows you to establish the domain.

Establishing the domain is an essential part of the whole process. The rest of the servers cannot be configured until this is done. On the Windows NT PDC, create all the users needed for the domain. Because this is a modified version of a master domain model, you want all of the users to log in to the Windows NT PDC. After installing the user database, you need to install a service to allow communication to the Novell servers.

The service that enables communication between the two operating systems is Gateway Services for NetWare (GSFN). Installing GSFN will enable users logging in to the Windows NT PDC to have access to the NetWare volumes and printers. For GSFN to work on Windows NT, you must install the NWLink protocol.

> **NOTE**
>
> NWLink is Microsoft's adaptation of Novell's IPX/SPX proprietary protocol. Previously, NetWare 5 IPX/SPX was the default protocol installed on NetWare servers. (TCP/IP was a module that needed to be purchased separately.) NWLink should install automatically when you install Gateway Services for NetWare. If it does not install properly, you can add it through the Network applet in Control Panel. Installation is pretty straightforward. Configuration is the tricky part.

Configuring Gateway Services for NetWare

After the service is installed on your PDC, proceed with your NetWare installation. After NetWare is installed, perform the following steps on the NetWare server:

1. Create a group called NTGATEWAY. This group will contain a user needed by the service.
2. Create a user who is a member of the NTGATEWAY group. This user should have rights to all the areas you want the NT users to access. This user will act as a security template for the NT users coming across the gateway. If this user can't access it, nobody can.

> **NOTE**
>
> Depending on which version of NetWare you are running, you may need to install OS/2 namespace on the volumes NT users save to. For most versions of NetWare, filenames are restricted to the old 8.3 file naming convention. However, if you want your NT users to be able to use long filenames, you must install OS/2 namespace for each volume to which NT users will be saving files.

Now that the user and group information is set up on the NetWare server, you can configure the Gateway service on the NT server.

The first step, as always, is to reboot the Windows NT server. Chances are the server prompted for a reboot after you installed the service, but if it didn't this is your time. Assuming that you log in to the NT server as an administrator equivalent, open Control Panel. In Control Panel you will find an icon for Gateway Services for NetWare.

Setting up Gateway Services for Netware is pretty self-explanatory, with no real surprises. For Novell bindery-mode servers choose the first option: Preferred Server. This drop-down menu should auto-detect the available bindery-mode servers. If the server you are connecting to is using a tree, select the Default Tree and Context option.

After finishing the installation, bring up the Configure Gateway screen.

This is where you need to enable Gateway. The screen will then allow you to enter the user information for NetWare. This is the user you created on the NetWare server in the NTGATEWAY group. Finally, add the NetWare shares to which your NT users will have access.

Summary

- Windows NT operates in a domain structure. Every user in one particular domain adheres to the same body of global rules and privileges.
- Windows NT can be configured into one of three domain models: the single domain model, the master domain model, and the multiple master domain model.
- Windows NT server can play one of three roles within these domains. Windows NT server can be configured as a PDC (primary domain controller), a BDC (backup domain controller), or a member server.
- A single Windows NT PDC is capable of accommodating 26,000 users.
- Member servers are optimal as application servers in environments where they risk moving from one domain to another.
- Before version 5.0 of Novell NetWare, NetWare's default protocol was IPX/SPX. NetWare versions 5.0 and higher now use TCP/IP as the default protocol.
- Novell's tree directory structure is considered the predecessor to Microsoft's Active Directory.
- To operate Windows NT and NetWare in a mixed environment, Gateway Services for NetWare must be configured on the NT server.

The Right Hardware for the Right Job

IN THIS CHAPTER

Your choice of an operating system will do little for you if it is not running on the right hardware. This chapter examines what the right hardware is under certain circumstances.

By now you're probably ready to take a break from ABCcorp and its network. Think of the next two chapters as a commercial break. We are going to step back from the big picture for a minute and look into some details. What hardware makes the server run?

You can put down your pen and paper for now, we won't be doing any specific designs in this chapter. However, we will cover some of the most important information in the book. Choosing the wrong hardware configuration could mean the death of your network. Using hardware that is underpowered or not up to the specifications of the software will result in a slow, unresponsive network. On the other hand, using a hardware configuration that is grossly above that which the software requires could be a waste of resources (technological and financial).

Many administrators look at the requirements for the operating systems they want to install and build their servers based on those specifications. While that is an important factor, operating system requirements make up only one-third of the total requirements of the machine. The other factors you need to consider are third-party software requirements and per-user requirements. This chapter covers all of these factors. The more information you have with which to make a decision, the better your network will be. This information will give you a template by which to gauge the exact hardware needs of your servers.

You may be wondering how complicated it is to find out the requirements for a server and build it. Actually it's not hard at all, but not every server is the same. A Windows NT PDC has different requirements than a BDC, which has different requirements than a member server, and so on. The point is that although the individual processes are not difficult, the act of orchestrating them is. This is a lot of information to digest, but with this information you will be able to design some pretty successful networks.

Overhead

This section deals with the requirements set forth by operating system vendors, in particular Microsoft's requirements for Windows NT 4.0 and Windows 2000. However, the vendor's requirements are only half of the story. The best part of writing a book like this is sharing the fist-hand knowledge of what it really takes to get a server running smoothly. Sometimes the vendors are right, oftentimes they are off a little. Regardless, you will get both sides of the coin here. Table 4.1 lists the requirements for a Windows NT server.

TABLE 4.1   Official Requirements for Windows NT 4.0 Server

Intel Based	RISC Based	Alpha Based
Pentium 133	MIPS R4xOO or equivalent	Alpha First Generation Processor at 150MHz
12MB of RAM	16MB of RAM	16MB of RAM

TABLE 4.1   Continued

Intel Based	RISC Based	Alpha Based
VGA video	VGA video	VGA video
A hard drive with 124MB free	A hard drive with 156MB free	A hard drive with 160MB of Free
3.5" floppy CD-ROM Keyboard		CD-ROM
Mouse		Mouse
Network Card	Network Card	Network Card

> **NOTE**
>
> I have never tried installing Windows NT on a RISC or ALPHA, but I included the specs for the RISC-based version of Windows NT in case you want to try.

Hopefully after looking at those requirements you realize why I haven't jumped on the Windows 2000 bandwagon yet. Even I have to admit I chuckle when I look at these figures.

These requirements were actually enough to get the product running when it was released. However, if you put a server meeting only these requirements on a client's network, your new job will be selling the only boat anchors to run Windows NT.

Following are some more realistic numbers whose only origin is in the trial and error of previous networks. Keep in mind these numbers are the base for the operating system only; we will be adding requirements for software and clients to this. The following are my recommendations for PDCs and BDCs:

- In a Single Domain Model, at least one (if not two) Pentium III 500MHz processor with 128MB of RAM and at least an 18GB RAID 5 array.
- For a Master Domain Model, an 800MHz processor with 128MB of RAM and at least an 18GB RAID 5 array. The requirements for the Multiple Master Domain Model should be the same.

Why the difference in requirements between Single Domain and Master Domain? A Master Domain is going to take a lot more punishment than a Single Domain. The processor is going to need that much more power to just keep ahead of the extra system processes. Things such as rights and authentications need to pass through the processor.

Why 128MB of RAM? This is even easier to justify and took very little job experience to come up with. The minimum amount of RAM you can get on most server machines today is 128MB. (Don't worry if you think that is too little memory, we will be adding to it.) That's it, no brain surgery on that one.

> **NOTE**
>
> RAID stands for Redundant Array of Independent Disks. The number appearing after the word RAID indicates the RAID level. A description of the different RAID levels is provided later in this section.

Why the RAID 5 array? (And what is a RAID 5 array?) Okay, first the "why." You should never put a PDC or BDC on a network without some form of hard drive fault tolerance. Therefore, it should be standard practice to design RAID 5 into all of your servers. A client is never going to yell at you for being too safe. (The exception to this is certain member servers and this is solely dependent on their function. If a member server is deemed non–mission critical, it may not require the added fault tolerance of a RAID 5 array.) However, because the margin separating the servers that need it from those that don't is very thin, I generally put RAID 5 in everything.

Now, what are RAID 5 and a RAID 5 array? When speaking about hard drive fault tolerance, there are seven levels of protection, or RAID. The most popular is RAID 5, also known as "disk striping with parity." In RAID 5 the hard drives (a minimum requirement of three) are divided into stripes. All information written to the drives is written in three parts. Parts one and two are the two halves of the data (just a theoretical example, the data isn't cut exactly in half), while part three is the parity information. The parity information is basically just a road map for reconstructing the data.

These three parts are written to the three drives in alternating order. The first time data is written, drive one will get part one, drive two will get part two, and drive three will get part three. The next time drive one will get part two, drive two will get part three, and drive three will get part one. This distributes all of the data and parity information over all three drives, so if one drive were to fail the others would have enough information on each other to rebuild the data.

RAID 5 is usually not supported by out-of-the-box server hardware. Normally it is either an upgrade to the standard hardware configuration or it requires the purchase of a third-party RAID controller. In most cases, the controller is a SCSI card that attaches to or replaces the SCSI back plane of your server. The controllers are also available in a myriad of configurations, including amounts of onboard cache, single or dual SCSI channel, and add-in software tools. (As with everything in the computer industry, the more bells and whistles you get, the more it will cost. A top-of-the-line RAID adapter can exceed the price of the server.) Make sure you get the drivers for the RAID controller. (This is why I am so adamant about using the Windows NT startup disks from the last chapter.)

> **NOTE**
>
> RAID 5 is not configured from within Windows NT (or Windows 2000 for that matter). The RAID controller will have a BIOS that you can access to configure it. Because there are many different RAID controllers, I can't give you an exact tutorial for configuring RAID 5, but in most cases the manufacturer's instructions are sufficient.

RAID Level Definitions

RAID 0—Disk striping without parity (no fault tolerance).

RAID 1—Disk mirroring (the same information is written to two drives at once).

RAID 2—Each bit of data word is written to a data disk drive (4 in this example: 0 to 3). Each data word has its Hamming Code ECC word recorded on the ECC disks. On Read, the ECC code verifies correct data or corrects single disk errors.

RAID 3—The data block is subdivided ("striped") and written on the data disks. Stripe parity is generated on Writes, recorded on the parity disk, and checked on Reads.

RAID Level 3 requires a minimum of three drives to implement.

RAID 4—Each block is written onto a data disk. Parity for same rank blocks is generated on Writes, recorded on the parity disk, and checked on Reads.

RAID Level 4 requires a minimum of three drives to implement.

RAID 5—Disk striping with parity (fault tolerance).

Each data block is written on a data disk; parity for blocks in the same rank is generated on Writes, recorded in a distributed location, and checked on Reads.

RAID Level 5 requires a minimum of three drives to implement.

RAID 6—Independent data disks with two independent distributed parity schemes.

RAID 7—Optimized asynchrony for high I/O rates as well as high data transfer rates.

4

THE RIGHT
HARDWARE FOR
THE RIGHT JOB

RAID 5 does have one drawback. The parity information requires one whole drive. This means that if you have three 10GB drives in a RAID 5 configuration, your free disk space is only 20GB. ($10 \times 3 = 30$, but one drive is dedicated to the parity information.) One very minor drawback to RAID 5 is that all drives in the array must be the same size. Therefore, you cannot have two 20GB drives and one 9GB drive in the same RAID 5 array. (There's always a catch.)

For a member server the requirements are the same as a PDC in a Single Domain model. I make a distinction because there are certain programs that should never be installed on PDCs. Therefore, if you were to add a member server to a Master Domain you would know the requirements.

The needs for Windows 2000 (as stated by Microsoft) seem a little more realistic. This is mostly due to the timeliness of Windows 2000 release. The requirements are listed in Table 4.2.

TABLE 4.2   Requirements for Windows 2000 Server

Intel Based	RISC Based	Alpha Based
Pentium 133	MIPS R4xOO or equivalent	Alpha First Generation Processor at 150MHz
	(Some Microsoft Literature lists RISC as being unsupported, however, presales support gives these system requirements)	
256MB of RAM	256MB of RAM	256MB of RAM
1GB hard drive	1GB hard drive	1GB hard drive
VGA display	VGA display	VGA display
Keyboard	Keyboard	Keyboard
Mouse	Mouse	Mouse
CD-ROM	CD-ROM	CD-ROM
3.5" floppy		
Optional Equipment		
Network Card	Network Card	Network Card

I have designed several Windows 2000 networks, and the requirements in this table are accurate. For most of us these requirements may seem to be a little on the low end, but keep in mind these are the bare minimums.

The next section looks at how these system requirements change as we add third-party software to the servers.

Evaluating Your Software Needs

When you deal with software, there are equations you should use. I use these two equations when trying to determine the hardware needs of my servers:

- (Total System RAM)= (RAM required for OS) + (Total RAM required by all Third-Party software)

- (Total Number of Processors)= (Processor Required by OS) + X, where X equals the positive whole number supplied by the following equation. (Any fraction less than 1 should be treated as 0 while any fractional amount greater than 1 should be treated as 1.)

  [(Number of Third-Party Programs on Server) / (3)] * [(Amount of RAM required by Third-Party Programs) / (Amount of RAM required by OS)]

For example, I have an Intel-based server running Windows 2000. I add to it three third-party programs with the following requirements:

- Program 1—64MB of RAM and a Pentium 233
- Program 2—128MB of RAM and a Pentium 500
- Program 3—64MB of RAM and a Pentium 500

What are the total requirements of the server?

RAM (equation 1) $512 = 256 + 256$

Number of System Processors (equation 2) $2 = 1 + X (1) [(3 / 3) * (256 / 256)]$

Here's how I explain the equation.

Above and beyond the need of the operating system, the software will add to the RAM, add a new processor for every three packages with the same requirements (causing you to double the RAM), and add to the hard drive space. This should seem pretty straightforward. If the OS calls for 128MB of RAM and you add a program that requires 32MB, bingo, you need 160MB of RAM. On the other hand, if your OS requires a 500MHz processor and you add a program that requires a 500MHz processor, you don't need to add another processor. However, if you add three programs that all require 500MHz processors and the total amount of RAM used by them causes you to double the amount of RAM on your server, add another processor.

> **NOTE**
>
> If you are using Windows NT you cannot add a second processor after you install the operating system. Physically you can install the processor, but Windows NT won't use it. Windows NT will only use multiple processors if they are installed on the server before the operating system. That is another reason why you need to plan this out first.

Keep this equation in mind when reading this section.

The requirements used by software manufacturers tend to be a little more ambiguous than those used by operating systems. Many software vendors can't take into account the cumulative effect software has on a server's memory. Most off-the-shelf software comes with a standard set of requirements much like those of the operating system. They tell you the bare minimum that the software needs to be installed, but this offers you little help in the real world. What you need is a way to figure out the cumulative requirements of the software.

Most of us don't just run one application per server. If we did, the guidelines on the side of the box would be sufficient.

Some of the most popular types of software packages on networks are database related. These can range from accounting packages to helpdesk tracking to e-commerce tools. They can be the most deadly applications a network will ever see. Most of the time the requirements for these packages are underrated by the vendors, so be especially careful when you are trying to gauge the system needs.

The main reason behind all of the confusion is the database itself. Most of the database programs on the market are really "database front ends." That is, they do not include a database server such as Oracle or Microsoft SQL Server, and because vendors have no idea what database you will choose they can't offer any extra guidelines. Their program, being a small interface for a larger database, has very small system requirements. You, as a designer, need to realize that these totals usually need to be added to those of a database server.

A database program generally installs itself as a front end to a large relational database such as Oracle or Microsoft SQL Server. The smaller program then builds the tables that it needs within the database and you're ready for business. So the first problem you run into is that you now have two programs to contend with instead of one. Let's take on the databases themselves first.

The following table lists the requirements for Microsoft SQL Server 7.0.

Processor	RAM	HD	Prerequisites
Pentium 166	32MB	180MB (full inst.)	Windows NT SP4, Internet Explorer 4.01

Now add that to the member server and your server looks like this:

Processor	RAM	HD	Installed Software
Pentium 500	160MB (I know that's not a logical number, but we're not done yet)	18GB	Windows NT 4 Internet Explorer 4.01 SQL Server 7

So far the picture hasn't changed too much, right? You still have to install the third-party software; things will begin to look different. The third-party software you choose for ABCcorp is Clarify. Clarify is a high-end helpdesk call tracking system that utilizes a relational database. Even though I am using Clarify as an example, you will find that in database programs the requirements vary little.

Clarify calls for the following:

Processor	RAM	HD	Prerequisites
Pentium 500	700MB	Varies by amount of use	Microsoft Office (for full use of all features) Windows NT SQL Server

You just added another prerequisite piece of software. The requirements for Microsoft Office are

Processor	RAM	HD	Prerequisites
Pentium 166	32MB	200MB (full inst.)	Windows NT SP4, Internet Explorer 5

Your little member server now looks like this:

Processor	RAM	HD	Installed Software
Dual Pentium 500	1GB of RAM	18GB RAID 5 array	Windows NT SP4, Internet Explorer 5 SQL Server 7 Clarify

That's a drastic change from its original configuration. The finished product is actually so different from the baseline specs that had you installed without regard for the software, it would not function. Situations such as this are the reason I will not install database programs on PDCs. They use too many of the resources that could be better spent on system processes. PDCs and BDCs need a lot of power just to do the job they were designed for. A database should not be installed on a controller (if it can be avoided). Some programs, however, specifically request to be installed on a domain controller. If you run across such a program, be careful and plan out your server ahead of time.

Not all programs are going to chew up and spit out resources like candy. I just chose databases because they tend to be the most intimidating.

What Other Types of Programs Should You Look Out For?

Another category of software that tends to be underrated (for system resources) is e-mail packages. To most administrators e-mail is one of those install-and-forget programs. E-mail normally spends the longest time on the drawing board; however, after installation it is all but ignored.

This couldn't be further from what e-mail programs need. E-mail can run on any number of configurations, from the lightest Linux server to the beefiest mainframe. Much of what determines your configuration is the number of users you have connecting to it.

If you plan to have hundreds of users on a single e-mail server, you need to keep an eye on it. Even though an e-mail itself is a flat text file (which does not degrade bandwidth very much), attachments can cause problems. On larger networks, you may want to limit the size of attachments that can be sent or received through your network. I tend to limit attachment sizes to 2 to 5 MBs.

Programs for performing network backups also pose threats to unsuspecting designers. I will discuss network backup software more in Chapter 11, "Securing Your Network," but there are some things you should be aware of. Backup software can, if unregulated, bring even the largest bandwidth pipeline to its knees.

A backup solution needs to be designed to utilize the strongest links when pulling data from remote devices. If this operation is performed during peak usage, both the servers involved and the network as a whole can be ground to a halt. I tend to configure backups to run during off-peak hours whenever possible, and (when it is not possible to run a backup during off-peak hours) I implement dedicated lines between devices.

Going by the Book

Now that I've scared you with tales of processor crunching and RAM eating databases, I think you're ready for the real world. This section goes over the hardware configurations for some popular programs and lists the software requirements, the software plus the operating system requirements, and a prerequisite software list.

Most likely you will need to install products such as e-mail, databases, and productivity tools on your servers. The following sections discuss the requirements for a few of those products, just to give you an idea of what to design for.

E-mail

One popular solution for corporate e-mail is Microsoft Exchange Server. This product is popular because of its general ease of installation and administration. If you are planning to implement Microsoft Exchange Server, you should be aware of the system requirements.

The following table illustrates the requirements of Microsoft Exchange Server:

Processor	RAM	HD
Pentium 133	32MB	250MB free

Microsoft Exchange Server cannot be installed by itself; it needs an operating system. The prerequisite software requirement is Microsoft Windows NT 4.0 or higher.

The following table shows the requirements for Windows NT 4 Server:

Processor	RAM	HD
Pentium 133	12MB	124MB free

If you want to install Exchange on Microsoft Windows 2000 your server needs to be a little stronger (than that needed for Windows NT).

The following table lists the system requirements for Windows 2000 server:

Processor	RAM	HD
Pentium 133	256MB	1GB recommended

NOTE

Pay close attention to not only the system requirements for the product you want to install, but also the requirements for any prerequisite software as well (such as operating systems).

Exchange Server is a very I/O-heavy application. This means that it reads and writes to the hard drive more than a normal application. To improve performance, it is suggested you keep the Exchange database on one physical drive. (This may not be practical in some cases. For instance, in large corporations you would need to balance hard drive performance with fault tolerance. In my experience, fault tolerance wins. I usually go with setting up my server with a RAID 5 array rather than keeping the Exchange database on one physical drive.)

Another warning about Exchange: It is recommended that you do not install Exchange on a PDC (I would even shy away from installing it on a BDC). There are too many systems processes fighting for space on a domain controller already; throwing Exchange on one is asking for trouble.

What will you really need to run this Exchange Server? Here are the specifications for a server that I just built to house 75 mailboxes:

Processor	RAM	HD
Pentium III 500	512MB	18GB

Over the past 5 years the Lotus Notes suite of products has gained popularity. You should be prepared to encounter more than one installation of the product during your time consulting.

Lotus Notes contains cc:Mail, which is a strong competitor for Exchange. The system requirements for Lotus Notes server R5 are

Processor	RAM	HD
(Not specified by vendor) I would recommend a Pentium 233	16MB	70MB

Databases

There are many database servers to choose from on the market today. Sybase, Oracle, and Microsoft SQL Server are the most popular offerings you will find (both in installation base and third-party support). I tend to use Microsoft SQL Server for two reasons: ease of installation and configuration. (Keep in mind that network implementation projects are very involved processes, and anything that can make the job smooth is welcome help.)

4

THE RIGHT HARDWARE FOR THE RIGHT JOB

NOTE

Before you select a database server, check the database requirements of any software you plan on running on the database. While many products support installation on multiple database platforms, some do not. You want to be sure you purchase the right database server for you needs.

The following table lists the systems requirements for Sybase's Adaptive Server Enterprise 12.5 running on Windows NT 4.0. (For more information about Sybase ASE 12.5 running on other platforms, visit www.sybase.com/products/databaseservers/ase/.)

Processor	RAM	HD
Pentium 166	46MB	442MB

Microsoft's relational database server product is SQL Server 7. This product has a strong installation base and a lot of third-party support. Many products today support MSSQL Server 7. The following table lists the system requirements for Microsoft SQL Server 7.

Processor	RAM	HD
Pentium 166	32MB	180MB

Microsoft SQL Server, like most everything here, requires Windows NT 4.0.

Productivity

Microsoft's productivity suite is known as Microsoft Office 2000. Microsoft Office contains multiple client-side products such as an e-mail client, a word processor, and a spreadsheet. While these products are not typically thought of as server products, you may want to consider installing them on at least one server. There are many times during a project when you may need a word processor or e-mail client on a server for testing purposes. The following table lists the requirements for Microsoft Office 2000:

Processor	RAM	HD
Pentium 166	32MB	526MB

Another popular productivity suite is Corel WordPerfect Office 2000 Network edition. This product contains all of the standard productivity tools (word processor, spreadsheet, and so on); however, one feature sets this product apart—its portability. Corel WordPerfect Office 2000 Network is one of the only productivity offerings available on Windows, Unix, and Linux platforms. The following table lists the system requirements for Corel WordPerfect Office 2000 Network on a Windows-based platform:

Processor	RAM	HD
486/86 (no kidding)	16MB	170MB

Antivirus Programs

Antivirus programs are a must have in today's business environment. After the Love Bug and Melissa viruses hit, focus began shifting from worrying about viruses after they became a nuisance to preventing further infections. It is almost inevitable that you will be asked to implement an antivirus solution. The following sections discuss some of the more popular programs on the market for virus protection.

Norton AntiVirus Enterprise

The Symantec site lists Windows NT 4.0 as its requirement for Norton AntiVirus. When a company does that it usually means that the minimum requirements for the operating system are more than enough for the software. I have had NAV Corporate Edition running for awhile now with only minor problems, such as failures shutting down some Windows 98 machines. (These could be possible memory issues, but Windows 98 is buggy like that.)

Mcaffee

Mcaffee's Virus Scan seems to be shifting to an online offering. From the information on its Web site it would appear that you pay a small fee for an Internet version of the scanning software. (Rather than install the product on your hard drive, the product now scans your PC over the Internet.) Given the description of the product and the lack of system requirements, one can only assume that (like NAV) it is not the biggest of memory hogs.

The Clients

This section covers something a little more elusive. Everyone knows it happens, but only few people document it. What is it? The more PCs you have attaching to the network and using programs, the more resources they use up.

Some of sections earlier in the chapter listed the calculations for determining how many resources you need on the server in relation to the number of people using the software. MAS90 by Sage Software is one program that comes with documentation explaining how the server systems requirements change as more people use the software.

MAS90 is an accounting program that runs a propriety database. This database has its own system requirements. The database front end that is installed on the client also has requirements. However, because the client portion of the software is a front end, all processing occurs on the server. Therefore, the server requirements change depending on how many clients are using the software. The database requirements on the server are 256MB of RAM and a 400MHz processor. This will fit into our member server specifications if we add more RAM. The calculation that Sage gives for the amount of RAM you need (above and beyond base) is 16MB of RAM per concurrent user.

You could spend hours calculating all of the different programs that run on the server, adding up the per-user costs, and coming up with long equations for how many resources you need. That is just impractical. I have come up with another formula that works in most typical situations.

For member servers I use this formula:

If (Total system RAM < 1GB) Then (Total system RAM) = (Total RAM required by OS) + [(Total System RAM required by client) * (Number of Clients)]

For example, if a member server is running a server-end program that needs 256MB of RAM and there are 10 clients (all of which require 16MB of RAM), I will add 160MB to the server.

> **NOTE**
>
> When using these calculations, keep in mind that most servers only allow you to add RAM in increments of 128MB. This means that even if you only need 160MB of RAM, realistically your server will have 256MB.

The next chapter covers in detail the factors you should consider when choosing your client hardware.

Summary

- Do not take the task of choosing your server's hardware lightly. Most factors that go into your hardware configuration are cumulative.
- The role of the server on the domain could also determine the base hardware configuration.
- RAID 5 is also known as *disk striping with parity*. RAID 5 offers fault tolerance, but at a price. You lose the capacity of one drive.
- All drives in a RAID 5 array must be the same size (RAID 5 requires a minimum of three drives to be implemented).
- Carefully research the system requirements of the specific software packages you plan on using.
- Databases tend to use the most system resources.
- Watch for applications that base their system resource requirements on the number of clients using the product. The numbers can get out of hand very quickly.

Considering the Client

IN THIS CHAPTER

Another often-overlooked portion of a network is the desktop PC. It is not by mistake that many designers tend to leave out the PC. In most cases, the client either has existing PCs for use on the network or will buy them after completion. However, because the PC is 50% of the client-server model, I felt that it was important enough to devote a chapter to the subject.

In the way the last chapter dealt with choosing the right hardware configurations for servers, this chapter will help you make the right decisions when choosing your client hardware. The client is one of the only "single points of failure" on a network. What does this mean? Most other components on a network can be supported with some form of fault tolerance. Almost every board, circuit, and drive in a server can have a hot standby ready to go. Network connectivity devices can be used in tandem to provide backup for each other should one fail.

This kind of technology, however, has been slow to hit the desktop market and for good reason. The technology is expensive and there has really been no call for it from the masses. Desktops are not servers; they don't require the same preventive measures that servers do. If a desktop breaks down, chances are there is enough information saved on the server to help the users regain what they lose. Users need to store as much data as possible on the server for this scenario to work. Try to design your servers to be as user friendly as possible. This will make it easier for users to store their data on the network. If you make the areas for user data storage easily accessible (and well marked), the clients will be more apt to use them. The first step in a successful PC recovery (reloading a PC after a system failure) is to have as much information as possible backed up. By putting the user's critical data on the server, you are taking the first and most important step to a successful backup/recovery plan.

Desktops are also thought of as expendable. Most companies will replace a desktop PC every few years (some even go so far as to lease PCs rather than buy them just so they are assured new PCs every two years). With this kind of mentality, it's not hard to see why a lot of the technology that makes servers more reliable has yet to find its way to the PC platforms.

This still does not change the fact that the desktop PC is one of the only single points of failure on a network.

What can you do? One of the things that makes PCs unreliable is the shoehorn methodology. Users tend to cram as many programs as can fit on a 20GB drive onto their PCs, expecting them all to run flawlessly. Unfortunately, in most cases, this does not work. In extreme cases it has adverse effects on the servers. One common problem in networks of any size occurs when rogue programs find their way onto client PCs. I suggest that you create a list of "supported" software for the client to distribute to the employees. This will help the client maintain a standard platform and let the employees know what should be on the PCs. Keep the PCs as clean as possible and they will be easier to maintain.

This chapter focuses on two parts of a PC: the hardware and the operating system. Hopefully by using the right configuration for your situation, you can minimize the effects of PC outages and troubles.

Choosing Client Hardware

Quentin Tarantino says there are two kinds of people in the world: those who like Elvis and those who like the Beatles. Everybody in the world can be divided on those lines because everybody likes one more than the other. The same holds true in the PC world. Everybody in the PC field can be divided along two lines: those who build their own PCs and those who buy off the shelf. While each has its own merits, they both have their shortfalls.

The people who build their own PCs do so for one of two reasons. The first is to prove that they can do it.

The other more fruitful reason behind building PCs is for customization. Industrious network administrators (and some just looking for a false sense of job security) build PCs for the workplace to make sure that each one is customized for the job it performs. If this job is done correctly it will work very well. I can't speak highly enough about it. One of the recurring themes of this (and the last) chapter is using the right tool for the right job. The ultimate way to ensure you have the right tool performing the right job is to build the PC from scratch. However, building PCs from scratch does have a dark side. Today you may be able to build five PCs for your network and have them all be identical. However, try building those same PCs two months from now and you may not be able to find exactly the same parts. Vendors rotate their stock and the availability of parts changes from day to day.

Another downside to building your own PCs is available support. You will have different warranty and support information for almost every part in the PC (that is, if they have any warranty at all). This can be confusing and frustrating for the client. Try to avoid situations like this at all costs.

The other side of this coin is the buy-it-off-the-shelfers. These people are generally looking for one thing: peace of mind. Peace of mind knowing that they can take it out the box, plug it in, and it works with minimal configuration. If it doesn't, it gets put back in the box and returned for a new one. Easy as pie. Most if not all of these PCs come with a warranty of some sort. This makes most companies very happy. Buying a PC from a vendor such as Compaq, Gateway, or Dell (to name a few) will give the client a single point of contact for support after you leave. The client will also be assured they can get the assistance they need when they need it.

So, which one is the best? That I can't say, but I suggest off the shelf. Remember, you are designing this network for somebody else. They need to know that after you walk out the door they can get the support they need in times of trouble. When a store-bought, brand-name PC fails, they should know where to turn. When a homemade PC fails, there is generally nowhere to turn. If you pay attention to the details, a store-bought PC can be just as customized and effective as one that has been built from scratch.

Most of the big name desktop PC manufacturers offer a variety of options. Selecting the right options can make all the difference.

The most popular options to choose from are hard drive size, RAM, video card, audio, removable media, and networking.

Let's look at all of these options and their uses in order. Don't go overboard on hard drive space. There are two reasons for this. The first is that it takes longer to find a file on a larger hard drive. The search times can be minimal and unnoticeable in most cases, but they do make a difference.

The second and more prevalent reason for not using a massive hard drive is the proper use of the space. In most situations, user information and data files are to be kept (for many reasons) on the servers. However, the more space a user has on his or her PC, the more temptation there is to use it. This could be saving files to the hard drive or adding programs that the company may not approve of. While I'm not advocating putting 600MB drives in all of the PCs, the standard 6–8GB (maybe 10–15GB by now) hard drives are more than enough.

> **NOTE**
>
> After consulting with the client, you may want to partition larger drives to mask a massive amount of space. Two to four GB of hard drive (in most situations) is more than enough. The client can then go back to using a tool like Partition Magic and reallocate more space as needed.

RAM is a different story. As far as I am concerned you can't have too much. I really can't come up with a compelling argument to take it easy on the memory. The only suggestion I have is to shop around if the memory sticks look expensive. This is not a green light to run up the client's expenses by putting 512MB of RAM in every machine. A good rule of thumb is to look at what the PC vendor is suggesting. The vendors (if they have an OS manufacturer's certification sticker on their PCs) are producing PCs that meet or exceed most operating system guidelines. Therefore, the PCs should have enough RAM (or be upgradable) to run what you need.

The video card can offer a first real decision-making chance. The average PC user does not need a 64MB video card capable of displaying eight trillion colors. However, for the users who do need it, such as programmers, graphic artists, or marketers, only the best will do. For everyone else, downgrade the video card to something generic. Choosing a card that is a little older and a little more established (offering fewer bells and whistles and fewer colors) will help stabilize the PC on the whole. However, when choosing your video card try to stick with one vendor. Vendors generally produce a variety of cards. This will help further your efforts to standardize the operating platforms.

If the user does not need audio, don't install it. Most motherboards have some form of onboard audio. This should be sufficient for listening to music at work (in companies that allow it). This is one point that should be discussed with the client. Most online music sources are bandwidth hogs and many clients will want to restrict (if not eliminate) the possibility of their pipeline being ground to a halt. Unless the company has users who work with audio as a job function, things such as wave tables and 64-bit sound just aren't needed. Another reason to stay clear of secondary sound cards is the IRQ situation. Plan ahead; every card you install requires another IRQ, and using two for sound (assuming the onboard sound uses one too) is wasteful. It also takes away from the available addresses you can expand with later.

What kind of removable media do you include in your client PCs? In my mind anything more than a CD-ROM is overkill. Most files can be transferred and stored on the network. The one thing I will suggest is one external LS-120 Superdrive for administrative use. The LS-120 has gotten very little publicity living in the shadow of the Zip drive. The LS-120 does have one clear-cut advantage—not only does it use 120MB disks, it doubles as a 3.5" floppy. It is a great Swiss army knife–type tool. My LS-120 has been very useful in situations where floppy drives have died. I have also used it when machines have lost network connectivity and I need to get large files either on to or off of the PC. I would buy one and let it float around the network.

Finally we come to the last piece in the PC puzzle, the network card. I've covered that enough already to let you make an informed decision; however, Table 5.1 is a quick reference to refresh your memory.

TABLE 5.1 Network Cards by Type

Network Type	Available Card Speed	Autosensing	Pros	Cons
Ethernet	10, 100, 10/100, 1GB	Most 10/100 speed cards are auto-sensing	Speed, software-enabled autosensing, available as an "on-the-motherboard" option from most PC vendors	Watch for the network speed of your connectivity devices
Token Ring	4, 16, 4/16	Some 4/16 autosensing cards are available	Most cards have software editable MAC addresses, available tool set makes administration easier	Expensive, autosensing is usually hardware enabled, limited PC vendor support

Client Operating Systems

Now that the PC hardware has been agreed upon, what operating system should it run? Until recently your choices were rather limited. Windows NT Workstation, Windows 95/98, and Windows 2000 Professional were your only choices (see a pattern here?). Now two more choices are available: Windows ME (big surprise there) and Linux.

Linux and a Viable OS Solution

Though the tools available for Linux make it more practical as a server operating system, I chose to put it here. Certain releases of Linux, such as Corel Linux, have an intentional Windows 98 look and feel to them. And now as software support for the platform is growing, it deserves a second look.

What are the drawbacks to putting Linux on a network? The major downfall of the system at the moment is support. Operating system support is starting to gain ground, as long as you purchase a major brand. The major Linux manufacturers, such as Corel, Red Hat, and Caldera, generally have the resources to properly support the products they release. However, where the support seems to be lacking is in the third-party driver support. It is still very hard to find hardware vendors that have Linux drivers available for their products. In some cases you can download them from the Net. In other (more rare) cases, you can find someone who has actually written a driver for the hardware in question. Whatever the situation, it still may require a little extra work on your part.

Where Should You Use Linux?

Linux's plethora of server-style tools and desktop-style ease of use make it ideal for the SOHO user.

> I will cover some SOHO (Small Office Home Office) design essentials in the WAN section of this book, but it is worth mentioning their growing popularity, especially among the traveling workforce.

Corel Linux comes bundled with one of the best Linux ports to date, Corel Office Suite for Linux. Corel WordPerfect, Quattro Pro, Corel Presentation, and Corel Draw are quite a powerful and well-rounded home office package.

Other major products available for Linux include extremely strong firewall protection and audio editors. A wide array of server and client products are available for the Linux platform.

The best part of Linux is its ability to thrive on PCs that are lacking in the power department. Linux works quite well on low-end Pentiums with baseline RAM. (Some versions of Linux can even work well on 486s.) The published requirements for Corel Linux are listed in the following table.

Processor	RAM	Hard Drive	Peripherals
Pentium	24 MB	800 MB	CD-ROM
			VGA Graphics Mouse

I've thrown away machines better than this. The point is, it really doesn't take much to run Linux.

The Microsoft Army of Client Operating Systems

So you're not going to go with Linux; rather, you choose to stay with a Microsoft product. Which product do you choose? As I see it the answer is easy. If you have no compelling reason otherwise, I would choose Windows NT Workstation or Windows 2000 Professional. (Even in early 2001, most PC vendors are releasing machines with Windows NT 4 Workstation on them.) Windows NT Workstation offers a more secure environment in which to operate. If you have Windows NT Server on your network, putting Workstation on the desktops should be a no-brainer.

What are the compelling reasons not to use Windows NT? The most compelling reason of them all is software compatibility. Not all software works on Windows NT. On the last project I completed we had some software that worked only on the Windows 95/98 platform. For those users we had to go with Windows 98. Everybody else got NT.

There are more Windows 95/98 and Windows NT books than you can shake a stick at, so I won't bore you with every detail of the installation process. Here are some pointers to keep in mind as you install:

- **Always install clean.** I prefer not to upgrade operating systems when I can avoid it. The first step in any OS install is to wipe the hard drive clean. This gives you an empty plate to start from and lessens the likelihood of outside interference.
- **Have the PC complete at time of installation.** Try to have all of the hardware that you will put in the PC there when you install the OS. Even though Plug and Play is better than it was at discovering hardware, it works better when it discovers everything at once. This allows the OS to properly assign resources to the hardware up front and makes for a smoother running machine.
- **Have the PC on a fully functional network.** This especially holds true for Windows NT Workstation. Have the rest of the network up and running before you start installing clients. When the network is functional, plug the blank PC into it and then install the OS.

In Windows NT this is important because NT needs to communicate with the PDC of the network to finish the install. In Windows 95/98, being attached to the network helps you determine whether all of the drivers are installed correctly. If your Plug and Play found and installed a certain network card but you can't see the network, chances are good that either the network driver is wrong or the card is bad.

- **Know your IP scheme ahead of time.** Have ready the address to assign to the PC. If you are using a DHCP server, have it up and configured. Anything you can do ahead of time is going to make the process easier.
- **Know your profiles.** In Windows NT, decide whether you will use static or roaming profiles. The profile is a collection of settings pertaining to one person. A profile is created for each person who logs on to a particular Windows NT machine. These profiles are normally stored on the local hard drive, but you can store them on the server if you want. This is known as a roaming profile. Then a user can log in to any machine on the network and have the look and feel of home. Another advantage to roaming profiles is file security. The profile can be locked down in such a way that if the user changes anything, as soon as he reboots the profile will revert back to the original.

Windows 2000 and Windows ME really haven't been on the market long enough for me to suggest either of them. I can say this: If you go with a Windows 2000 mixed-mode server network, try to have a few Windows 2000 workstations around. This will help you get used to the platform and observe its workings. There is nothing that can compare with real experience. No matter how many books you read, it's just not the same. As for Windows ME, as tempting as it is to install the newest operating systems, try to stick with the ones that were meant for network use. Windows 95, 98, and ME (all being based on the same kernel) were all meant for the home user. Windows NT and Windows 2000 are considered the network products. Try to use these whenever possible.

Summary

- One of the biggest decisions about desktop PCs facing a network designer is whether to buy off the shelf or build from parts.
- To be fair to the client, buying off the shelf gives them more support.
- Don't underestimate Linux as a plausible desktop operating system, especially for the SOHO user.
- When installing a Microsoft client operating system, follow the guide to installing a clean system.
- Try to use Windows NT Workstation whenever possible.

Choosing a Protocol

IN THIS CHAPTER

To understand exactly how protocols work, you first need to understand *where* they work. Because different protocols work on different layers of the OSI model, one computer may use a suite of protocols to accomplish a job. Two protocols that work together are TCP and IP. These protocols work on separate layers of the OSI model to aid in computer communication. The following sections will help illustrate the roles of the seven OSI model layers.

The OSI Model

The seven layers of the OSI model are numbered from the bottom up. For information to get from one PC to another, the data must traverse these layers on both the sending and receiving devices. Information originating on layer 7 of one machine would

1. Travel from layer 7 to layer 1 on the machine of origin
2. Travel across the network media to the recipient
3. Travel from layer 1 to layer 7 on the recipient

Each layer of the OSI has a very specific function. Information traveling from one layer to another is altered slightly to make it readable by the next layer. When this data reaches the receiving computer, it travels the layers in reverse to undo the alterations made by the originating computer.

The following sections look at each of the layers and their functions to get a better understanding of the role protocols play in PC communication.

The Application Layer

The Application layer (layer 7) is concerned with coordinating communication between applications. This layer of the OSI model synchronizes the data flowing between servers and clients by handling functions such as file transfers, network management, and process services. Other duties of the Application layer are

- The World Wide Web (WWW)
- E-mail gateways
- Electronic Data Interchange (EDI)
- Chat services
- Internet navigation utilities

The Presentation Layer

The Presentation layer (layer 6) is the C3PO of the OSI model. The function of the Presentation layer is to translate the information from the Application layer into a format that is readable by the other layers. All data encryption, decryption, and compression take place at the sixth layer of the OSI model. The Presentation layer also controls all audio and video presentation functions. Services provided by the Presentation layer include

- MP3
- Real Audio
- Real Video
- Jpeg
- Gif

The Session Layer

The Session layer (layer 5) coordinates communications between network devices. The Session layer (working with the Session layer of another device) establishes a session between two applications. The two Session layers monitor the "conversation" and, when appropriate, terminate the session. Other Session layer responsibilities include

- SQL (Structured Query Language)
- X Windows
- NFS (Network File System)

The information that is sent (or received) from the three top layers (layers 5, 6, and 7) is known as *user data*. However, not every protocol understands user data (in fact, only layers 4 through 7 can work with user data). Therefore, as data moves through each layer of the OSI model, protocols translate it into a format the next layer can understand.

The Transport Layer

The function of the Transport layer (layer 4) is to take user data from the upper layers and break it (or reassemble, as the case may be) into chunks of data that can be easily transmitted.

The chunks of data formed by the Transport layer are known as *segments*. These segments are then passed to the lower layers for further processing.

The Transport layer also provides services for data flow control. Flow control helps this layer ensure the reliable (connection-oriented) transmission of data from one device to another. It does this by taking user data from the upper layers and segmenting it. These segments are then transmitted (one at a time) to the intended recipient. The recipient (after receiving a segment) sends back an acknowledgment. If the sender does not receive an acknowledgment, it retransmits the segment. After several retries, the sending device attempts to re-initiate a connection with the recipient. If the recipient proves to be unresponsive (the receiving device is no longer on the network), an error is generated and the remaining segments are not transmitted.

The Network Layer

Layer 3 of the OSI model is one of the most important layers for PC communication. Most connectivity devices (routers, layer 3 switches, and bridges) work on the Network layer of the OSI model.

For routing to work correctly, the Network layer builds a network map. This map serves as a guide to route data across the network.

The Network layer builds this map by first taking segments from the Transport layer and converting them into packets. These packets are then passed to the Data Link layer where addressing information is added. The packet (eventually becoming a frame) is sent across the network. When a device receives a packet, the sender's information is stripped from the packet and stored in a table. As this table grows, the Network layer builds a clearer picture of the network environment. Other protocols and devices can use this information to route data in a more efficient manner.

For example, if a device on Network A wanted to send data to a device on Network B, it would send a broadcast across its local network (A). This broadcast would act as a scout, searching for the address of the recipient. Because the receiving device is not on Network A, no reply would be sent to the broadcast. The device on Network A would then assume the intended recipient is on Network B and send the data there. The sending device notes this on its network map and any further data intended for the same recipient is sent directly to Network B.

The Data Link Layer

Whereas the Network layer holds the map of the network, the Data Link layer (layer 2) ensures the information on the map is correct through addressing. The Data Link layer accepts packets from the Network layer and frames them, thus converting them into data frames. These frames contain the following information:

- Preamble—signals the start of the frame
- Destination Address
- Source Address
- Length Field (in a standard Ethernet Frame)—Indicates the size of the data contained in the frame
- Type Field (in Ethernet_II frames)—Indicates which protocol will receive the data
- Data
- Frame Check Sequence—A verification number corresponding to the checksum of the frame

For routing purposes, the Data Link layer has been broken into two sub-layers: the MAC and the LLC.

The MAC Sub-Layer

The MAC (Media Access Control) sub-layer is in charge of framing the packets from the Network layer. In framing the packets, the MAC sub-layer attaches the addressing information to the packet. This addressing information includes the MAC address.

Another function of the MAC sub-layer is to provide connectionless services to the upper layers. Connectionless service takes place when data is sent to a device without a session being open. In other words, the sending device ships the data through the network without alerting the recipient beforehand.

The LLC Sub-Layer

One function of the LLC (Logical Link Control) sub-layer is to provide connection-oriented service (the MAC is connectionless). Connection-oriented service provides for the establishment of sessions prior to the delivery of frames. By opening a session first, the sender is guaranteed delivery of frames through acknowledgments.

The Physical Layer

The first layer of the OSI model defines the physical connection between devices. The Physical layer accepts frames from the upper layers and transmits them as bits over the media.

Figure 6.1 illustrates how the entire process works.

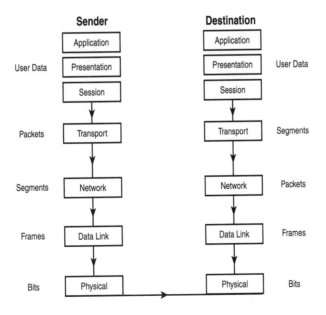

FIGURE 6.1

Encapsulation path of data.

Understanding how the OSI model works will help you understand how protocols function. This chapter focuses on three of the more popular routed protocols: TCP/IP, IPX/SPX, and AppleTalk.

> There are two types of protocols in network engineering: routed and routing.
>
> A *routed* protocol is what we most often associate with network communications. IP is an example of a routed protocol.
>
> A *routing* protocol, on the other hand, is a protocol used by a router (or other connectivity device) to carry routed protocols. RIP and OSPF are examples of a routing protocol.
>
> This chapter covers routed protocols. Routing protocols are covered in Chapter 7, "Connectivity Devices."

TCP/IP

TCP/IP is by far the most popular protocol in use today. Therefore, it is the protocol you are most likely to come across in your designs.

> **NOTE**
>
> TCP/IP actually isn't a protocol; it is a suite of protocols. TCP is a Transport layer protocol and IP is its Network layer counterpart.

The routed protocol stack TCP/IP is the major protocol stack used on the Internet. But how does TCP/IP work, and why is it so popular? The following sections take the two protocols apart and discuss each separately.

TCP

TCP (Transmission Control Protocol) is the Transport layer protocol in the TCP/IP protocol stack. All of the functionality of TCP resides in the fourth layer of the OSI model.

The Transport layer of the OSI model is responsible for the conversion of user data into segments and the reliable delivery of those segments to their intended recipient. TCP (like any protocol that resides on the fourth layer of the OSI model) must be able to perform these duties. How does TCP comply with the functions outlined by the Transport layer?

TCP takes user data from the upper layers of the OSI model and breaks it into segments. These segments are numbered by TCP before delivery across the network. (The segments are numbered as a form of checks and balances to ensure that all segments for a particular session are delivered.)

Once all of the segments are ready for delivery, TCP requests a session with the Transport layer of the destination device. (Knowing the destination is the function of IP, which is covered in the next section.) When the connection is established, TCP sends off the segments.

The destination sends an acknowledgment for every packet it receives. The destination device then reassembles the segments into user data (based on the numbering of the segments). If any segments are missing the destination, TCP simply re-requests the specific segment from the sender.

> **NOTE**
>
> TCP is considered a connection-oriented protocol because it opens a session or connection with the destination before sending segments. By doing this, the sender can be assured that the destination is active and ready to receive any segments.

This form of guaranteed segment delivery is one of the features that make TCP a very desirable protocol. If a segment is lost in transit, TCP simply resends it.

When TCP numbers segments for delivery, they are placed into a queue for transmission across the network. TCP then builds a virtual circuit to the destination devices. This ensures that the segments arrive in the correct order.

The destination device's TCP reassembles the segments by number and requests the sender resend any missing packets. If you were using a connectionless protocol in this example, any missing segments would be lost. This could result in lost or corrupt data.

TCP seems like a very good, reliable protocol on its own; however, TCP is just half of a dynamic protocol stack. How does TCP know where to send those segments? The second half of the TCP/IP protocol stack addresses this issue.

IP

Everyone is familiar with IP and IP addressing. It is almost impossible to work in the computer industry today and not know what IP is. However, do you really understand how it works, or why it is so popular? This section covers how IP works and addresses some common issues such as addressing and subnetting. It also covers when you should include IP in your designs and how to implement it.

The most popular Network layer protocol is IP. One of IP's responsibilities is to address the host machine.

A standard IP address looks like 128.95.95.178—four sections containing four bytes each. An IP address is made up of 32 bits or four bytes. Because the bits are in binary, the largest achievable value for one set of four bytes is 255 (actually 254 since 255 is set for broadcasts). This means that the achievable range of IP addresses is 0.0.0.0 through 255.255.255.255. (These numbers are achievable but they are not all valid.)

Table 6.1 is a list of IP addresses that are considered reserved.

TABLE 6.1   Reserved IP Addresses

Address	Binary	Reason Address Is Reserved
0.0.0.0	00000000.00000000.00000000.00000000	An address cannot be all 0s.
		Used by RIP for routing.
255.255.255.255	11111111.11111111.11111111.11111111	An address cannot be all 1s.
		Used for broadcasts.
127.0.0.1	01111111.00000000.00000000.00000001	Reserved for internal loop-back testing.

Depending on the class of the address, anywhere from one to three bytes are used to identify the host, and anywhere from one to three bytes are used to identify the network. The first part of an address is used to identify the network, whereas the second part is used to identify the host.

IP addresses are divided into three classes. These classes were created to keep track of the number of addresses being allotted to certain sized institutions. The classes for IP addresses are class A, B, and C. There is also a lesser known (and even lesser used) class D that we will not be discussing. (Class D is primarily used for multicasting.)

Class A Addresses

For class A addresses the first byte of the address represents the network and the last three bytes represent the host.

Figure 6.2 shows a class A address divided into its network and host parts.

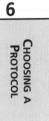

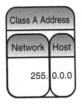

FIGURE 6.2

The host and network portions of a class A address.

Class A addresses have a network range between 1 and 127. Therefore, an IP address starting with a number between 1 and 127 will be a class A address.

Class B Addresses

In class B addresses, the first two bytes represent the network and the remaining two bytes represent the host. A valid class B network range is 128 through 191.

Figure 6.3 shows a class B IP address divided into its network and host parts.

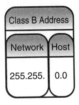

FIGURE 6.3

The host and network portions of a class B address.

Class C Addresses

In class C addresses, the first three bytes represent the network and the last byte represents the host. A valid class C range is 192 through 223.

Figure 6.4 shows a class C IP address divided into its network and host parts.

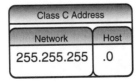

FIGURE 6.4

The host and network portions of a class C address.

> **NOTE**
>
> You may have noticed that the valid range of addresses for class C only goes up to 223, but IP addresses can reach 256. This is to leave room for class D (223 through 239) and class E (240 through 255). Don't spend too much time worrying about these addresses; they are not used very often.
>
> However, for troubleshooting purposes it is good to know about these ranges. For example, if you are designing a class C network and assign it an address of 230.230.230.0 with a subnet mask of 255.255.255.0 (the valid subnet mask for a class C network), you may run into problems.
>
> In this particular case, the device would not be able to communicate with any other devices in the 255.255.255.0 subnet. However, on the surface the address 230.230.230.0 appears to be valid, even though it is actually class D.

The Subnet Mask

The subnet mask is used by IP to distinguish the host address from the network address. To understand how the subnet mask works, convert an IP address to binary. Here is the class C address 198.68.85.114 in binary:

11000110.01000100.01010101.01110010

The subnet mask for a class C IP address is 255.255.255.0. In binary the subnet mask looks likes this:

11111111.11111111.11111111.00000000

How does this help IP tell the network address from the host? As you can see from the binary representation of the address and the mask, the binary 1s mark the network portion. Conversely, the 0s mark the host portion of the address. This may seem obvious now, but it becomes harder to see when you start subnetting your networks.

> **NOTE**
>
> The class of IP addresses you are using will determine the subnet mask you need. Following are the default subnet masks for the three classes of addresses:
>
>   Class A = 255.0.0.0
>
>   Class B = 255.255.0.0
>
>   Class C = 255.255.255.0

How Do You Design for IP?

Luckily, most common server operating systems provide either default support for IP or offer it as an add-on. Therefore, you should not have any problems setting up the network to run IP. However, how do you develop an IP scheme that works for you?

In most situations you will not have access to a full license of IP addresses. (Licenses are granted through most WAN providers. These are usually large communications providers such as telephone companies.)

NOTE

Because there is a finite number of IP addresses to go around and demand keeps growing, many providers are very careful when granting licenses. Many people will be given only the addresses they need (or can prove they need). Don't be surprised if you request a large block of addresses and only receive a fraction of what you wanted.

Because you will only have access to a small range of addresses, you must use them wisely. Here is an example from a network I designed.

A couple of years ago I designed a small network for 80 people. When we turned to our WAN provider for a block of IP addresses, we were granted 16.

The solution I implemented was to use a private IP scheme on the internal network (see the following sidebar for an explanation of private addressing).

The 16 public (routable) addresses could then be used on the Internet interfaces (more than enough addresses for a network of that size).

On the internal network (any machine that does not need to be accessed from the Internet) I used a set of IP addresses that are considered private. The most common set of private addresses is 10.x.x.x.

RFC 1918

RFC 1918 defines which IP schemes have been reserved for use on private networks (networks that will not access the Internet) and how they should be used. These IP addresses are free to use, and you can subnet them as needed. These addresses are

10.0.0.0

172.16.0.0

192.168.0.0

I try to use these addresses as much as possible in my designs because they are free and there is no concern about whether you will have enough addresses. Using the free addresses on your internal PCs will cut down on the number of routable addresses you need to purchase. The purchased addresses can then be assigned to only those machines that need a direct interface to the Internet. As long as your router's routing tables are configured correctly, you should have no problem assigning these addresses to the PCs on your network.

These addresses were used on all of the devices that were not directly connected to the Internet. The only devices that were given the public addresses were the router to the Internet and the e-mail server.

In this example I was able to use private addresses to make up for a shortage of public addresses. However, what do you do if you have more than one logical network that needs to be addressed? You may need to subnet.

Subnetting an IP Network

When a network is subnetted, bits are passed from the host portion of an address to the network portion. This allows for the addressing of more networks (or subnetworks) from one IP license. Figure 6.5 shows a network that would benefit from subnetting.

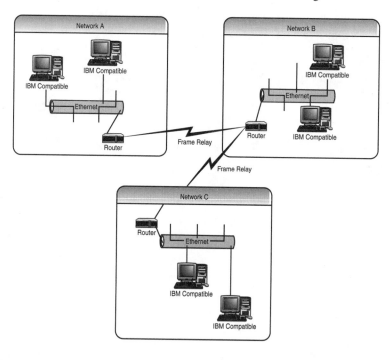

FIGURE 6.5

A non-subnetted network.

You need to subnet the license 10.0.0.0 to fit three subnets. Where do you start? You should start by looking at the subnet mask. (Even though you are creating three networks, they need to share one subnet mask.) By converting the subnet mask into binary, you can easily see how subnetting is accomplished.

The subnet for 10.0.0.0 is 255.0.0.0. 255.0.0.0 in binary is

11111111.00000000.00000000.00000000

You then need to determine the number of bits that need to be given to the network address to allow for three more networks. For example, if you were to pass two bits from the host portion of the mask to the network you would create two networks (with a possible 4,194,302 hosts on each one).

11111111.11000000.00000000.00000000

As you can see, you passed one bit from the host to the network. This gives you a new subnet mask of 255.192.0.0. Your new networks would have the addresses of 10.64.x.x and 10.128.x.x.

You can figure this out using the following equations.

2^x-2 = Number of addresses (where x equals the number of bits in the address)

Therefore, in the third byte of the example, you used two bits for the network ($2^2-2 = 2$) giving you two networks. That left a total of 22 bits for the hosts ($2^{22}-2 = 4,194,302$).

> **NOTE**
>
> Why do you subtract 2 from the total number of addresses? You cannot use all 0s or all 1s as an address; therefore, you must subtract those two possibilities.

The second equation is used to figure out the network addresses.

$256-x = y$ limit x (Where x is the new subnet mask y will equal the interval between networks until y reaches x)

$256-192 = 64$, so the valid networks are 10.**64**.0.0 and 10.**128**.0.0(64+64). If you were to add 64 again you would get 192, which is your subnet mask.

You need three networks to successfully subnet the example in Figure 6.4. Therefore, you should use a subnet mask of 255.224.0.0. This would give you six networks with 2,097,150 hosts each. You would obviously never need that many hosts, but it is the number of networks you are concerned about.

By subnetting the networks you can better direct the traffic around the three networks. Had you not subnetted the networks, the traffic (produced by broadcasts and CSMA/CD packets) would start to degrade the performance of the network. Now that the networks are subnetted, the traffic stays on its particular subnet, creating a less hectic network environment.

Novell and IPX

Prior to version 5.0 of Novell's NetWare server, IPX was the default protocol. (IP is now the default.) Therefore, there is an overwhelming chance that if you encounter a Novell network it will be running IPX.

IPX differs slightly from IP. An IPX address is 10 bytes long (as opposed to 4 in an IP address). This allows for a much greater range of addresses.

IPX is much easier to administer than IP for two reasons. The first reason is that there are no classes or subnetting in IPX. The first four bytes of an IPX network always represent the network. The second reason is the last six bytes (the host portion) are usually the MAC address of the particular device. (The host portion is changeable, because you never know when you might get two devices with the same MAC.)

> **NOTE**
>
> Finding two network devices is extremely rare, however it is not out of the realm of possibility. As you know, MAC addresses (for the most part) are burned (hard coded) into the NIC by the manufacturer. However, some manufacturers produce cards that allow you to change the MAC with software. (Thus increasing the chance that you could have duplicate MAC addresses on one network.)
>
> Why would you want to change your NIC's address? Most of the time you wouldn't. However, on one job I was working the PCs needed to connect to a large array of AS/400s. The access to the AS/400s was granted by MAC address. Therefore, all machines on the network had their MACs changed to fit the access they needed. We would routinely encounter duplicate MAC addresses.

There are some drawbacks to using IPX. Because the major protocol of the Internet is IP, you must run a protocol converter before hitting the Internet. This can be as simple as using a router with two interfaces: one IPX (for the local network) and one IP (for the Internet). However, this is an extra step, and there may be some tricky programming required on the router to get traffic flowing correctly.

Another drawback to using IPX is more evident in mixed networks. If you have a mixed network with Novell and Microsoft servers you may have multiple protocols running around. You could have Novell IPX/SPX on the NetWare servers and NWLink and Novell IPX ODI protocol on the Microsoft machines.

Try to standardize on one common protocol if possible. The more protocols you have on your network, the more chances you have for errors and incompatibilities.

This brings us to our next protocol, NetBEUI.

Microsoft and NetBEUI

Until Windows 2000 came along, IP was not the default protocol installed on Microsoft platforms either. Microsoft installed its own little protocol known as NetBEUI. NetBEUI is a great, lightweight, reliable protocol.

NetBEUI has one major drawback, however; it's not routable. In today's operating environments, most companies will have routed networks, even if the routing is just for Internet connectivity. This really limits the practical uses for NetBEUI.

However, like everything, NetBEUI does have its place. If you are designing a small to mid-sized Microsoft-based network with no planned router needs, NetBEUI will work very well. How many networks will you encounter that fit that description? Not many, but enough to warrant mention here.

Choosing Your Protocol

Which protocol you choose for your network depends on the environment you are designing. There are definite instances when you would use any of the protocols we discussed in your designs.

Clearly, the protocol of choice for most networks you encounter will be TCP/IP. If you are designing a large network (multiple subnetworks over any number of WAN links) with a connection to the Internet, you should consider IP. Because IP is the routed protocol used on the Internet, you will have no issues sending or receiving data over any public switch.

You should choose IPX if you are working with a Novell (or Novell/Microsoft mixed) network, where the version of NetWare is older than version 5.0. Versions of NetWare older than version 5.0 used IPX by default. IP was offered as an add-on to the original operating system. In a situation where you are only running NetWare, use IPX. Novell implemented the protocol very well, and it works with little configuration.

If you are running a mixed Microsoft/Novell network, you should use Microsoft's NWLink to interface with NetWare's IPX, rather than Novell's IP to interface with Microsoft's IP. Prior to version 5.0 of NetWare, the version of IP you could add on to the operating system was Novell IP. This version of the protocol differs slightly from Microsoft's IP. You may get sporadic (unexplainable) anomalies if you mix the two IP stacks.

As for NetBEUI, I would have no problem designing a small network using the protocol. If you are designing a small, private network (no routing, no Internet connection) NetBEUI will be a good choice. This protocol is small and fast, fitting many non-routed designs very well.

Summary

- The seven layers of the OSI are
  - Application
  - Presentation
  - Session
  - Transport
  - Network
  - Data Link
  - Physical
- TCP/IP is the most common suite of protocols in use, and the major protocol of the Internet.
- TCP is a connection-oriented protocol.
- IP provides 32-bit addressing of networks and hosts.
- There are 3 classes of IP addresses: A, B, and C.
- IP addresses can be subnetted to allow for more networks.
- IPX is a Novell-supported protocol allowing for 80-bit addressing of networks and hosts.
- The Microsoft protocol NetBEUI is not routable.

Connectivity Devices

IN THIS CHAPTER

Connectivity devices are "required equipment" for inter-computer communication. Each device performs a specific function in a network environment. What device do you choose for your network?

Devices can range from the very simple in technology (hubs and MAUs) to the very complicated (routers and switches). All connectivity devices can be divided into two categories: intelligent and un-intelligent. *Intelligent* connectivity devices such as routers and switches perform the most complicated tasks. These tasks can include routing by IP address or blocking access to a part of the network. Some devices can even monitor and allocate bandwidth on demand. Complicated tasks such as these can only be performed by intelligent devices.

Routers and switches perform these "intelligent" tasks with the help of a processor and an operating system. In most cases, these devices use a proprietary operating system that was created for specialized functions. However, because these devices are designed to perform such complex tasks, they tend to require some amount of configuration before deployment. Administrators will typically need to configure a router or switch for their particular network (or network segment), making them hard to port from network to network. Unlike hubs, if a router dies on one network you can't replace it with another router (from another network) and expect it to work without configuring it.

Implementing and configuring devices such as routers, switches, and bridges requires a greater amount of networking knowledge than hubs and MAUs. Before implementing these devices, make sure the client has a complete understanding of the skill set required to successfully maintain all of the devices on the network.

Un-intelligent devices, on the other hand, generally have no processing capability or operating system. They perform easier tasks without discretion for any network criteria. These devices tend to deliver information in a linear fashion (that is, there is one physical path the electronic signal can take to its destination). Hubs, MAUs, and other un-intelligent devices are "plug-and-play." You can port these devices from network to network, segment to segment, and they will work just as well on one as they will on the other.

There are many reasons why you would want to use an un-intelligent device over an intelligent one. All connectivity devices have a place in today's network environments. Many people base their decision on cost; others look only at the speed of the device. Un-intelligent connectivity devices tend to be less expensive than those with the capability to process complex data. However, that is not the only reason people choose to implement hubs over switches.

Portability and ease of configuration are two factors that make hubs (and other un-intelligent devices) popular. These devices can be shuttled from place to place very easily and work just as well on one as on another, because there is little or no configuration involved.

By the end of this chapter you will be able to effectively use all routers, hubs, MAUs, and bridges in your designs.

MAUs and Hubs

This section focuses on two of the most popular un-intelligent devices: MAUs (Multiple Access Units) and hubs. Although you will see many more hubs during the course of your projects, I included a small section on MAUs to prepare you for any mixed networks you encounter.

MAUs

MAUs are used on Token-Ring networks. These devices help create a ring for the "token" to travel around. They look and function similarly to hubs, however the two are not interchangeable. MAUs function only in Token-Ring environments.

Because Token-Ring networks are quite limited in the speeds they can achieve, MAUs are only capable of moving data at 4Mbps or 16Mbps. (Remember that in a Token-Ring network it is the NIC that determines the speed of the network, not the connectivity device.)

MAUs employ the simplest of technology. MAUs operate by taking bits of data and releasing it down one set path. Information on a MAU travels from the first port to the second port (and so on) in order until the data reaches the end. The data has no other paths to choose from (unlike a router) and a standard MAU has no processing capability to make complex routing decisions.

> **NOTE**
>
> Companies such as Nortel and 3Com have created MAUs that perform other, more technologically advanced functions than the average MAU. These functions can include monitoring networks or port activity. However, the technology behind what a MAU does as a connectivity device has not changed. The overall purpose of a MAU is still to move data in a logical ring.

If this form of data routing sounds familiar, there is a good reason. By connecting the last port on a MAU to the first port of another MAU, a physical loop or ring can be created (see Figure 7.1). All of the workstations participating in the network are then connected to the remaining available ports.

7

CONNECTIVITY
DEVICES

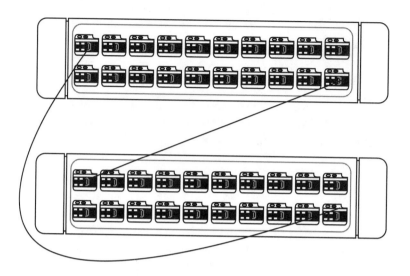

FIGURE 7.1

MAUs connected in a ring.

MAUs are available in a number of different port configurations. The most common are 12- or 24-port RJ45 MAUs.

CAT5 is not the only cabling option you will see in MAUs. I have also worked with devices that use IBM type 1 cabling. These devices (because IBM type 1 cabling is larger than CAT5) tend to be larger than RJ45 MAUs with less port capacity. A typical IBM type 1 MAU can accommodate eight ports per device.

NOTE

The speed of a Token-Ring network (unlike Ethernet) has nothing to do with the connectivity device. There are no speed requirements or specifications for MAUs. A single MAU will work just as well on a 4Mbit network as it will on a 16Mbit network.

When you are designing your Token-Ring environment, try to have the best idea possible of the total number of ports needed on your network (before ordering any equipment). There are two reasons for this.

First, MAUs are very expensive per port. You will want to know exactly what you need before you order too many or too few devices. (You don't want to have a very expensive piece of equipment sitting around doing nothing.) On the other hand, you don't want to order three expensive MAUs, only to approach the client later and ask to purchase more.

The second reason for knowing an exact number before ordering equipment is the configuration of the RI/RO (Ring In/Ring Out). On some devices, the RI/RO ports are separated from the workstation ports, therefore a 12-port device will really be a 12-port device. However, on some devices the RI/RO ports are included in the total number of ports on the device. On a device like this, a 12-port MAU would really have only 10 usable ports.

Both of these reasons illustrate the fact that you need to have a well-thought-out plan before you attempt to move in a more permanent direction (such as ordering equipment).

> RI/RO stands for Ring In/Ring Out. These are the ports used to connect MAUs and form a physical ring. The Ring Out port of the first device is connected to the Ring In port of the second device. This continues until you reach the last device. The Ring Out port of the last device connects to the Ring In port on the first device, thus forming a ring.
>
> Some newer MAUs have separate RI/RO ports (usually on the back of the device). However, older devices (especially older IBM type 1 MAUs) have RI/RO ports included in the port configuration of the device. (On an 8-port device, one port is designated for Ring In and another for Ring Out, leaving six usable ports.)

Token Ring uses an access method known as *token passing*. The main function of a MAU is to facilitate the act of token passing.

When a workstation sends a token onto the network, it leaves the NIC. The first device it encounters is the MAU. The token passes from port to port (being processed by every device connected to the MAU). Once the token reaches the last device on a particular MAU, it is directed to the Ring Out port. The Ring Out port of one MAU is directly connected to the Ring In port of another. (This allows the token to continue moving in a ring.)

NOTE

> Older MAUs are actually wired (internally) like a circuit. This means that information can physically only travel from one port to the next.
>
> Newer MAUs use a small amount of processing capability to send the token to the next available port.

The workstation receiving the token processes it and sends it along to the next port. This scenario works great physically but has one logical drawback.

If a workstation attached to a MAU is not functioning properly (for example, it can accept a token but it does not process it), every machine attached to a MAU from that port forward will cease network operation. This is a common problem with Token Ring in general.

7

CONNECTIVITY
DEVICES

Even though problems like this are difficult (if not impossible) to avoid, you can take measures to help you get your network back up as soon as possible.

Label your MAUs in a clear and logical fashion. When a machine goes down, you'll want to be able to find it and remove it from the MAU as quickly as possible.

Another thing you can do is to populate your MAUs logically. Don't put three people from accounting on one MAU with five people from HR, and then put the remaining six people in accounting on another MAU with the two people in IT. Try to keep everybody geographically together. This ensures that if everyone in HR is having a problem, you know exactly what MAU to look on.

Hubs

A hub refers to an un-intelligent device that has no discretion whatsoever as to where or how it sends information through a network. A switch (or switching hub), on the other hand, is an intelligent device capable of many more functions, including port management, anti-broadcasting, and protocol options. Switches are by far the premier choice for today's networks; however, I have included a section on hubs because there are instances in which you may need to implement them.

Hubs are to Ethernet networks what MAUs are to Token Ring. That does not mean they work the same way—they are actually quite different, but they do allow workstations to communicate with each other with minimal overhead.

Hubs are a popular solution for network designers because of their cost and their ease of installation. Hubs are extremely inexpensive per port. You can generally find a 5-port, 10Mbit hub for about $30. However, these (less expensive) hubs tend to offer no management capability at all. (Some hubs, even though they offer no routing or switching capability, do have a management feature.) Some hubs allow the administrator to view and control aspects of the hub's functionality through SNMP (Simple Network Management Protocol).

If you are going to choose a hub (over a device like a switch) you should try to choose a vendor known for its consistency and stability. (Vendors such as 3Com have made un-intelligent hubs that continue to provide consistent results.)

NOTE

When considering a connectivity device, price is usually discussed as a "per-port" value. This is because connectivity device configurations can vary greatly from vendor to vendor. Therefore, to have a common basis for comparison you need to break the device down to its smallest part, the port. Many vendors will openly offer you a per-port price comparison of their product versus those by other vendors.

A hub accepts incoming information from any port and "broadcasts" it to remaining ports. This can cause some undesirable results. The act of broadcasting data to as many as 36 simultaneous ports can reduce the amount of available network bandwidth. Why do hubs transmit data in broadcasts? Hubs do not have the processing ability to make complex routing decisions. This lack of discretion causes the hub to broadcast information to all ports, thus ensuring the intended destination receives the information. The other machines on the network just disregard the information.

Ethernet hubs (unlike MAUs) are available in different speeds. Hubs can be rated for 10 or 100 megabits per second. However, this bit rate is not a guaranteed per-port bandwidth (only switches guarantee a per-port bit rate). Rather, it is the approved bit rate for the device as a whole. The per-port speed can vary with the amount of network traffic.

Switches (or switching hubs) are discussed later in this chapter. Switches offer a more desirable alternative to hubs, with many more features.

Hubs are better suited for small networks or network segments. Because hubs offer nothing in the form of traffic management, their use is best reserved for low-traffic situations. However, they are extremely cost effective, so you may be using them more than you expect. Many designers use hubs (not switches) on small network segments where only four or five workstations need to be connected to the rest of the network.

7

CONNECTIVITY
DEVICES

Check the hub vendor's online documentation before designing any Ethernet networks. Almost all stackable hubs (hubs that can be chained to each other to provide more ports) restrict the number of hubs you can chain to each other. In some cases you can only connect four hubs, creating a network of 96 ports. In others the numbers are greater, however almost all hubs have a limit to the number that can be interconnected.

Switches

A switch can be thought of as an intelligent hub. Switches (like hubs) have ports to deliver data directly to the workstation (unlike other intelligent devices, which only deliver to networks). This means that switches (or switching hubs) pass data directly to a workstation or other devices, whereas a router will only pass information to a specific network.

From the outside a switch may be indistinguishable from a hub. The difference between the two is on the inside. Switches (like routers) have a processor and an operating system to help them make decisions on routing data. Even though they do not use complex calculations to route data across vast networks, switches do perform some of the same functions as routers.

How Do Switches Work?

Switches have the capability to query the workstations attached to each port. This information is placed in the switch's internal cache. This cache stores all of the MAC addresses of workstations in memory and changes them as workstations are added and dropped.

When the switch receives data, it opens the packet and reads the destination. The switch can then match that information to the addresses in its cache and route the data to the correct port. Reading the MAC address off of each particular packet and routing it to the correct port eliminates the need to broadcast data to every port.

Switches have a great advantage over hubs because they do not broadcast information like hubs do. This also means that switches can guarantee per-port bandwidth. When you purchase a 10Mbit switch, each port is guaranteed a throughput of 10Mbit. (Depending on network traffic, a 10Mbit switch can be faster than a 100Mbit hub because of the lack of broadcasting.)

This technology does come at a price. Switches can have a per-port cost double or triple that of an un-intelligent hub. Even though prices are coming down, some companies will find switches to be cost prohibitive.

When Would You Use Switches?

Switches are best utilized on large networks where bandwidth usage is critical. Examine your designs carefully and ask yourself these questions:

- Will my network need to support high-bandwidth applications such as streaming video?
- How many subnets will my network have? (Some subnets may need switches while others may get by on hubs.)
- Is the per-port cost justifiable on a larger network?

Switches offer more stability and overall bandwidth to networks than hubs do, and you should always consider using switches in your designs. Switching allows the client to grow at a rate that hubs will not stand up to.

You need to design the best network for your client's needs. If your client consists of five people in an office who need to send files back and forth, by all means give them a hub. However, if the client is a business with a growing network and multiple bandwidth concerns, there should be no hesitation in using a switch.

Routers

Routers are perfect examples of intelligent connectivity devices. Routers have a processor and an operating system to aid in the delivery of information to specific places. The combination of the processor and the operating system enable the router to make complex decisions based on multiple criteria. (Criteria are provided by the administrator. Routers require a greater deal of configuration than hubs, or even switches.) This capability makes the router an intelligent device.

Routers deliver data to specific destinations through a series of "best paths." The router can either be told explicitly what the best path is (*static routing*) or it can use any number of criteria to figure out the best path (*dynamic routing*). Which type of routing is best for your network depends on the level of administration the client is willing to provide. Dynamic routing requires more administration and configuration to both implement and maintain than a static routing environment.

> **NOTE**
>
> You may choose not to include a router in every network you design. In some networks they are just not needed. Some networks you design will use a third party to implement routing solutions. However, you should realize where routers are best utilized and how they work.

Static Routing

In some networks you design you may have a set path for information to travel. In other words, the network is fairly predictable. You know that for information to get from point A to point B it needs to travel over path C. Figure 7.2 is an example of a network that would use static routing.

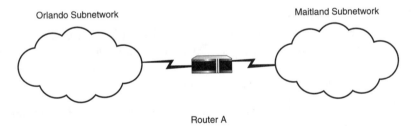

FIGURE 7.2

A static routing environment.

In this example, if a user on subnet Orlando needs to access the server in subnet Maitland, there is only one path the information can take. The user sends his information to Router A. The router then forwards the information to the subnet Maitland.

This example may seem a bit elementary (in fact, a router would not even be necessary in this situation), however, Figure 7.3 shows another example based on the same idea.

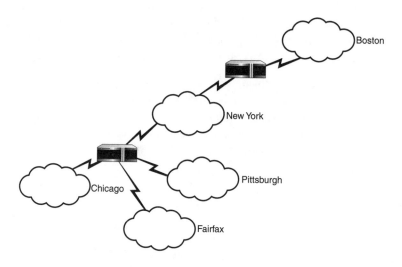

FIGURE 7.3

A more complex routing environment.

This network has five subnets. If a user in subnet Boston needs to access a file in subnet Chicago, the router uses a static path to send the data. The frames would travel from Boston to New York to Chicago. The router would not make any decisions concerning multiple paths to a destination. Information leaving Boston bound for Chicago would always travel the same path.

The following section discusses how static routing is accomplished.

Before Implementation

Before you implement any routing solution you absolutely must have the clearest possible picture of what the finished network will look like. Make a network map that shows your network segments with any protocol information you can include. Figure 7.4 is an example of a network map that I would use to plan my router implementation.

This map allows you to see exactly where you need to make routing decisions. One thing you want to avoid is router overkill. Routers tend to be causes of bandwidth bottlenecks (masses of information passing from one network to another through one port). For this reason you want to choose your router placement carefully. Not every network segment needs a router.

The most common areas for router placement are between IP subnets. Here the router can direct information that otherwise cannot travel between the networks. However, if you have two separate networks (using the same IP subnet), there may not be an overwhelming reason to route data between them.

Another factor to keep in mind is that routers can be expensive and complicated to configure. When planning your router placements, explore the skill set of the client's administration team. Can they maintain the routers after they are implemented?

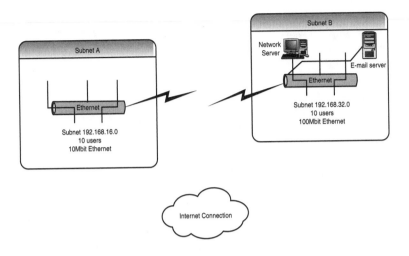

FIGURE 7.4

Pre-router network map.

Implementation

Routers operate through the use of tables. These tables are stored in the router's internal memory. Routing tables store the network addresses of any destination network to which it has access.

> **NOTE**
>
> Routers do not route information directly to a workstation. Routers only send data to the network the destination device is on. Once the data is on the correct network, the hub, MAU, or switch takes it to the workstation.

These routing tables can be populated one of two ways: statically or dynamically. The administrator manually populates a table that is static. The static table data includes source and destination network information. This information does not change without input from the administrator.

> **NOTE**
>
> If a static routing environment needs to be changed, every routing table on every router needs to be modified manually. (In a dynamic routing environment, this is not the case.)

How would you statically map the routing tables for the network illustrated in Figure 7.5?

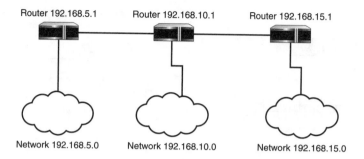

FIGURE 7.5

An unconfigured static routing environment.

Here are the static routing tables for the routers in Figure 7.5.

Router 192.168.5.1

Source Network	Destination Network	Destination Router
192.168.5.0	192.168.10.0	192.168.10.1
192.168.5.0	192.168.15.0	192.168.15.1
192.168.10.0	192.168.5.0	Local
192.168.15.0	192.168.5.0	Local

Router 192.168.10.1

Source Network	Destination Network	Destination Router
192.168.5.0	192.168.10.0	Local
192.168.5.0	192.168.15.0	192.168.15.1
192.168.10.0	192.168.5.0	192.168.5.1
192.168.10.0	192.168.15.0	192.168.15.1
192.168.15.0	192.168.10.0	Local
192.168.15.0	192.168.5.0	192.168.5.1

Router 192.168.15.1

Source Network	Destination Network	Destination Router
192.168.5.0	192.168.15.0	Local
192.168.10.0	192.168.15.0	Local
192.168.15.0	192.168.5.0	192.168.5.1
192.168.15.0	192.168.10.0	192.168.10.1
192.168.15.0	192.168.15.0	Local

> **NOTE**
>
> Notice the differences in the static tables for the three routers. Notice there is no entry in the table on router 192.168.15.1 for routing data originating on network 198.162.5.0 bound for network 192.168.10.0. That data should never reach the 192.168.15.0 network.

As you can see, even with a routing environment of only three routers, configuring static routing tables can be very time-consuming. The administrator needs to keep up with changes in the network environment and modify the routing tables as needed.

> If you choose to use static routing tables in your network designs, document the entries for each router. This will help the administrator get a better idea of what is happening on the network and help her keep track of changes.

Static routing is most effective on networks that do not change very often. If you can be fairly sure that the network you are designing will not change, and you have a couple of subnets that need to be connected to each other, try using static routers.

Even though connecting your network to the Internet is discussed in greater detail in Chapter 10, "Internet Connectivity," you should know how to add this option to your designs. Figure 7.6 shows our static routing environment with an Internet connection.

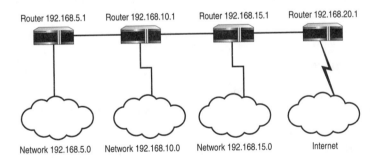

FIGURE 7.6

A static routing network with an Internet connection.

After adding the new router 192.168.20.1 (connected to the Internet) you need to modify the static routing tables. Most brands of routers allow for an entry know as the "router of last resort."

By configuring a table entry for the router of last resort you are effectively telling the router to forward any frames for which it has no table entry. These frames get sent to whatever router is listed as the router of last resort. Therefore, if a frame is sent from network 192.168.5.0 to www.marzdesign.com, rather than have a static table entry for www.marzdesign.com, the router just looks in its table and forwards the frame to the router 192.168.20.1. That router then forwards the frame to the Internet.

One major advantage to static routing is that the routing table itself is not shared. In dynamic routing the device sends a copy of its routing table to its neighboring device. Static routers do not send their tables to anyone.

Because the routing tables are not shared, static routers are more secure. If you are designing a network in an environment where security is critical, you should consider static routing. For a larger network this could mean you have more work to do, but it may be worth it.

Another advantage to not sharing your routing tables is cutting back on network overhead. Static routers can route data faster than their dynamic counterparts. This is due to the lack of complex routing algorithms that can use up processor time. The amount of general network traffic is reduced (though not by much) due to the lack of table updates floating around the network.

Static routing has two major drawbacks. The first drawback is in administration time. Even if the environment does not change very much after installation, setting up the routers can be extremely time-consuming. Great effort needs to be put into ensuring that all possible paths are accounted for or the network will not function correctly.

The other drawback to static routing is down time. If a router becomes unavailable (unlike dynamic routing) there is no way for the network to heal itself. In other words, because the only path to a destination is hard coded on the device, when that path is unavailable the network can no longer function. To compound matters, if there are other functioning routers on either side of a dead device, they are invisible to each other.

Dynamic Routing

Dynamic routing allows devices to update their own tables, unlike static routing. This allows routers to keep up with changes in the environment and pass frames more efficiently.

Dynamic routing involves the sharing of each router's routing table with other devices on the network. This lets other routers know what the status of the network is at all times. By using dynamic routing routers can constantly update a "best path" to any destination.

This best path may not be the same each time. As you can see in the example in Figure 7.7, there is more than one path data can take to get from Subnet A to Subnet D. Dynamic routing would let the router decide which path is best. (Depending on network conditions, it may not always choose the same path.)

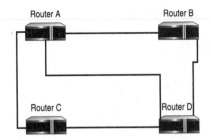

FIGURE 7.7
A dynamic routing environment.

Dynamic routers populate and share their routing tables through the use of routing protocols. (Routing protocols are used by routers to carry information between devices.) These protocols enable routers to communicate with each other and share such information as network status and table entries. Popular routing protocols used today are RIP, OSPF, and IGRP.

> **NOTE**
>
> Each vendor has a different way of implementing RIP, OSPF, and IGRP (IGRP is a Cisco protocol, but some vendors support it). Therefore, I will not go into detail on implementing the protocols. However, I will discuss the limitations of each protocol because this is what will impact your designs.

Routing Protocols

This section discusses the different routing protocols in use today and how they can affect your designs. The routing protocol you choose for your environment may impact the future growth of the network.

RIP

Routing Information Protocol (RIP) enables routers to send updates to other routers. (These updates include the routing table.)

RIP uses *metrics* to calculate the best path to a destination. The router makes decisions based on these metrics and routes data accordingly. The metrics used by RIP are known as hop counts.

> A *hop count* is a numeric value that represents the distance between routers. Generally, the distance from one router is a hop count of 1.

Figure 7.8 is a network map showing just the routers for a sample network.

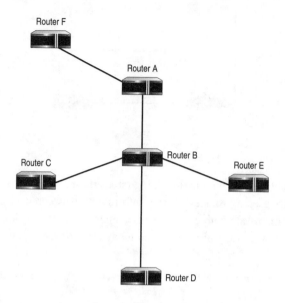

FIGURE 7.8

Sample RIP update from Router A.

The following table illustrates the RIP update for Router A.

Destination Network	Hop Count
B	1
C	no update sent
D	no update sent
E	no update sent
F	1

RIP updates are only sent to a router's direct neighbors. Because routers only send updates to their direct neighbors, until the update circles the network and returns to Router A, it will not know where Routers C, D, or E are. Therefore, only Router B would receive the update. Router B would then send the following update to Routers C and D. (If it looks confusing refer back to Figure 7.8 and it will make sense.)

Destination Network	Hop Count
A	1
C	1
D	1
E	no update sent
F	2

Finally, when the RIP update makes its way around the network, Router A's RIP table will look like this:

Destination Network	Hop Count
B	1
C	2
D	2
E	2
F	1

RIP does have its limitations, most notably a 15 hop count restriction. RIP was designed when nobody thought a network would ever need more than 15 routers. Therefore RIP will not route data to more than 15 hops. Figure 7.9 illustrates what happens when a router dies on our sample network.

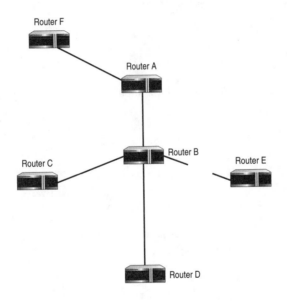

FIGURE 7.9

A network with a down router.

Looking at Figure 7.9 you can see how Router E is situated in the network. Normally this router would have a hop count of 2; however, now that it is offline, the router is automatically assigned a count of 16. This makes the router invisible to the rest of the network.

Destination Network	Hop Count
B	1
C	2

Destination Network	Hop Count
D	2
E	16
F	1

Rather than set the hop count to 0 to indicate that Router E is off the network, RIP sets it to 16. Because the RIP hop limit is 15, setting Router E to 16 makes it unreachable. Therefore, no routers will try to send packets to Router E.

IGRP

IGRP works much like RIP, but the metrics it uses are different. IGRP does not use hop counts to calculate the best path, rather, it uses delay, bandwidth, load, and reliability.

All of these metrics (unlike RIP) are set by the administrator:

- Delay can be any number from 1 to 16,777,216
- Bandwidth can be 1,200bps to 10gps
- Load can be a value from 1 to 255
- Reliability can be a value from 1 to 255

The router takes all of these values for each path, puts them together, and calculates the best path.

OSPF

OSPF (Open Shortest Path First) is another popular routing protocol. OSPF, like most other routing protocols, utilizes metrics to calculate routing options. This particular protocol uses the metric of "bandwidth" to calculate the shortest distance between two points. (The shortest distance being the one with the highest available bandwidth.)

The administrator needs to configure the bandwidths of every port (or link) on the router. OSPF then uses this information as its metrics.

NOTE

OSPF is a "link-state" protocol. This means that the protocol only shares information with neighboring routers about the ports (or links) they are directly connected to.

In other words, if Router A has two ports (port 1 and port 2) and Router B is connected to port 1 on Router A, Router B will only receive updates from Router A concerning port 1.

OSPF is attractive to administrators of larger networks for a few reasons. The first reason is that there is no hop count limit. OSPF can be scaled to networks of any size. This factor makes OSPF very useful in large networks where more than 16 router hops may be possible.

Another reason OSPF is a good choice as a routing protocol is the fact that it uses bandwidth very well. OSPF has two built-in tools for working with and conserving bandwidth. The first tool is a load-balancing mechanism. If you have two paths (from two different links on the same router) leading to the same destination, OSPF will distribute data between the two.

OSPF also helps to limit the amount of bandwidth being used by only sending updates to neighboring routers when a change has occurred in the environment. RIP and IGRP send updates periodically, regardless of whether the network has changed since the last update. This cuts down on the amount of updates being sent, thus cutting down on network bursts.

7

CONNECTIVITY
DEVICES

> All of the protocols discussed in this section are only addressed at a very high level. I have tried to give you enough information about each one to help you decide which would be best for your network. After you have found the one that fits your environment best, I suggest you look further into that particular protocol.

Routers can be used on a network of almost any size, but they are best utilized on network segments. Use routers to segment large networks into smaller, more manageable pieces. By breaking a larger network into small subnets, you give the administrator more control over each segment.

The administrator will be able to ensure that information meant for a particular subnet is sent only to that subnet. Routers can be used to distribute data based on IP (network) address, cutting down on the amount of traffic on certain segments.

If you are using a protocol such as IP, and you have to subnet your network, use routers to connect the subnets. Routers will easily connect the different IP schemes to create a seamless network.

Bridges

Bridges work much like routers because they connect networks. However, unlike routers (which work on the Network layer of the OSI model) bridges work on the Data Link layer. This makes bridges "network type" transparent.

Why is this important? Bridges can be used to connect networks that may be dissimilar. For example, a bridge can be used to connect a Token-Ring network with an Ethernet network.

As router technology has improved over the years, many routers can perform the same functions as bridges. You may not use bridges as much in your new designs, but you will definitely see them on many older networks.

Bridges were very useful in connecting not only Token Ring to Ethernet, but also interconnecting Token-Ring networks. A bridge would be used (like a router) to connect many Token-Ring subnetworks. However, unlike routers, bridges are very streamlined. They do not have to calculate metrics to route data. (In fact, bridges do not *route* data at all, they merely pass it from one side to another. This form of network connectivity can be viewed as a great security risk. Bridges do not discriminate between what information should or should not be shared between networks. Bridges can also be the source of network bursts. One side of the bridge may not be able to handle the amount of bandwidth being sent across, which can cause massive traffic issues on the smaller segment.)

Look at the network design illustrated in Figure 7.10. Where would you place connectivity devices? What devices would you use?

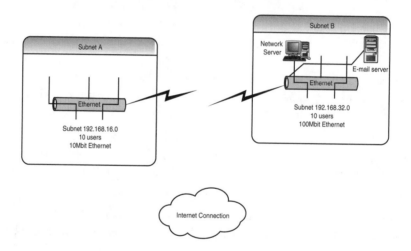

FIGURE 7.10

Network with no connectivity devices.

There is no definite answer here, but Figure 7.11 illustrates what I would use.

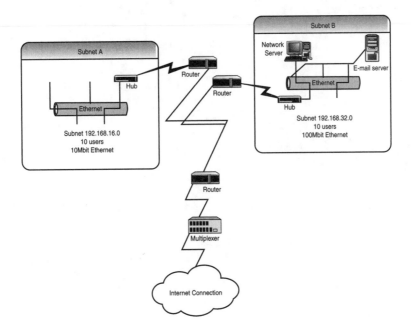

FIGURE 7.11
Author's solution for connectivity device placement.

Summary

- Connectivity devices can be divided into two categories: intelligent and un-intelligent.
- Un-intelligent devices include MAUs and hubs. These devices (most commonly) lack the processing required for making complex routing decisions.
- MAUs are used on Token-Ring networks to create a physical ring of computers.
- Hubs connect Ethernet PCs to each other.
- Intelligent devices include routers, switches, and bridges.
- Routers can pass data using calculations based on metrics to determine a "best path."
- Switches act like hubs; however, they obtain addressing information from individual frames to provide direct delivery.
- Bridges act as connectors for un-like networks.

WAN Technologies

IN THIS CHAPTER

By this point you should have all of the knowledge required to design a fully functional LAN. Your designs utilize hardware, software, protocols, and connectivity devices to support almost any business need.

However, you need to expand your designs from LANs to WANs. WANs open and expand LANs. Internet access, e-mail, telecommuting, and expanded office interconnecting are all functions of WANs.

WANs and LANs are built from the same base components. Hardware, software, network types, and network protocols are all common between the two. Therefore, this discussion of WAN design begins at the point of LAN/WAN divergence: the WAN protocols.

WAN protocols function (technically) like their LAN counterparts. They are designed to work on specific layers of the OSI model and they assist in the transportation of information from source to destination.

WAN protocols are extremely streamlined. They are specialized to carry information in a quick and efficient manner. However, because the information is carried across WAN links (usually a high-speed connection, possibly public access), they have to be aware of bandwidth issues that LAN protocols do not need to worry about.

> **NOTE**
>
> The specific function of a WAN protocol is to encapsulate and "carry" LAN protocols, thus acting as a transport mechanism for LAN data across wide networks.

WAN protocols are written to make the best use of bandwidth. Most offer administrative tools for the control of bandwidth that LAN protocols do not.

WAN protocols also serve different source and destination points than LAN protocols. Where LAN protocols carry data from PC to PC, WAN protocols carry data between networks. What happens when a PC on one network wants to send information to a PC on another? The LAN protocol carries the data to the network's border (the WAN connectivity device). The WAN protocol carries both the LAN protocol and the data to the destination network where the LAN protocol resumes its journey.

The WAN protocol covered in this chapter is Frame Relay. However (as in LANs), the protocols are just a fraction of the picture.

> **NOTE**
>
> The term Frame Relay can be used to describe two things. Frame Relay is a topology (a Frame Relay circuit), and Frame Relay is the protocol that carries data across the circuit. You cannot have one without the other.

This chapter also discusses high-speed WAN connections and the local carriers that provide them. Finally, you will work these concepts into your designs by creating some WANs of your own (on paper).

Frame Relay

One of the more popular WAN protocols is Frame Relay. Frame Relay is effective in connecting remote LANs for a seamless networking environment.

To put it simply, a Frame Relay network is a giant switch interface. When you connect two sites with Frame Relay, the protocol forwards your information to a switch (or series of switches). These switches carry your data to the destination site.

The advantage of Frame Relay is its ability to forward data to the switch. Frame Relay as a protocol allows for the creation of virtual circuits between two points. These virtual circuits allow the information from a single session to travel one path to a destination, regardless of the switch's desire to route along different paths.

To get a better understanding of what this means, take a look at Figure 8.1. This figure illustrates a typical switched network.

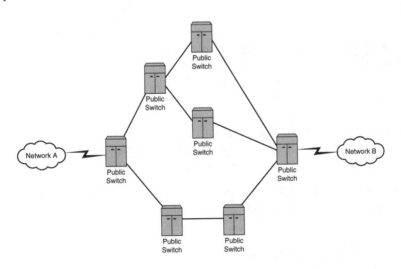

FIGURE 8.1

A typical switched network.

In this example, data must travel through four switches to get from Network A to Network B. The information leaves Network A one packet at a time. Because each packet is its own entity, the switch can send each one along a different path (eventually leading to the same destination).

Even from this rudimentary description of a switched environment, you can see how undesirable a large switched environment can be in WAN networking. Your data will follow multiple paths to one destination, often arriving out of order. Frame Relay eliminates the problem of multiple paths by using Permanent Virtual Circuits (PVCs).

> A Permanent Virtual Circuit is a direct end-to-end path that is unchangeable. To create a PVC, an administrator maps a static routing path on every switch between the source and destination. This allows the information to always follow the same path from end to end.

When you place an order for a Frame Relay connection the vendor will map the PVC on all of the switches between you and the destination. This will ensure the information always travels the same route.

Another aspect of Frame Relay (making it so desirable) is the variety of speeds in which it is available. Frame Relay as a service is available in fractional increments from 56k up to a full T1 (1.544Mbps).

NOTE

> A T1 is divided into 24 channels. Each channel is 64k, making the entire T1 1.544Mbps. Why is the lowest speed 56k and not 64k? There is a 1-bit header on every transmission, thus lowering the 64k to 56k.

When ordering Frame Relay you need to specify how many channels you want between your end points. For example, if you ordered a Frame Relay between New York and Chicago, and you wanted 256k in both directions, you would order four channels.

There is one more factor that you need to pay attention to when ordering Frame Relay service. Read the contract carefully and find out what the CIR is.

> CIR stands for Committed Information Rate.

The CIR is discussed ahead of time with the vendor. You can order a 256k Frame Relay circuit, but it may only have a CIR of 128k. What does that mean? Any network traffic that exceeds the CIR is discarded (in a PVC).

In a Switched Virtual Circuit (SVC), the CIR is adjustable. This allows the traffic to exceed the CIR, but you will most likely be charged a premium for doing so.

NOTE

Most vendors' PVCs will allow for "bursting." This allows your traffic (depending on the overall network usage at the time) to temporarily burst information above the CIR. However, you may be charged for doing so.

Why would you want a CIR that was less than your bandwidth? The lower the CIR is on your circuit, the less expensive the circuit is. Therefore, if you have a 256k circuit between Miami and Orlando, but you only need 128k from Orlando back to Miami, you would set the CIR to 128k on that part of the circuit.

Broadband DSL/Cable/ISDN

For some companies, the services of a high-end WAN link such as Frame Relay may be more than they need. Whether you are connecting SOHOs or providing a quick WAN for a small company, consumer-end broadband may be a plausible choice.

DSL, Cable, and ISDN

DSL, cable, and ISDN services are considered consumer-end solutions because their bandwidth offerings will not support the needs of most larger companies. However, for companies looking to connect small remote offices they are a cost-effective alternative to a full WAN link.

DSL and ISDN lines can provide a good link between two offices. Many connectivity devices provide support for DSL and ISDN links (either as standard equipment or through an add-in). Figure 8.2 shows a network that would benefit from an ISDN connection.

The network in Tampa has four users who are acting as a remote telephone support staff. They need a connection to the main office in Orlando. The users in Tampa plan on accessing some publicly stored files and printing to network printers in Orlando.

8

NOTE

Read your service agreement carefully before signing up for any consumer-end broadband products. Some products will charge for usage (either a per-minute or per-bit rate). This can get very expensive over a WAN link.

Most consumer-end products will not guarantee performance or uptime availability. For this reason, it is not advisable to use DSL, cable, or ISDN lines for a mission-critical link.

If the link goes down, the users can still offer telephone support, which makes them a great candidate for this product.

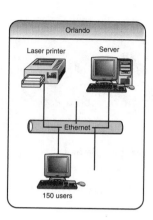

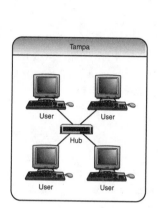

Figure 8.2

Network use of ISDN.

Consumer-end and business-end products (such as Frame Relay) can coexist on the same network. Figure 8.3 illustrates adding another segment to the network shown in Figure 8.2.

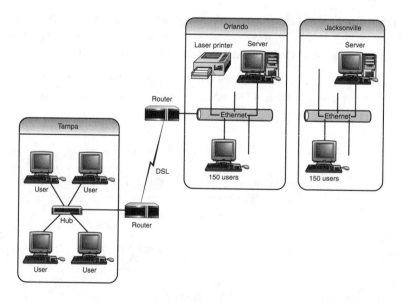

Figure 8.3

Adding another segment to the network.

Our sample company added a new 120-person call center, complete with its own billing, accounting, and HR staff. This new network will use a 128k Frame Relay. Figure 8.4 shows what the new network would look like.

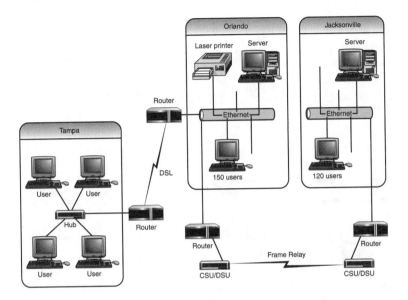

FIGURE 8.4

Connecting the new network with Frame Relay.

Why mix the two technologies? The major factor is cost. Whereas yearly WAN links (Frame Relay) are calculated in the thousands to tens-of-thousands of dollars, DSL and ISDN are in the hundreds. This makes them very appealing to cost-conscious enterprises.

Cable

Would you use cable connections in the same situations you would use DSL or ISDN? No, cable is better suited for a different segment of the user population.

Because most connectivity devices do not offer support for cable connections, it is best reserved for home users. Cable is a good connection medium for users who work from home to connect to a main office.

How can a cable user connect to a main office if no connectivity devices have cable connections? They can't, directly. However, cable works great in cooperation with VPNs over Internet connections where the office network and your PC can connect. VPN (covered in Chapter 9, "Remote Connectivity") offers home users access to their offices via the Internet.

There is one drawback to using cable; it is not the most secure solution. When you use a cable connection you are actually participating in a network with everyone else in your area. This means that the potential is there for others to gain access to your information through your own connection.

For this reason I will generally place a software-based firewall or router between the users and their cable modem.

> **NOTE**
>
> Because software-based firewalls can be tampered with (by well-meaning, but precocious, users) I tend to lean toward using routers.

Figure 8.5 shows a typical home office using a cable modem and router.

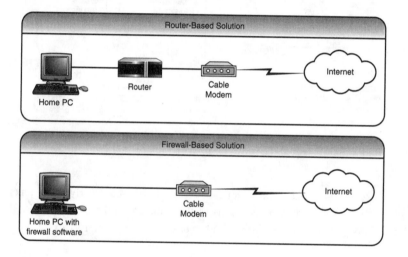

FIGURE 8.5
SOHO with cable connection.

You can configure an access list through your router, which tells the router specifically what IP addresses can get through in either direction. (Consult your specific router's documentation for more information.) Access lists are not foolproof, but they do offer more security than an open connection.

Keep in mind that routers can be quite expensive, especially for home use. In some cases a router may not be economically (or administratively) feasible for a particular home user. You should research the number of low cost (sometimes free) PC-based firewalls if you cannot implement a router-based solution.

Local Carriers

WAN links can be obtained through a number of sources. Knowing who these sources are, and what services they provide, is the key to successfully choosing the right one for your project. Many times you will not be making this decision on your own. The client may have a previous relationship with a provider or they may want final approval over your choice. Either way you will have to do a fair amount of research and provide some good documentation for why you should or shouldn't use a particular vendor.

To help you decide what WAN provider is best for your needs, I divided the available services into two categories: full/managed and a la carte.

Full/Managed	*A La Carte*
Single point of contact for support	Multiple points of contact issues
One monthly service fee	Multiple fees to multiple companies
Equipment is provided "turn key"	You need to configure most of your own equipment
Typically more expensive	

Full/Managed Services

Suppose your network has the layout illustrated in Figure 8.6.

Your job is to link the sites L.A. and Denver with Las Vegas. You have decided to use a 128k Frame Relay with a 128k CIR between Denver and Las Vegas and a 256k Frame Relay line with a 128k CIR to L.A. After some discussions with the client, you find they have no preferred vendors and want to use a fully managed solution. What's your next step?

> **NOTE**
>
> When discussing the client's WAN needs, ask them who their current TI (telephone) provider is and whether they are happy with the service. Because many companies provide WAN and telephone services, you may get a discount for using the same company.
>
> However, some companies don't like to use one company for everything. These companies like to build relationships with multiple vendors in the event anything happens to an existing provider.
>
> While both views are valid, you will need to discuss all options with your client before making a decision.

Start by doing your research. In most cases you won't have to look far; many vendors' telemarketers will find you at the client site. However, I like to start my research on the Web, but not in the obvious places.

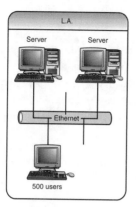

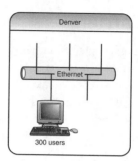

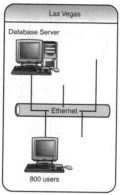

FIGURE 8.6
A typical network.

When I start researching any third-party solution (for any service) I start by searching the Usenet newsgroups. People tend to speak up when they have an issue with a vendor in these groups. I have found a good way to search these discussions is through www.deja.com.

NOTE

As with anything on the Internet, you have to be careful with what you read. However, if you read in 14 different newsgroups (by 14 different people) that a particular vendor has an issue with customer service, then you should consider looking into it.

After using the newsgroups to narrow my field of choices, I move on to the company Web sites. Here I can get a better idea of exactly what services the companies provide and whether they are provided where I need them. I try to end this process with three strong candidates.

With the three possible providers in hand, I will arrange meetings (or sales pitches) between the vendors, the client, and myself. (Even if the client does not insist on being present for the meetings, I will urge them to attend. Because they will be left to work with this vendor after my job is done, their view on the choices is very valuable.)

After one or possibly two meetings, a decision is made. Then it is time to arrange services.

> ***Important*** You may want to start arranging WAN services as soon as the paper network designs have been approved. In other words, do not wait until the LAN portion of the network has been finished to start working on the WAN.
>
> As you may have gathered from the description of the vendor selection process, it can take a while. To put it in perspective, many vendors have a standard (inflexible) 45-day delivery time on local loops (or WAN circuits). That means after you have picked a vendor and agreed on services there is a 45-day wait before they can start installing equipment.
>
> For this reason, the earlier you can begin the process, the better.

Most full/managed solutions will include the following (some of which may be provided by a fourth party):

- Local loop
- WAN equipment
- Installation
- Configuration
- Internet services
- Line monitoring
- DNS hosting
- IP licenses

These services are generally provided transparent to the client (if one or more fourth parties are involved) and will appear on one bill.

You should ask the vendor for these key pieces of information when you are arranging services:

- *What equipment do you provide?* The vendor will usually insist on a standard router or switch type. Generally the client will be charged a monthly fee for the equipment. This can be very cost prohibitive. If the vendor allows you to purchase the hardware, you may want to look into it.

- *Who is my point of contact?* This may sound like it would have a simple answer, but you might be surprised. Many vendors do their best to have a single point of contact for issues, but you may find yourself with a list of people for different problems. In some cases you might have a Web site as the first point of contact instead of a person.

- *What is the escalation path for an issue?* You need to know whom you talk to if your issues are not getting resolved.

- *What is the time frame for completing the work?* You might not get a straight answer for this immediately (because there are other parties involved), but keep asking. You may have to be a little flexible when planning WAN implementations. Expect at least 60 days for full service.

- *What management solutions do you provide?* Management packages can vary greatly. Some vendors will watch for outages, whereas others will monitor your links for outside attacks.

- *What is the down time response?* If your line does go down, what is their obligation for bringing it back up in a timely manner?

A La Carte WAN Services

If you do not have a lot of time on your hands, do not even attempt to order your WAN services in pieces. The process is extremely time-consuming. You may not have the time in the project to spend with multiple WAN vendors working out a solution.

The client will not see immediate cost savings over a managed service. You will be buying all of the equipment up front. However, the lack of major recurring rental charges will eventually make up for the costs.

Another thing you should consider before putting together a WAN solution is administration. Will the client have someone to manage the WAN after you leave? Read over the questions you asked the managed providers, and make sure the client will be able to handle that on their own.

If the client is ready to manage the WAN link, you can begin ordering services.

The first step is to order your circuit from the telephone company. The telephone company is typically responsible for dropping a T1 (or *x* number of channels) between two points. While you are waiting for the circuit (generally 30 to 45 days), you can begin purchasing equipment.

The minimum amount of equipment that you will need (for Frame Relay service) is

- Two routers (one for each side)—The router is going to sit between your network and the CSU/DSU. The router will actually run the Frame Relay protocol and push your data over the link.

- Two CSU/DSUs (Channel Service Unit/Data Service Unit)—The CSU/DSU will sit between the router and the multiplexer. (Some routers have built-in CSU/DSUs, so read your documentation carefully.) The CSU/DSU takes the Frame Relay packets and converts them to bits for transmission over the T1.

- Two multiplexers (optional)—If your T1 is going to be utilized for more than Frame Relay (combining Internet access and Frame Relay on the same T1) the multiplexer will separate the two portions of the T1. The Frame Relay portion can then go to the CSU/DSU and the Internet portion can go to your Internet router.

> **NOTE**
>
> Even though CSU/DSUs have their own inner multiplexers, many of them do not give you the capability to split off a portion of a T1 and use it external to the CSU/DSU. The multiplexer built in to most CSU/DSUs is for the internal use of the CSU/DSU only.

> **NOTE**
>
> Consult your hardware vendor's documentation before installing any hardware.

LAN Considerations

We sometimes take for granted the luxury of designing a complete network from scratch. Implementing a WAN on a network that exists only on paper is much easier (and allows for more error) than implementing one on an existing network.

You must you take several things into consideration when turning an existing LAN into a fully functional WAN.

First and foremost, look at the existing equipment. Will it handle the added burden of a WAN link? Figures 8.7 and 8.8 illustrate two existing networks. The client wants to connect these networks with a Frame Relay.

Your first step in approaching this task should be to draw out your plans. Figure 8.9 shows my solution.

First I moved the server from Memphis to Atlanta (there are more people in Atlanta who need access). I can now set up the Frame Relay.

I suggest a 128k circuit with a 56k CIR from Atlanta to Memphis. Because most of the traffic is now flowing from Memphis to Atlanta (after moving the server), we can save some money by dropping the CIR to Memphis.

Is that all that needs to be done? No, we will need to reconfigure some network services such as DNS and other IP-related software to reflect the changes in the environment.

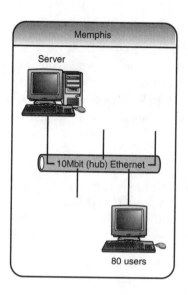

FIGURE 8.7
Network 1.

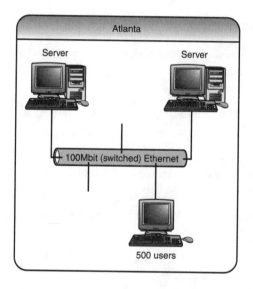

FIGURE 8.8
Network 2.

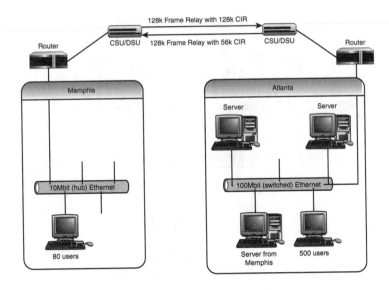

FIGURE **8.9**
Author's solution.

Scenario

Try to link the three networks shown in Figures 8.10, 8.11, and 8.12 with a Frame Relay circuit. I will not offer a solution for this scenario because I have given many solutions for similar issues throughout this section. You should be able to map this network though (it's really quite basic).

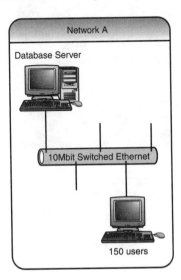

FIGURE **8.10**
Network A.

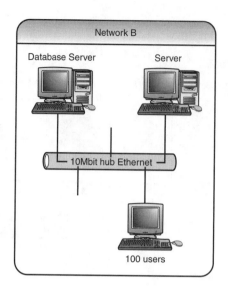

FIGURE 8.11
Network B.

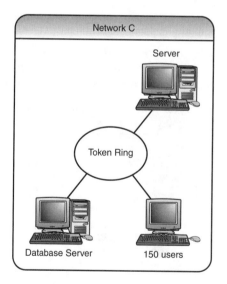

FIGURE 8.12
Network C.

Summary

- WAN protocols carry information from network to network (rather than PC to PC).
- Frame Relay is capable of speeds from 56k to 1544k.
- The CIR (Committed Information Rate) is the maximum data rate your link can carry.
- A CSU/DSU converts the Frame Relay packets to bits suitable for transmission.
- DSL and ISDN are inexpensive broadband solutions for smaller companies.
- Cable modems are suitable for home users (using VPN). Some businesses may find security and bandwidth an issue using cable as an enterprise solution.

8

WAN TECHNOLOGIES

Remote Connectivity

IN THIS CHAPTER

Within the past 5 years, the number of people working from home offices has skyrocketed. Telecommuting is an ever-expanding part of the network user community, and you need to be able to accommodate them in your designs.

Many companies have entire departments working from remote connections, such as an outside sales force. Other companies, as a corporate incentive, may allow users to work from home offices a few days a week. All of these remotely connected users can be placed into two categories: roaming or grounded.

Grounded users are based in one location, such as a home office. These users tend to have the same needs as users on the local network. They will typically require access to most (if not all) network resources, e-mail, the Internet, and printing. Grounded users also tend to have desktop PCs rather than easily transportable notebook computers.

Roaming users, such as a sales force, face issues that grounded users may not. Roaming users almost always have notebook computers. Depending on the nature of the job, the notebook computers can face differing amounts of abuse, leading to sporadic (unforeseeable) issues. However, users who travel tend to require less from their network connections. These users generally only require access to one or two applications and possibly the Internet (although all of these requirements can vary).

Important applications for these users include PIM (Personal Information Management) software and e-mail. Such applications can generally be run from the user's notebook (offline) and synced with the server at a later time. Syncing allows users to conserve bandwidth and telephone costs by using the least amount of (online) time possible.

You may encounter a third type of user: hybrid users. This type of user works at the main corporate office (local network) and from a home office. Hybrid users will typically have a laptop that they use in both locations.

Depending on the remote connection solution, these hybrid users can pose particular problems. The users will need different network settings for each location, and balancing them can be tricky.

There are two main forms of remote connectivity: direct (dial-in) and VPN (Virtual Private Network). Dial-in access is usually provided through a server (or other local device). The user establishes a connection directly to the remote network. VPNs, on the other hand, require the participation of a third party. VPNs utilize the user's Internet connection to attach to the remote network. VPNs also require some firewall configuration (see Chapter 11, "Securing Your Network," for more information).

This chapter discusses all of the issues related to implementing a remote connectivity solution.

Dial-In Connectivity

Direct dial-in access is accomplished through the use of a dial-in host. These hosts are generally specialized servers, such as Microsoft Remote Access Server (a service of Windows NT). These servers accept modem connections and authenticate the users as though they were connecting locally.

Dial-in access is relatively inexpensive. If the user is within local calling range to the host there are no recurring costs. The only required hardware (other than a PC) is a modem.

On the server side of the equation, dial-in server software is either packaged with or available as an inexpensive add-in to the server operating system. As with the client, the only additional cost is a modem (or multiple modems in the case of the server).

I will not cover setting up a dial-in server. However, I will discuss where it is appropriate to use one.

Dial-in servers (as opposed to VPN solutions) are best utilized in small, fairly localized, non–bandwidth-intensive environments.

Each modem you have on the server will require an analog phone line and a phone number. However, the client may have physical limitations on the number of incoming phone lines they have (without the purchase of an additional T1). For some companies purchasing new T1s for analog service may not be a big deal, other companies may not have the resources to expend on 24 phone lines.

Another form of dial-in service is digital dial-in service, also referred to as ISDN (Integrated Services Digital Network).

The equipment used to implement an ISDN connection is a little different than that used for analog dial-in. The server (host) side of the network needs a router. This router is configured with a network number (the network number serves as the phone number for the client to dial). The client then needs ISDN service on their end to complete the connection.

One good thing about digital service is that the service quality tends to be much more reliable than analog. However, roaming users will not be able to use digital services because they are bound to a specific location.

9

REMOTE
CONNECTIVITY

One issue with analog dial-in service is location. Unfortunately, not every user who needs the services of a dial-in solution is going to be within the same local calling area as the host. Imagine if every time you needed to work you had to make a long-distance phone call (possibly for hours at a time). Many users would not appreciate needing to run up unnecessary charges like that. (Even if they route the charges back to the employer, it can be very expensive.)

The client can use an 800 number as a dial-in and eliminate the long distance charges, but that still leaves the third (and most important) factor: bandwidth.

The highest speed possible on a standard dial-in line is 56k. On today's networks, 56k is not fast enough to run many applications. Users will have particular trouble running databases over a dial-in connection. Keep in mind that 56k is the *maximum* speed. However, to accomplish this speed the signal can only be converted from analog to digital once. In a standard environment the signal is switched from analog to digital then back to analog. To ensure a digital environment on the server side, you will need to implement an ISDN solution on the server side. (There are connectivity devices that can handle both analog and digital dial-in connections.)

You will best serve your business client by designing solutions using analog dial-in service for roaming users. However, before committing the resources, examine the needs of these users. Here are some questions to ask about roaming users and dial-in service:

- *What kind of (and how many) applications do the users need to run over the connection?* Remember that the users may not need to be connected to the network to run certain applications.

- *How long will the average user need to be connected?* The longer a user needs to be connected could result in the need for more resources on the server side. You could need more modems, phone lines, and a bigger budget (for higher phone bills).

- *Can the application required by the users run over a 56k connection?*

- *Where does the user normally travel?* Try to keep these connections local (or use an 800 number).

- *Can the client utilize the connection for a secure transfer of data?*

Examine the answers to these questions closely. The two questions that could tell you if analog dial-in service is right for your roaming users are "Can the application required by the users run over a 56k connection?" and "Can the client utilize the connection for a secure transfer of data?" If the client answers no to the either of these questions, an analog dial-in solution may not be what the client needs and you should consider another form of remote connectivity.

For now, assume that an analog dial-in solution is the best solution for your client.

How do you design it? Regardless of the dial-in software you are using, the following guidelines will get you through most situations. We will discuss each point later.

1. Do not use a server on your network that is being utilized for another role as a dial-in server. Especially if you need to accommodate more than 10 users, the resources needed for dial-in access may warrant a new server. Using an existing server on your network for remote access can also open that segment of your network to outside attack.

2. Try to place the server on a subnet (or other network area) that would restrict it from seeing other network areas. Dial-in servers can be large, gaping security holes. Try to restrict as much physical network access to the machine as possible.

3. Try to have more modems than possible concurrent connections. If you have 20 users, but you know you will only have 10 on at any one time, plan on having 12 to 15 modems online. In most cases you will not need as many modems as users (unless each of them will be connected every day, all day). However, you should have extra modems around—modems tend to break (more so than other types of network equipment), so plan on having extras.

4. Define the access speeds needed. Dial-in access can support regular analog lines, ISDN, and special digital lines.

Not only do dial-in servers use many system resources, they tend to be great security risks. Therefore, I try to design dial-in solutions in a way that addresses both concerns. First, try not to use an established server as a dial-in server. In other words, don't install dial-in services on a server that is already performing a role on your network. Second, try to separate the actual network segment that the dial-in server is on. This will limit the amount of network exposure for an attack.

Figure 9.1 shows a typical dial-in solution.

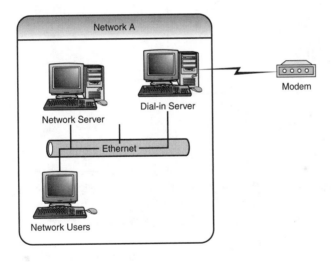

FIGURE 9.1

A typical design for a dial-in solution.

9

REMOTE
CONNECTIVITY

Notice how the dial-in server opens the network to anyone with a modem. Because the users dialing in require access to resources across the network, the entire environment is open to attack. This is what you want to avoid.

Securing a Dial-in Solution

This section discusses the process of securing a dial-in network. The first thing you should do is create a new subnet for the dial-in area. This area can then be separated from the rest of the network with a router. Create an access list on the router to allow access from the main network to the dial-in area, but not from the dial-in area to the main network. Separating your dial-in access to another subnet can lead to the formation of a DMZ. (This scenario requires some extra work and expertise in areas such as advanced routing. A process like this may be too much to go through for a smaller network. Discuss your client's level of comfort and security before endeavoring on a project like this.) Figure 9.2 illustrates the process of implementing a separate subnet for dial-in access.

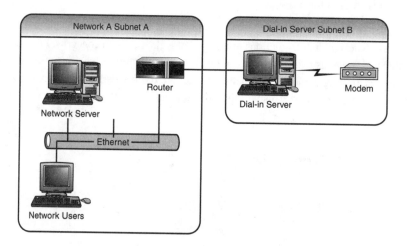

FIGURE 9.2

A separate dial-in subnet.

DMZs (Demilitarized Zones) have come into existence fairly recently in networking. They mark off areas of public access on a network. DMZs tend to be in areas not needing the security of a firewall (or needing just the security of a weak firewall).

The weak firewall (or other access point) allows access to the area of the DMZ. A second, stronger firewall resides at the back of the DMZ to fully restrict access from flowing farther into the network. The firewalls allow users from the host network to access the DMZ freely.

Figure 9.3 shows a true DMZ.

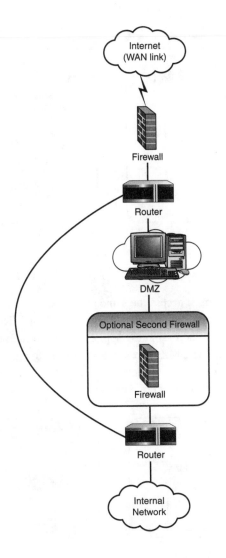

FIGURE 9.3

A standard DMZ design.

Set up the dial-in server in the DMZ. The dial-in server should have its own user list and not participate in the host network in any way (that is, PDC-to-BDC replication).

The next part of the process is tricky, but it may be necessary. If the dial-in users have access to server-based programs that nobody else in the company needs access to, put those programs on another server in the DMZ. See Figure 9.4. (In the figure the dial-in subnet is a DMZ.)

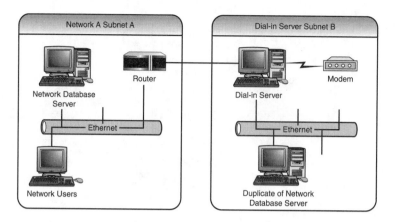

FIGURE 9.4

Separating application servers in a DMZ.

However, if the dial-in users must access the same programs as the remaining user community (that is, a shared database), that program must be put in the DMZ. The DMZ will allow users on the host network to continue accessing the application as normal; however, the tricky part could be adding the server to the DMZ. You might only need to rearrange your server's cabling, but in some cases you might still need to physically relocate the server. See Figure 9.5 for the finished diagram. Notice how I removed the duplicated server from the DMZ.

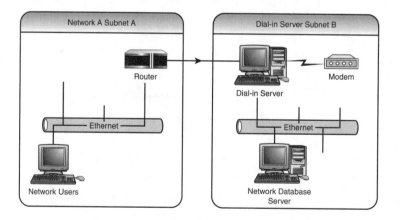

FIGURE 9.5

Network with application server placed in DMZ.

If relocating the server is not possible, you do have another option. The following scenario works best if you need to share a database (as opposed to any other networked program).

Rather than move the server into the DMZ (for dial-in access), set up a new server running the same software. Now you will have two database servers running identical pieces of software. Next, replace the router with a firewall. A firewall will give you more control over specific IP ports.

By reading through your database vendor's documentation, you can find out what ports are used for replication. You can then open those ports using the firewall and close all other points of entry. This will allow you to replicate the database for the dial-in users with the database for the remaining user community, keeping the data intact.

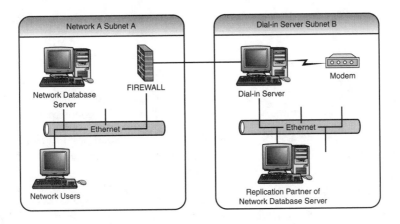

FIGURE 9.6
Using a firewall in a DMZ.

Keep in mind that these scenarios can be expensive to implement (in terms of both time and money). If your client is working with a very sensitive database, or there is information on the network database that remote users should not see, this scenario may work for you.

However, if you only have a small group of users who need access there is an easier, more cost-efficient solution than setting up an entire dial-in server. There are small, personal pieces of software that allow users to work on remote machines via modem connections.

Software packages such as Symantec's PC Anywhere allow a user to dial in to a specific machine and take control of it. This is a good, temporary solution. (Perhaps for a user who is going on leave but still needs access to network resources.)

NOTE

I want to stress the word *temporary* here. Remote control software is considerably less secure than any other (properly installed) solution. (However, it is less expensive and easier to install.) If you feel the client is going to need a more permanent solution, even for a handful of users, try to go with a dial-in server.

Another, more secure solution is to have the users authenticate to the network through a RAS (Remote Access Server), such as Windows NT 4. This option offers you more control over the parameters surrounding the connections and considerably more security.

What if dial-in service is not an option for you? (You possibly need more bandwidth, or have more users than can be served efficiently by a dial-in server.) Your other option is to implement an Internet-based VPN connection.

VPNs

Another solution for granting users remote connectivity is VPN (Virtual Private Network) access. However, VPNs offer the network administrator more control over who accesses the network. They also provide a more secure solution over their dial-in counterpart.

One option for implementing a VPN solution is to contract for a part or a full/managed WAN implementation. If you plan on contracting for VPN services, you may want to read this section anyway for some insight into what makes VPN work.

Consider a VPN solution over dial-in when your number of remote users exceeds a point at which dial-in is no longer cost effective. A VPN device can be more expensive initially than a dial-in server. However, with a dial-in server you have other recurring costs that you do not have in a VPN. For every x number of users you need to purchase more modems and telephone lines. At some point the prices of VPN compared to dial-in will begin to even off. (With a VPN solution there are no added costs per user.)

There are several ways to implement a VPN solution. The solution you choose depends on the budget of the project and the level of technical expertise involved. A firewall-based solution such as a Cisco PIX or the firewall version of CheckPoint Secure Remote (Firewall 1) can be very expensive to initially set up. An OS-based solution such as Microsoft's Windows 2000–based VPN will only cost as much as the operating system itself.

NOTE

It is hard to say exactly how many dial-in users you can have before VPN is your most cost-effective option. The prices of the two can vary greatly. You really have to do some homework here and price different modem options.

Required Equipment (Host Network)

To implement a VPN solution you first need a connection to the Internet (see Chapter 10, "Internet Connectivity"). Next, you will need the VPN software and an authentication device. A firewall is also recommended, but you can use your own discretion when deciding whether to use one on your project. (You will also need a corresponding piece of VPN client software.)

The listed pieces of equipment are available in a myriad of configurations. You can purchase an all-in-one hardware unit that includes the router for the Internet access, the firewall software, the VPN software, and a built-in authentication mechanism. You can also break out all of the components onto their own hardware (a separate router, firewall, VPN device, and a passthrough authentication device).

I tend to gravitate toward the all-in-one devices. I have implemented two—a Cisco PIX and a Nokia 330 running CheckPoint's Secure Remote (Firewall 1). I find these devices easier to manage and there is less hardware to complicate matters and clutter tight wiring closets. However, these devices do provide a single point of failure.

> What is an authentication device? VPN solutions can be authenticated to your network in a couple of different ways. You can have the VPN software provide all of the authentication (the VPN will allow network access based on VPN user rights), the VPN software can pass all users to the network operating system for authentication, or a combination of the two.

The VPN software (if you choose not to go with an all-in-one device) can usually be installed on any number of operating systems. Most VPN software is available for Microsoft Windows 2000 (NT), Unix, and even Linux. However, these products might work in conjunction with built-in firewall software (check with your vendor to see if your VPN software has a firewall component). Microsoft's solution is a built-in component to its newer operating systems (Windows 2000 and Windows ME).

9

REMOTE
CONNECTIVITY

NOTE

> When choosing the hardware for your VPN device, use the same criteria you would use in choosing a PDC. The VPN hardware will be performing roughly the same tasks. However, keep in mind that you will need an extra NIC. One interface of the device must accept users from the Internet while the other passes users to the network.

Figure 9.7 is a diagram of a VPN solution broken into separate hardware devices.

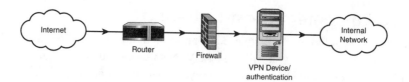

FIGURE 9.7

A VPN solution hardware diagram.

All-in-one devices and separate hardware devices both have their good and bad points. With an all-in-one device there is less hardware to worry about (or break). However, if that one piece of hardware does break, then four services will be rendered useless. All-in-one devices also tend to be more expensive than their piecemeal counterparts.

A good point to note about all-in-one devices is that you will only need one point of contact for customer service. Making a customer service call relating to any aspect of an all-in-one device can be easier than that for a solution housed on multiple platforms.

Required Equipment (Client PC)

The client PC needs two things to implement a VPN solution: an Internet connection and a piece of VPN client software (corresponding to the host network's VPN device). The client can use any method available to connect to the Internet. This includes cable, ISDN, and DSL.

The fact that the client can use broadband connection methods is one of the appealing features of a VPN solution. In some cases, VPN users will have an almost seamless connection to the host network and be able to perform almost any network function.

Designing for VPNs

One of the more important impacts VPN will have on your network is in the IP scheme. You will need to have a number of routable IP addresses to implement a VPN solution.

One option is to assign a routable IP address to the Internet router and NAT the remaining addresses.

> NAT (Natural Address Translation) is a process in which a router has a single routable IP address configured to it. The same router also has a table containing the complete range of non-routable IP addresses that are on its network. Any outgoing packet is re-addressed to appear as if it is coming from the routable address. Any incoming packets are broadcast to the correct non-routable address.

You will face a few issues with using NAT. The first will be apparent if you are using a Microsoft-based network operating system (and your VPN is set up to authenticate to Microsoft server). In this situation you may have trouble gaining access to network resources unless you assign a routable IP address to your WINS server.

I have had some trouble using NAT for WINS. In most cases, the VPN vendor has instructed me to assign routable IP addresses to the WINS server to help authenticate users. The reason for this is simple. If the users have no network access until they are authenticated, but they can't get authentication until they are on the network, you will have a problem.

A second issue you will face using NAT is a little harder to deal with. Consider the following scenario. If you have implemented a VPN solution and you are using NAT for all of your host addresses *and* the client is connecting through a NATed connection, some VPN devices will not function. Most implementations of NAT will not allow an incoming packet from a source that cannot be verified. (That means that if the network cannot send and receive an acknowledgment from a particular address, it will not allow any incoming packets from that address to reach the host network.) Because the client's router re-addresses the packet from the client PC, the host's router cannot verify the packet.

The easiest way to resolve this issue is to purchase a static IP address from your client PC's Internet provider. This will clear up the problem, but will most likely cost you an extra surcharge. If the Internet provider is unable or unwilling to provide you with a static IP address, contact your VPN vendor. Many VPN vendors do have workarounds for this issue. I have encountered this issue twice and both times the VPN vendor did have a workaround. There was a downloadable patch available for the particular software I was using, which resolved the issue.

Scenario

The following scenario examines how to implement a VPN solution.

ABCcorp wants to allow 150 members of an external sales force to access a sales ordering database. These users will be a mix of roaming and grounded users. Figure 9.8 is a diagram of ABCcorp's current network.

In the finished diagram, I added my VPN devices and I had to change the IP scheme as shown in Figure 9.9.

I needed to add a routable IP address to the WINS server and add the remaining addresses to the NAT table.

This will provide the proper addressing scheme for the VPN to function correctly.

I did not have to move around too much of the hardware (unlike the dial-in solution). However, there is also no e-mail connectivity at this time. Notice how the VPN (Internet) router and firewall are attached to the same multiplexer as the WAN link. This allows the two devices to share the same T1. The multiplexer separates the channels used for the WAN traffic from the channels used for the Internet (VPN) traffic.

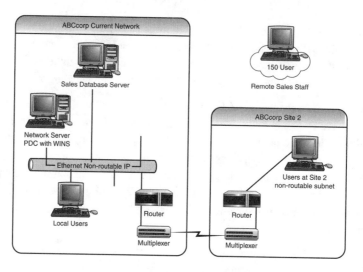

FIGURE 9.8

ABCcorp's current network.

If you use less than half of the bandwidth of a T1 for a WAN link, it is possible for you to use the remainder for your Internet service. Anything less than half for your Internet service may not be enough to also provide you good VPN connectivity.

At the beginning of this chapter I mentioned hybrid users who utilize the same laptop from home as at the office. How do you deal with them? If you are using a dial-in solution you do not have to do anything extra. Dial-in users will use the same network settings as local users. However, if you are using a VPN solution, you might have some issues to contend with.

With a VPN solution, the user will encounter a different IP scheme at home and at the office. If the two locations use static IP addresses, the user needs to be instructed on how to change her address to suit the network she is on (which could cause more headaches than it is worth). The other solution is to equip the user's laptop with two NIC cards. (This may require some fiddling around on your part, but it does work.)

If the user is using DHCP on both networks, the DHCP client should take care of the dirty work for you.

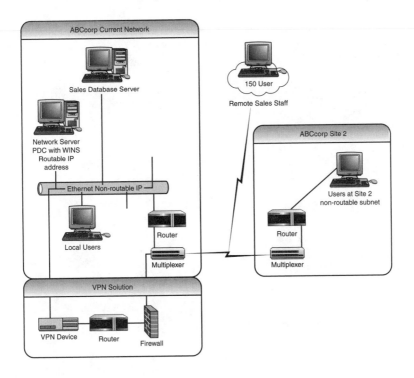

FIGURE 9.9

Author's solution.

Summary

- Dial-in servers are relatively inexpensive (for an initial setup).
- Dial-in connections are subject to recurring monthly charges.
- The highest speed available on a dial-in connection is 56k.
- Dial-in solutions are better for small, localized populations of users.
- VPN services are more expensive initially but are subject to little or no recurring charges (unless the service is part of a full/managed WAN package).
- VPN will not allow a connection that passes through two NATing devices.

Internet Connectivity

IN THIS CHAPTER

Internet connectivity can be a double-edged sword. On one hand, you put all of the information in the world at your client's fingertips. Your client can use this information to expand their business and keep ahead of the competition. By opening your client's network to the Internet, you give them access to e-mail and other tools that can be used for enhancing business and communications.

Chapter 11, "Securing Your Network," discusses the other edge of the sword, which concerns security. Opening your network to the Internet also opens it to attack from the outside.

The purpose of this chapter is to help you implement Internet connectivity at your site. Installing Internet-related equipment can be a complicated and confusing task. However, by the end of this chapter you will have a better understanding of the tasks and devices involved in integrating Internet access with your project.

This chapter looks into the role of connectivity devices in the Internet. Specifically, it discusses how routers, firewalls, and multiplexers are used in providing connections to the Internet. These devices are all used in a different capacity and your network needs to accommodate them.

Third-party vendors will play a large role in getting your network on the Internet. These vendors provide varying degrees of service and sorting through them can be confusing. However (as in the last chapter), not everything needs to be done through a vendor. You might be better off doing many things on your own.

This chapter also covers what makes up a good DNS strategy and how to implement e-mail. Putting all of these components together should produce a functional network that will serve your client's needs.

Working with Internet Providers

As discussed in the previous chapter, the role of vendors in providing services to your network can vary greatly. Most vendors offer services that are customizable to fit the needs of you and your client. You need to research what offerings will best fit those needs.

Take into consideration the skill sets of any administrators the client may have (or that they may be trying to hire) and the type of applications you will use before interviewing vendors. This information will help you formulate a better picture of the needs your client has as pertaining to their Internet services and give you a better idea of what service you need from the vendor.

Following is a list of questions to ask your client before you start looking for Internet providers. Generally (as with everything to this point), these questions should be asked during the design (documentation) process. You should not wait until any portion of the network is constructed to have this conversation with your client.

- *Will the client be considering the use of a vendor in providing a WAN connection?* If the client has plans to install a WAN circuit such as a Frame Relay, the same vendor may be used for the Internet service (some vendors may insist on providing Internet service with their WAN service). If you plan on using the same vendor for both services you may save on implementation time. (I would recommend against splitting the two services. If the client is implementing a WAN link, try to use the same provider for the Internet connection.)

- *What are the bandwidth needs of the client?* If the client wants to use the Internet solely for Web browsing, a smaller pipe may be suitable. However, if the client plans on implementing a VPN and wants to run Web-enabled applications, then larger amounts of bandwidth will be needed.

- *Does the client have any relationships established with vendors for other services?* This could be useful information to have. Most companies will have phone service (I hope). The vendor for the phone service will most likely provide WAN/Internet services as well. Most of these vendors will offer some kind of discount when using them for multiple services.

- *What kinds of skill sets can the client provide after the job is finished?* You don't want to implement a very administratively intense architecture if the client does not have the staff to support it. In such cases, you would want to consider a managed solution.

- *Will the client plan on hosting their own DNS?* We will cover this more in the next section, but you will need to know this information now. Some vendors may charge a small fee for hosting your DNS.

- *Will the client need e-mail services?* E-mail and Internet services do not need to be provided by the same vendor. For instance, if the client already has a Web site hosted by an ISP, their e-mail is already being handled (whether they realize it or not). However, the number of addresses they have (through the vendor) may be far from enough to support a business). If the client already has a registered domain name, all of the e-mail addressed to that domain is being sent to the ISP hosting the name.

DNS, or domain name system, is a service for translating hostnames into IP addresses. Because IP works on numeric addresses, a method needed to be developed to convert the numbers into names that people could remember.

For example, when you type www.marzdesign.com into a Web browser, a DNS server actually translates that name into the address 207.217.96.38. (Even though it is easier to remember the Web sites by name rather than by address, routers still route by address only.) Without a DNS server to translate the name into an address, the browser would never find the site (unless you typed in the numeric IP address).

Here are some scenarios to show you how the answers to the preceding questions can help you.

If the client is planning to implement a WAN link to another site, a T1 will need to be installed. (Depending on the type of WAN link ordered, this could be a dedicated T1 or lease line.) This installation may take around one and a half months.

10

INTERNET
CONNECTIVITY

If the client then chooses to use another vendor for their Internet service (rather than the vendor who supplies the WAN link), the Internet provider may not want to run their service over the proposed T1. In this case, the Internet provider would then have to install his or her own T1. This means the client will have two T1s being run to their site: one for WAN traffic and one for Internet traffic (this will also double the cost of the original T1 installation).

For this reason some WAN vendors will provide Internet service over the same T1. Splitting WAN and Internet providers may result in a redundancy in services and major headaches.

If the client has 400 people using the Internet and another 100 using a VPN service, you will need more bandwidth than you would for a 50-user business using the Internet purely for surfing the Web. The majority of companies that implement an Internet connection need it for more than Web surfing.

Whether the client plans to host their own Web site, allow remote access, or distribute information, you will need to have a formula to justify the amount of bandwidth needed for an Internet connection.

I use the criteria in Table 10.1 to figure out how much bandwidth to use.

TABLE 10.1 Internet Bandwidth Usage

Number of People	Bandwidth Used
Up to 500 people (Web surfing)	128k
Over 500 people (Web surfing)	256k
Up to 150 people using VPN	256k
Over 150 people using VPN	512k
Web hosting company site	128k (average "informational" usage)
	512k to T1 (for e-commerce)
E-mail (up 1000 people standard usage)	128k
E-mail (up 1000 people marketing and distribution)	256k (depending on the size and amount of distribution)

The numbers in Table 10.1 take into consideration application usage under normal business situations (including simultaneous usage). These figures should be added together to arrive at a good estimate for the amount of bandwidth you will need.

In some cases you may be designing a network for a company that has no clear idea of what its staffing needs will look like in the near future. Many of the "dot com" startups will begin with one picture in mind and end up with a totally different one. You should be able to get a rough idea of how big the staff will be and its needs by the other elements of your design. Take a look at the applications you are designing for. Are they high-bandwidth applications? Look at the number of sites you are connecting. Are there servers at every one? By examining your designs, you should be able to foresee the bandwidth needs of the company.

Internet providers, or WAN providers, will generally offer their services together in packages. For example, if a company needs a 256k Frame Relay (requiring a fractional T1 to be run to the site) it makes sense to use the remaining channels (or a portion thereof) for Internet access. For this reason many Internet providers offer the same categories of service as their WAN provider counterparts. It is not uncommon to see full/managed and a la carte Internet service offerings.

Full/Managed Internet Service

Managed Internet service can include any or all of the following:

- Vendor-provided equipment
- Managed firewall
- Intrusion/attack detection
- Some form of technical service
- VPN (can be included as part of the Internet service)
- IP licenses
- E-mail services
- DNS hosting
- Some type of service (up-time) guarantee

The kinds of equipment the vendor needs to supply can include any (one or more) of the following (either for an upfront cost or a monthly lease):

- Multiplexer (separates the channels of a T1). If a T1 is dedicated for data only (no voice), the vendor may just supply a CSU/DSU.
- Router.
- Firewall.

Many vendors will supply a router that contains a firewall. These devices generally save room and equipment costs. However, you may want the vendor to only install a standard router while you implement a firewall of your own.

As with WAN services, managed Internet service is an out-of-the-box package. After coordinating the service issues between your client and the vendor, you can expect to place the order and give the client the contact names; the vendor handles everything else. However, managed solutions do have their drawbacks:

- Managed solutions can be expensive (due to equipment costs and monitoring).

- Many vendors will also require the use of an analog phone line. This line will be used to dial in to the equipment in case of network connectivity failures.

- Making a technical service phone call and waiting a specified amount of time for a response (as outlined in your contract) every time a change needs to be made can be frustrating (especially if it takes multiple calls to fix one problem). Most vendors do have responsive, very well-trained technicians. However, some companies will experience "growing pains" and need to tweak their network for the first few months. These companies may find it tiresome to wait 2 to 6 hours for a network change.

A La Carte Internet Service

The definition of a la carte Internet services is slightly different than that of a la carte WAN services. The main difference between a la carte Internet services and managed Internet services will generally be control over the firewall. The client will most likely retain control of the firewall with a la carte services. (You can also retain control over the VPN service and the DNS hosting; however, those services are optional, even in managed service.)

Why would you want to retain control over the firewall? If your client has an administrator experienced with firewall management, it may be a good idea to implement your own. Policy changes on a firewall tend to require a quick turnaround time, which is something you may or may not get with a vendor. If your client is in a position where waiting for a policy change to occur is not an optimal situation and the skill set to manage the firewall is available with existing staff, then I suggest letting the client handle the firewall.

The following is a list of things you should expect from your vendor:

- Periodic Reports. Many vendors will offer periodic reports (depending on the amount of services) that could include anything from line usage statistics to intrusion attack notifications.

- Low Response Time. Try to negotiate for the fastest response time you can from trouble calls (especially if the client will not control any features of the service). Average standard response times range from two hours to one business day. However, some vendors will let you "buy up" to responses of 30 minutes (on emergencies).

- Flexibility. When purchasing your circuit, make sure that you have enough room to expand. If you are using 512k of a T1 for Internet service, find out what the process is if the client wants to use the remaining portion. (Whom do they call? How long do they need to wait?)

- Single Point of Contact. Many vendors are just now moving to a "single point of contact" customer service model. However, some companies still have separate contacts for different issues. Having a single point of contact to leave with your client is going to make a big difference to them.

Internet Connectivity Equipment

There are two pieces of equipment that play a major role in providing Internet access to your network: the CSU/DSU (Channel Service Unit/Data Service Unit) and the router. Each has a very important role to play. The CSU/DSU is a pretty specialized connectivity device, whereas a router is used throughout your network for different purposes.

Multiplexers and CSU/DSUs

A multiplexer takes all of the information from your network (arriving over separate channels) and passes it over a broadband link. All broadband links are made up of channels (T1, T3, ISDN, and so on). The multiplexer ensures you are using the correct channels for your services.

Most multiplexers have a display panel to inform the administrator which channels are being used and how many are available. Some advanced multiplexers will even display line statistics, such as available bandwidth on certain channels.

The multiplexer should be the first device attached to your network from the T1. Without the multiplexer, your information would not travel through the broadband link. Figure 10.1 shows the placement of the multiplexer in relationship to the telephone company's equipment. However, in most cases you will only use a separate multiplexer if your T1 is carrying both voice and data or if your T1 is being split between two services (such as Frame Relay and Internet). If your T1 is dedicated to just data, you can use a CSU/DSU.

A CSU/DSU not only has a built-in multiplexer, it also translates the data flowing across it. A CSU/DSU will encapsulate the data from the local network for transmission over the WAN link.

In the example in Figure 10.1, the T1 originates from the telephone company. The line then runs to the demarc (the demarc line can be internal of external to your facility). From the demarc the T1 extends to the multiplexer and on to the network.

A *demarc* (demarcation point) marks the line where control over a circuit is transferred from the CO (central office) to the CPE (customer premise equipment). This will be the end point for your physical network.

Routers

A router's basic role in providing Internet services can be explained very easily. The router acts as the traffic director for the entrance of the network. The router knows two pieces of information: the address of the internal network and the location of the Internet. This router will take any information not destined for an address on the local network and throw it in the general direction of the Internet.

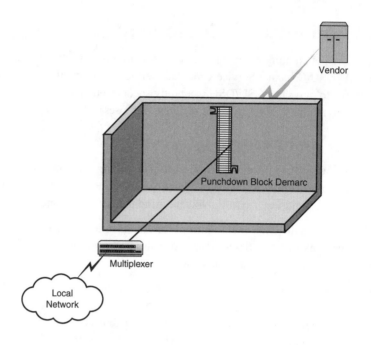

Vendor

Punchdown Block Demarc

Multiplexer

Local
Network

FIGURE 10.1

WAN design with multiplexer.

This piece of equipment will usually be the default gateway (on PCs) or the router of last resort (for other connectivity equipment). If a packet is not deliverable on the local network, it is sent to this device to see if it can be delivered over the Internet.

There is one item that will set a router intended for Internet use apart from all other routers on your network: An Internet router needs a routable IP address. (You can assign routable IP addresses to routers that do not access the Internet; however, a router that is directly connected to the Internet needs a routable address.)

For traffic from the Internet to reach your network, the router needs to be "seen" from the Internet. Making a router visible from the Internet is a two-step process. First, the router must be assigned a routable address from the Internet provider.

The address assigned to the device does not need to be the same address other devices use to refer to the router. This address can be NATed. In other words, if the vendor assigns your router the address 207.123.42.5, but your internal addressing scheme is 192.168.64.x, you can NAT the external address to the internal one. By doing this you tell the router "your address is 192.168.64.x. However, I want you to accept any data from the Internet addressed to 207.123.42.5 and route it to the rest of the network."

The second step in making your router visible to the Internet is to have its address associated with your domain name in your Internet provider's DNS. Your Internet provider needs to do this step for you, and it should appear completely transparent to you and your client. Keep in mind that this process is only required if you want your network to be accessible by name (for example, www.marzdesign.com).

If you only want traffic to reach your network by IP address, the vendor only needs to add you to their routing tables. After adding you to their routing tables, you will be able to receive information through your Internet connection.

Figure 10.2 shows a WAN with a connection to the Internet.

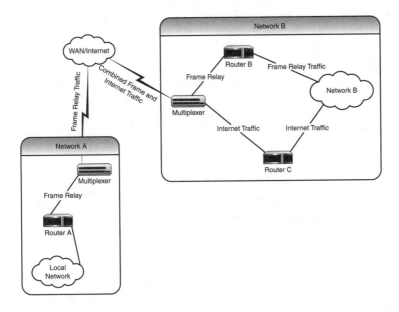

FIGURE 10.2
WAN design with Internet connection.

Here we have two networks connected by Frame Relay. Network A is also connected to the Internet. Look at the configuration for the routers. Router A is used to bridge the Frame Relay, whereas Router C is used for Internet connectivity.

Because of their operating systems and processing ability, routers can be used for other functions pertaining to Internet access. Most commonly, the router can also be used as a firewall.

Most routers can be set up with third-party firewall software. (If you order a managed service from an Internet provider, you will generally receive an "all-in-one" device like this.) You can save in equipment cost by installing the firewall on the router itself. (Separate firewalls can be

10

INTERNET
CONNECTIVITY

expensive depending on platform.) You also rule out any equipment failures between the router and the firewall. However, by giving the firewall "frontline" access, you also create a single point of failure on the network.

I personally recommend an all-in-one device for clients without a dedicated firewall or an Internet security administrator. (See Chapter 9, "Remote Connectivity.")

NOTE

In some areas of your network, single points of failure are going to be unavoidable. Not all routers, servers, and other network systems will have redundancy. The router connecting your client to the Internet may be one of them. Unless your client is large enough to afford redundant connections to the Internet (two separate Internet links, routers, and possibly vendors), you will need to accept this device as a single point of failure.

For most companies this is not a problem. Most companies view the Internet as a non–mission-critical platform. However, if your client's core business function is on the Internet, you will definitely want to explore redundancy in your connections.

Implementing a DNS Solution

We are all aware of the function of DNS: It acts as the road map for our networks. However, when you start dealing with the Internet, that road map changes.

Imagine you are traveling through a foreign country. You have a map of the area to help you get around. However, the map is written in the native tongue (which you do not speak). Right now that country is how your network appears to the Internet if you do not have DNS. Unless you know exactly where you're going, chances are you won't be going anywhere. If you add DNS, the map is translated into something you can understand, and all of a sudden you can travel around with ease. DNS translates the foreign (local) addresses into something easy for you to understand.

When you host your own DNS server, you are creating a map of your network for PCs to refer to when sending information. However, when those PCs want to send information outside the network, where do they look? You certainly wouldn't want to map out the Internet yourself. Therefore, you have two options. You can let the Internet vendor host your DNS for you, or you can become a secondary site to the vendor's DNS.

Primary Versus Secondary DNS

There are two types of DNS servers you can have (in some cases you may have one of each): primary and secondary. A primary DNS will generally have information relating to your internal network. The reason this is termed a primary DNS is that this is the first DNS your PC will look to when it needs to get information. A primary DNS will contain host names for your internal devices such as 192.168.100.55 = MyPrimaryServer1.

A secondary DNS is a copy of somebody else's primary DNS. You cannot make changes to this DNS and (in most cases) you don't hold an actual copy of the DNS table. When you set up a secondary DNS you are basically telling your PCs, "If you cannot find what you're looking for in the primary DNS (if you even have one) try looking to this secondary DNS address." Generally, your secondary DNS will be a mapping to an ISP's primary DNS, which contains information for navigating the Internet.

For a small client with no real in-house expertise, vendor-hosted DNS is a possible alternative. If the client is small enough and the environment will not change very often, talk to the Internet provider about hosted DNS. The vendor will make a couple of entries for the client in their DNS database for the PCs to refer to. In effect, the PCs will only have one database to look to whether they want to route internally or route to the Internet.

However, if you have a larger client in a changing environment, you should consider hosting your own DNS. This will give the client access to make the changes they need to, when they need to.

Do you really need DNS? Depending on your network, you might not. If your network is fairly small or you have no plans for connecting to the Internet, you may want to skip DNS altogether. Actually, it may be easier for me to tell you when you would need DNS rather than when you wouldn't.

If you register your domain (with Internic, Network Solutions, or any of the other approved registrants), you create a name that corresponds to a particular IP address. Therefore, when I registered the name "marzdesign.com," I registered it to 207.217.96.43. By registering that name to that particular address I put "207.217.96.43 = marzdesign.com" into my ISP's DNS. Before I had done this, you would have had to use my IP address alone to find me.

The main reason for registering a domain name is for e-mail. If you want your client to be able to receive e-mail at "TheirCompany.com," that address needs to be registered. (One problem that we face today is the dramatic shortage of domain names. You may want to warn your client to be flexible when considering a domain name because the exact one they want may be taken.)

Many individuals and companies register names with the intent of selling those names to other companies. If your client has a common name like "ACME Motors," they may find that the domain (acme.com) is already registered. (A search can be conducted on www.networksolutions.com.) However, the client can attempt to retrieve the registrant's information (through a "whois" search) and contact them concerning the use of the domain name. It may turn out the registrant simply bought the name, yet has no desire to use it.

> **NOTE**
>
> Many times, if you simply point your Web browser toward your desired domain name (and it has been registered by someone willing to release it to you) it will bring you right to the registrant's ISP's Web site. From here you can get most of the information you need to obtain the address you want.

Is DNS only needed for the Internet? No, if your network is large enough that remembering multiple IP addresses is not efficient, you may want to consider DNS. Many large companies have an internal DNS to help users navigate the local network.

If you host your own DNS, the vendor will need to make some provisions to accommodate you.

The vendor will still need to enter at least one record into their own DNS for you. An MX record will need to be added at the vendor's site to route e-mail to you correctly. The MX record simply supplies the vendor's DNS with the DNS name and address of your e-mail server (which must be a routable address). This will enable messages from the Internet (or any place not local to your network) to find you.

The vendor will then supply you with the name and address of their DNS server. You will need to add a reference to their DNS in your DNS. Adding the Internet provider's DNS as a reference in yours will allow your users to access their DNS entries (and those of the Internet).

A DNS server does not necessarily need to be an entity unto itself. Most companies will operate efficiently with a DNS server installed on another domain controller (or other primary authentication server). However, if the company is very large, or has a high volume DNS resolution, you may want to use a dedicated server.

Pay close attention to where you place your DNS server. Take a look at Figure 10.3. The diagram shows a network with a DNS server that is not in the perfect place.

In this example, the majority of users must travel through three routers to get to the DNS server. Place the DNS server on your largest subnet; that's where it will be most effective. If this adversely affects the other subnets, they may be large enough to have their own secondary DNS servers. Figure 10.4 shows a better placement for the DNS server in the previous example.

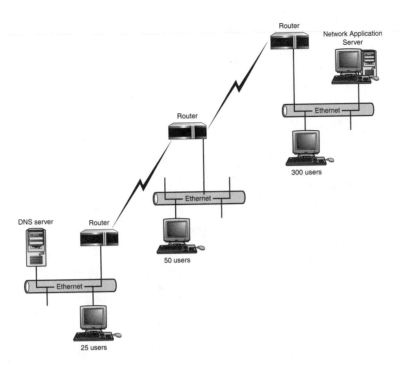

FIGURE 10.3
Incorrect DNS server placement.

> Most situations will have you putting your e-mail server in a DMZ (discussed in the following section). Putting a DNS server in a DMZ could be very bad for security. Remember, DMZs allow less secure access to certain parts of your network. Putting a DNS server in such a situation could compromise the addresses of all of your local servers and routers.

In this example, the DNS server is within a router hop of both the e-mail server and the Internet; however, it is not with the DMZ.

A DNS server is not your only option for implementing DNS. If your network is fairly small (at least small enough that implementing a full DNS server is not practical, but you want the convenience of DNS), you can use hosts files. Hosts files are flat text files that contain all of the DNS mappings for your network. (If you are using a Windows-based PC, do a search for Hosts.sam (every Windows machine has one). This file is the sample hosts file. (To make that file the actual hosts file, remove the sam extension.

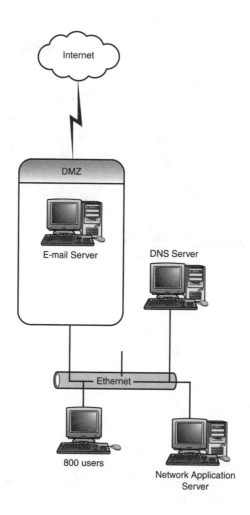

FIGURE 10.4

Good DNS placement.

Hosts files do have a drawback: they need to be manually edited when changes are made to the network architecture. However, this may not be a bad price to pay if you do not expect your network to change very much.

Preparing for E-mail

When you are still in the design phase of your network project, try to begin naming your servers on paper. When you get to the point of designing your Internet access and e-mail areas, you want to have as much information (on paper) as possible.

Remember, you will be ordering your services before you even begin constructing the network. The Internet vendor is going to want two key pieces of information from you (concerning your e-mail): how many routable IP addresses you need and the name/IP address you will assign to your e-mail server.

The vendor will need this information for the work they need to do on their end. They need to make provisions in their DNS and they need to gather free IP addresses to supply to your network. You will be supplying this information to them weeks in advance. Therefore, you need everything drawn out accurately on paper, so as not to provide information that is incorrect.

There are two theories on placing e-mail servers on networks. One theory is that a good firewall offers all of the protection you need. Simply allow for mail traffic on a specific firewall port and your network is finished. A network diagram based on this theory would look like Figure 10.5.

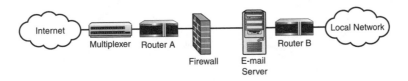

FIGURE 10.5
E-mail protected by a firewall.

The mail traffic would enter with the rest of the Internet traffic through Router A. The mail would pass through the firewall to the mail server (and the rest of the network).

This option is definitely the most cost-effective; however, it is also the least secure.

> **NOTE**
>
> By saying this option is the *least* secure, I do not want to insinuate that it is *not* secure. It is still as secure as the firewall you put in place. Remember that a hole in a firewall is an entry point to your network. Can port 25 (the port needed for SNMP traffic) be exploited? (If you have a firewall between your e-mail server and the Internet, IP port 25 needs to be opened to allow e-mail to pass through.) Yes, but to what extent?
>
> Opening port 25 is a very small security breach, and most times it cannot be avoided. If the network you are designing lends itself to placing an e-mail server in this setting, don't lose any sleep over it.

This design works best on smaller networks, especially those with no need for a VPN solution. However, if your client is a larger (security minded) enterprise (possibly with a need for a VPN solution), you may want to model your design after the following scenario.

The second scenario of e-mail placement has the e-mail server going into a DMZ. We discussed DMZs in the last chapter as they pertain to VPN service. The same DMZ can be utilized for your e-mail server.

The DMZ will allow less secure access to only those parts of the network where outside information may be stored. E-mail definitely fits this description. The e-mail and remote access servers will be the two most unsecured entities on your network. You need to design around them carefully.

There are two different ways to set up a DMZ around an e-mail server. The first way to set up a DMZ is almost like a floodgate (see Figure 10.6). In this example, the e-mail server acts as a pass-through.

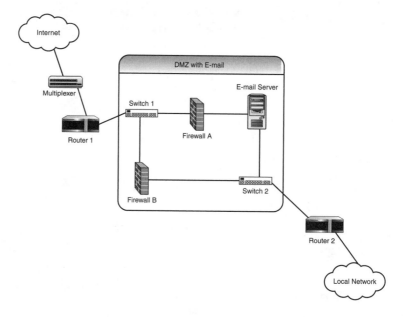

FIGURE 10.6

E-mail within a DMZ—option one.

The second way to set up a DMZ for e-mail is to have the e-mail server originate from a separate interface on the Internet router. See Figure 10.7.

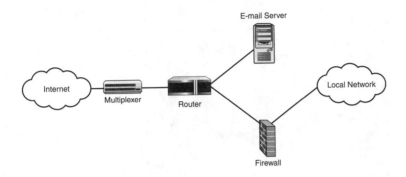

FIGURE 10.7

E-mail within a DMZ—option two.

This example is a little friendlier to VPNs.

I find this example to be easier to manage. If you use an all-in-one device, the administrative picture is a little more refined. You generally do not need to mess around with multiple firewalls and IP ports. Even though there are now two distinct network segments, they can be served from one firewall.

Scenario

Design an e-mail solution for the following company showing DNS and WAN placement information.

ABCcorp has two offices. Office A has 450 employees. Office B has 50 employees. You are hired to design a network for ABCcorp. They have already decided on a 128k Frame Relay link between Offices A and B. However, they still need Internet access (mainly for some browsing and software update downloading) and e-mail access (mainly for direct marketing). Figure 10.8 illustrates my solution.

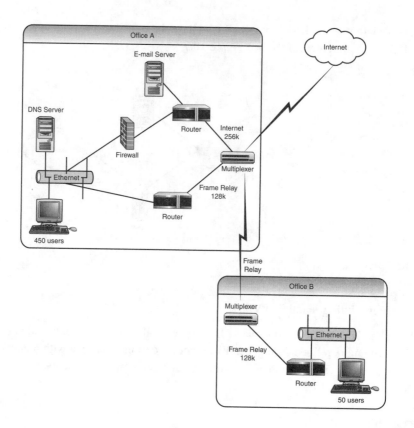

FIGURE 10.8
Author's solution.

Summary

- As with WAN solutions, Internet providers can offer managed and a la carte services.
- Use the same provider for WAN and Internet services whenever possible.
- Begin planning for Internet services before building your network.
- If the client has a network that you feel will change often, discuss with them the possibility of retaining control of DNS and firewall servers.
- DNS can be hosted locally or through your Internet provider.
- Try to keep your DNS server closest to the majority of your users and the WAN circuit.
- If you have VPN service (placed in a DMZ) you can put your e-mail server on the same network segment.
- When you start planning Internet access and DNS, you need to discuss domain name registration and hosting.

Securing Your Network

IN THIS CHAPTER

One of the most important issues companies face today is network security. Threats such as viruses, denial of service, and internal attacks are common enough in enterprise networking to warrant preventive measures.

In recent times some of the largest companies in the world have fallen victim to the crippling effects of viruses. Viruses, such as Trojan horses or worms, are received in e-mails and propagated through networks like wildfire. Such virus attacks can cost a company tens of thousands of dollars in lost productivity, lost data, and overtime charges.

Denial of service attacks have hit even the largest, most elaborate e-commerce sites on the Web. Some say these are the most devastating security breaches that can occur on a network. Denial of service attacks tend to shut down the one source of revenue for a company.

Our view of the lone hacker sitting behind his computer in a dark loft meticulously hammering at a network until he gets in is not the only threat we are dealing with. A little-discussed (and potentially more destructive) form of network terrorism comes from inside the local network. With everyone enforcing the barriers against outside attacks, many people forget about the attacks that come from inside the boundaries of the network.

Corporate espionage, disgruntled employees, and users with too much curiosity can all be serious issues for companies of any size. Internal attacks can be the hardest to combat. How do you prevent high-level employees from selling trade secrets over the Internet? Do you restrict their access to those secrets, or do you restrict their ability to access the "market places" while at work? These issues need to be discussed with your client during the design process.

Large corporations are spending more money than ever to ensure the safety of their investments. However, enforcing network integrity does not necessarily equal spending a lot of money. While corporate-wide antivirus solutions and firewalls can quickly add to the budget of a project, there are a few low- or no-cost options you can deploy.

Educating your users can be one of the greatest tools at your disposal in enforcing network security. The first section of this chapter deals with educating your user base and implementing network security standards and policies.

The best part about these network standards and policies is that they do not necessarily need to be planned at design time. While you should discuss the potential of using network policies during you initial meetings, the actual procedures should not be written until the network is in its final stages. This will give you a better idea of what you need to secure.

Network Standards and Policies

This section departs from the strong technical discussions we have been engaging in throughout the previous nine chapters. Rather, we will be focusing on security strategies and policies.

These strategies and policies lay the groundwork and set the direction for network security as a whole.

Discussions concerning security should start while you are holding your initial meeting with the client. The level of security desired by a client will dictate some of the design elements in your network. One example of this is remote networking. Based on the client's desired level of security, you could use a dial-in server on a common subnet, or you could implement a DMZ. You would obviously need this information beforehand to start designing your solutions. However, if the client chooses to use network standards and guidelines to help enforce network integrity, these policies should not be written until the latter stages of network development.

Such policies will dictate (in great detail) what systems users can and cannot access, what functions they can perform on those systems, and the penalties for straying from the policy. For this reason it is better to wait for a clear picture of the network environment to develop before outlining any standards.

Not every client will look to you for guidance in implementing a security policy. In some cases they will have a preliminary (very basic) idea of the level of security they need. For instance, the client may come to you during design time and say that they don't want their employees to have access to sexually explicit material on the Internet. In this example, they have given you a general idea as to the kind of security they want on their Internet connection; the implementation of that idea is up to you.

In other cases the client may approach you at design time and introduce you to the security officer for the company. You may be asked to work in conjunction with the security department to develop feasible standards and policies as a starting point. The policies will then be turned over to the security office for refinement and implementation.

In either case you will need to know the difference between a standard and a policy and how to implement them. In this context, standards relate to the integrity of network applications and equipment, while policies govern the information passed through the environment.

Implementing Standards

Standards are an important factor in network security. Network standards will outline what hardware and software can (and should) be used on the network. This is crucial information for administrators joining the network after you leave. Future network administrators need to know what they have to work with when adding to or replacing components of a network.

Without the leverage of a formal hardware and software standard, the company has no real recourse if a user installs foreign or infected programs on his machine. Such programs can be games, pirated or unlicensed software, or hacking tools.

NOTE

Discuss these standards carefully with your client before committing them to paper. Some clients may be more lax about some programs than others. For example, games seem to be the big gray area of foreign programs.

On one hand you have the ultra-tight security models that provide for the removal of Solitaire from the client operating systems. Such strict standards are usually implemented in areas where a PC is used in a secondary role to a person's job, such as a security guard at a gate. The guard uses the computer to monitor access through the gate; however, if the guard were to become distracted by an involved game of chance, the gate may be compromised.

On the other hand, you have the clients who will say, "Well, if it keeps employees happy and drives productivity let them play a game here and there." These companies tend to focus on intensive computer work such as programming where employee burnout is a looming factor.

I have written standards for both extremes, and both do work if enforced properly.

How do you create and enforce a network standard? Let's look at this from two different sides. First we'll discuss creating the standard. Then we will look at enforcing it. The reason I am breaking the two apart is that you will most likely have a smaller role in enforcing the standard than you will in creating it.

Creating a Network Hardware Standard

Creating your network will start during the design process; however, it really won't take shape until you begin ordering equipment from vendors. Remember our discussion of off-the-shelf PCs versus home-built PCs? Buying a bulk of off-the-shelf PCs is going to help you create a network standard. Why?

Your goal here is to have every PC on the network (aside from any that need to perform specialized tasks) identical to the next. Each PC should (ideally) be the same model, by the same vendor, and meet the same specifications as every other PC on the network.

NOTE

This will become more apparent as you begin to order your equipment, but you may not be able to obtain all of your PCs at one time. Because of this, you may end up with different models in the first batch than you have in the second batch.

This is perfectly okay for network standards; you really just want to limit the overall number of differences between PCs.

After you have all of your PC hardware ordered, you can begin to write up your Network Client Hardware Standard. This is going to be an actual form that you will turn in to the client at the conclusion of the project. This form will outline the minimum hardware requirements (as related to the PCs that have been purchased) for future PC procurement. You should be documenting everything you do up to this point (and beyond). This specification should be fairly easy for you to create if you keep good documentation.

> The Network Client Hardware Standard document should be formatted like the rest of your documentation and you should include it in your documentation folder.
>
> I mentioned that this document will outline the minimum hardware requirements for network PCs. This is not the same minimum that you need to run your software (see Chapter 5, "Considering the Client"). Rather, the minimum outlined here is to ensure all future PC orders will be greater than or equal to what is already on the network.

Following is an example of what information should be in your Network Client Hardware Standard.

Network Client Hardware Standard

To maintain the highest level of hardware integrity and interoperability, <Company Name> has implemented a corporate hardware standard relating to all network clients. All purchases that require a hardware profile differing from the one outlined below must be approved by <Department, or title>.

The PC issued to you by <Company Name> should meet or exceed these standards.

<Hardware Standard>

<This is a Sample:

- Compaq Pentium 500 (use the brand if you know the client will try to make all further purchases from the same vendor)
- 128MB of RAM
- 15GB hard drive (Manufacturer is important here!)
- CD-ROM (Minimum speed)
- 17" monitor
- ATI Pro video card
- 10/100 Ethernet card> (Manufacturer is important here!)

Any modifications made to a PC without the consent or permission of <IT Department or other governing body> will be deemed in violation of this standard and subject to <Whatever expressed or implied penalty the client wants to mention here, usually "subject to termination">.

All future hardware purchases will meet or exceed this standard.

Hardware standards are not just for client PCs. You should also create an identical standards form outlining the server hardware in use. However, because servers can tend to be specialized, you either have to create a couple of standards for servers (based on server role) or just list the specs of each server and its function.

Software Standards

The software standard will serve the same purpose as the hardware standard. However, clients will tend to gravitate more toward enforcing software standards when it comes to infractions.

It is much easier for users to load software on their machines than install a DVD-ROM. Users will tend to install games and other shareware packages onto their systems, usually with good intent (at least not a malicious one). However, games are not the only foreign software to look out for.

Another good reason to implement a software standard is to ensure the IT staff has a good grip on the applications they are expected to support. If the vice president of marketing wakes up one morning and buys Quicken to help with the budget for his department, who will support it? Even more important, what adverse effects will it have on other installed programs? A standard must be enforced to keep the network manageable and conflict free.

This document is easier to prepare after you have ordered your equipment and the network is near completion. The network should be functional before you start working on the software standard. Why wait?

You want to actually use the software for a while in a functional environment. This will give you time to work out any kinks or conflicts before you commit your choices to paper.

> **NOTE**
>
> While you want to test your software recommendations before committing them to paper, you should have a preliminary version of this document before you order your hardware. This ensures that you order hardware that is at least capable of running the software you need.

Your software standard should be set up the same as your hardware standard. Because the wording of the documents is so similar, you may want to combine the two into a Network Standards Form. Following is an example of a Network Standards Form:

Network Standards Form

This document represents the Network Standards Form as set forth by <Company Name>. To maintain an acceptable level of compliance and manageability, these standards will apply to all hardware and software owned and purchased by <Company Name>.

...

All purchases that require a hardware, or software, profile differing from the one outlined below must be approved by <Department, or title>.

Approved Network Hardware

<Hardware Standard>

<This is a Sample:

- Compaq Pentium 500 (use the brand if you know the client will try to make all further purchases from the same vendor)

- 128MB of RAM

- 15GB hard drive (Manufacturer is important here!)

- CD-ROM speed

- 17" monitor

- ATI Pro video card

- 10/100 Ethernet card> (Manufacturer is important here!)

Approved Network Software

<List all approved network software packages>

Any modifications made to a PC without the consent or permission of <IT Department or other governing body> will be deemed in violation of this standard and subject to <Whatever expressed or implied penalty the client wants to mention here, usually "subject to termination">.

If you are having trouble finding the right wording for this, or any of the documents outlined in this book, fear not. I have included the entire document packet from a sample job in the back of the book.

Network Policies

Network policies differ from network standards in that they define an acceptable code of conduct rather than an operating platform. Policies give the client leverage in situations that may be more legal, or moral, than business related. Other, non–network-related policies include sexual harassment and attendance guidelines.·When you begin writing your policies, think about it as trying to educate the users rather than punish them.

Education can be one of the best security tools at your disposal. Create the groundwork for an educated user base by writing policies that help them become aware of network security issues, rather than merely threatening them for breaking arbitrary rules. Helping the client gain the respect, attention, and assistance of the users (especially in a large enterprise) can be a difficult but rewarding task.

We have all seen policies that state "The Internet is intended for work-related use only. No sites with pornographic, racist, religious, sexist, or otherwise offensive content are to be viewed at any time." That is a good policy, but it leaves some wiggle room. We all know that the Internet is more than just the World Wide Web. If your client is large enough (or corporate secrets pose a great enough security risk), you should consider a more complete policy. Here is a better Internet policy:

> The Internet, as supplied by <Company Name>, is intended for work-related use only. No sites with pornographic, racist, religious, sexist, or otherwise offensive content are to be viewed at any time. At no time should any information pertaining to <Company Name> (including but not limited to files, programs, passwords, and or usernames) be exchanged over the Internet to unauthorized recipients, unless approved by the <Governing MIS> department. At no time should an employee of <Company Name> (in chat or on a bulletin board) state or otherwise imply affiliation with or approval by <Company Name> to discuss business (or other) related matters without permission from the <Governing MIS> department.

Other topics to include in network policies are e-mail, Internet, and other "group related" Internet activities. However, not every security hole has something to do with the Internet. There are other security risks closer to the users than they may think. One good policy to enforce is a password policy.

To be secure, passwords should be changed on a regular basis. (We all know the rules for good passwords: unique words, a mix of capitals and numeric characters.) However, having the most unique password in the world does the user little good if he or she keeps it on a post-it note under the keyboard.

A good policy for passwords offers guidelines explaining password security to the users, as well as offering suggestions for how to keep them secret. You should also include a statement like the following:

> A member of management or the IT department of <Company Name> will never ask for a specific user's password. If you are approached for your username, password, or any other information pertaining to the network and/or systems at <Company Name> by an employee of <Company Name> or otherwise, contact a member of the IT department immediately.

This will help the user to understand that passwords are meant to stay secret and even the IT staff should not be asking users to reveal them.

You will soon find that policies and standards can become very verbose, and reading them can be very intimidating. Users can tend to become disenfranchised and unsettled if they feel they are being punished before they even do anything.

To avoid a situation like this, try using language that is less harsh. For instance, rather than saying "punished" say "action will be taken." We all know what both of those phrases mean;

however, the latter is easier to digest. Another technique you can use is to intersperse particularly long policies with items relating to the company's responsibility to the employee. For example, after bombarding the users with line after line of what they shouldn't do, throw in a line that states "<Company Name> will be responsible for ensuring the safety of all employees as pertaining to work-related equipment and its correct uses."

Implementing Routers and Firewalls

There are, obviously, more technical ways to implement security on a network. One of the most common, and most effective, security devices on a network is a firewall. Firewalls can be extremely effective if used correctly. However, if the person implementing the firewall does not do so correctly, it can be a risk to the network.

You should be designing firewalls into your projects at an early stage. Most of the time you will include firewalls in your plans just as you would any other device. However, you will not be configuring security on that firewall until the network is near completion.

Firewalls Versus Routers

With router technology growing at a quicker rate than ever before, many routers (even without firewall software installed on them) can perform many of the functions of firewalls. Routers, through access lists, can deny or allow access to network segments based on rules (most commonly an IP address).

Routers can be best utilized in implementing internal security. Static routes and access lists can be very effective in allowing or deterring traffic through and around certain segments of your network.

Many larger corporations may have network segments that not everybody should have access to. Research and development is a good example of such a segment. Most companies with research and development groups do not want the average user to have access to the devices and information on that network segment.

An access list could be implemented on the router that separates the research and development segment from the rest of the network. This access list could be structured to allow users from within the research and development segment (designated by a separate IP subnet) to access the remainder of the network. Conversely, the same access list would not allow the users from the remainder of the network (based on IP address) to access the research and development segment.

If you are dealing with multiple segments that need to be secured from both the remainder of the network and the outside world, static routes may help you. Static routes are very effective in ensuring that data flows in a set, secure path. By using static routes you can ensure that Network A only accesses Network C, and Network B only accesses Network C, but Networks A and B never interact.

Another security feature of static routes is that they do not advertise their routing table. This feature ensures that no one from outside (or inside) the network can get access to the routing tables and exploit the network. However, static routing does have one very big drawback: it has no built-in redundancy. If a router with a static route were to go down, no routers on either side of that router would be able to communicate.

Firewalls and Rules

Firewalls operate by implementing sets of rules. These rules spell out the addresses that can and cannot pass (in either direction) through the firewall. Firewalls are a good tool for enforcing the policies implemented earlier in the section "Network Standards and Policies." The rule-based system that drives these devices can be strong and effective, but it is only as strong as its weakest link. If the firewall is not configured correctly, any hole can be exploited.

The rules you write for your firewall will depend on the firewall's location. If your firewall is located between your network and a DMZ, it will need a different set of rules than it would if the firewall were the gateway to the Internet.

When you are designing your rules, try to structure them in accordance with the policies you established. If the client is interested in blocking out certain Web sites, do so at the firewall.

NOTE

Some firewalls will block access to Web sites based on the site's name. However, manually entering each restricted Web site can be next to impossible. There are several services a client can subscribe to that can provide a "pre-fab" list of questionable Web sites. These services usually charge a nominal fee, and many work in conjunction with specific firewalls.

One important factor to watch when you are implementing your firewall is software port values. Every piece of software that needs to communicate with another does so on IP ports. When you establish a firewall rule (for example, "nobody from any external IP address <the Internet> can access any device on the internal network") there is an implied "deny" on all IP ports affected by that rule. Therefore, if you have a piece of software that is automatically updated by a vendor, you need to find out what IP port they use and allow access on that particular port.

Another security method that can be implemented by firewalls is authenticated access. If your client is concerned with tracking users' Internet usage, or denying access to entire segments of the user population, you should consider using firewall authentication.

Firewall authentication works by implementing a user list on the firewall. The firewall then acts as any other network authentication device by asking the user for a valid username and password. Access to the Internet is then allowed or denied based on the authentication.

Enterprise Antivirus Solutions

Computer viruses are one of the greatest threats to large networks. Viruses can attack (almost) any computer regardless of role or location. Devices can be attacked from the Internet, through e-mail, or from infected media. In other words, viruses can gain access to PCs by any input to the device.

The damage caused by viruses can range from barely noticeable to absolutely disastrous. For this reason, enterprise antivirus solutions should be a design essential for all of your projects. However, depending on the client, "enterprise antivirus solution" can mean many things.

This section covers three different antivirus scenarios. We will discuss the pros and cons of each scenario and why you would use a particular solution. Most of the scenarios discussed should be available through any commercial antivirus platform.

This section deals with three types of antivirus software. Just in case you are unfamiliar with them, here are the differences. *Client scanning software* is exactly that, client PC software. *Server scanning software* is designed to scan server operating systems. Although server software can be purchased separately, it is most often found bundled with either network or enterprise software. (Client and server scanning software can generally be found in bundles labeled "Network Scanning Software.") However, most network scanning packages allow for the scheduling of client (PC) scans from the server. *Enterprise scanning software* works much like network software; however, it usually includes an e-mail scanning solution and generally allows for more licenses.

Scenario A: Client-Only Scanning

The next sections provide different antivirus scenarios and how they are addressed by different software packages. Each scenario includes a list of the pros and cons of that particular solution.

Scenario A is client-only scanning. Antivirus software is installed only on the clients (PCs) and each user is responsible for the maintenance of his or her machine. The user will generally scan the PC and update the virus software (with the latest definition file) on a regular basis.

The theory behind the client-only scanning method is that if the clients are clean, the servers will stay clean (as they are only repositories for information from the clients). Scanning the clients will clean all of the infected files on the PCs as well as any files they place on or retrieve from the servers. However, depending on the client virus software, you may not be able to scan incoming or outgoing e-mails (check your vendor's documentation).

Table 11.1 lists the pros and cons of client-only scanning.

TABLE 11.1   Pros and Cons of Client-Only Scanning

Pros	Cons
Client-only scanning software generally costs less than enterprise, server, or network software.	Your client machines are only protected when the client runs the software.
The users can scan their PCs at their own convenience. (Unlike network or enterprise software, where "client scans" are scheduled by an administrator.)	The user *must* update the software regularly with the latest virus definitions.
Network traffic (due to network scanning) is cut to a minimum.	The servers are not protected at all, leaving the potential for infection.

Client-only scanning works best when implemented on small networks where the users can be expected to keep up the maintenance of their machines. If you are implementing a network of around 20 to 50 users and server usage is expected to be low, you might consider client-only scanning. However, it is the least protective of the solutions and should be used with caution. You want to avoid this scenario on large networks.

Scenario B: Network Scanning

Network scanning is the most common form of virus protection. Network scanning involves loading both client and server software into your environment. Most antivirus vendors offer a "network" option. These packages usually consist of a bundle of client and server software (and some volume licenses for the clients).

This option gives the administrator the ability to automate much of the virus protection process for the network from one central location. The administrator can establish a set time when both server and client scanning should begin. The software will then scan all devices and report its findings back to the administrator.

Table 11.2 lists the pros and cons of network scanning.

TABLE 11.2   Pros and Cons of Network Scanning

Pros	Cons
Scanning the client machines is no longer the responsibility of the user.	Network scanning can generate a lot of network traffic.
The software generally needs to be updated (virus definitions) in only one place. The update will propagate itself to the other clients.	One missed definition update can leave an entire network unprotected.
	Network scanning offers little to no support for scanning e-mail (with expensive add-ons).

Network scanning is most effective on medium-sized networks (generally 100 to 300 users). However, network scanning can only be effective if the scanning is performed at a time when network traffic is low (generally at night). Scanning for viruses at night does pose some issues, however.

To scan a PC it does need to be turned on (obviously). Be sure your users are aware of the scanning schedule and leave their PCs on during the scan. Another issue with scanning for viruses at night is, believe it or not, traffic. Most companies run their network backups at night. Network backups (discussed in the section "Designing and Implementing a Backup Solution") take up massive amounts of bandwidth. This can severely cripple any attempt to scan for viruses.

Schedule your scans carefully for the best results.

Scenario C: Enterprise Scanning

Enterprise virus scanning software works much the same way network scanning does with one notable exception: e-mail server support. Many client antivirus packages will support scanning e-mails as they are sent or opened on the PC. However, you should be scanning the e-mails as they arrive on the network, not the PC. By the time an e-mail reaches a specific PC it has already touched at least one server (the e-mail server). This message may have even been backed up (by a network backup system) by the time the intended recipient reads it. Therefore, scanning e-mail for viruses after they are received on the PC may be too late.

Most network viruses arrive through the company's e-mail system. Enterprise scanning offers the best solution for stopping infected messages from reaching clients.

Table 11.3 lists the pros and cons of enterprise scanning.

TABLE 11.3 Pros and Cons of Enterprise Scanning

Pros	Cons
Support of e-mail servers (not just clients).	Enterprise packages tend to be expensive.
Scanning the client machines is no longer the responsibility of the user.	Enterprise scanning can generate a lot of network traffic.
The software generally needs to be updated (virus definitions) in one place. The update will propagate itself to the other clients.	One missed definition update can leave an entire network unprotected.
Most enterprise solutions have more (if not unlimited) server licenses.	Can be expensive, especially when you start having to pay for each mailbox.

Any network consisting of more then 300 users should consider enterprise antivirus software. The cost of enterprise scanning packages alone may deter some smaller companies. However, if the client has enough servers that require scanning, the expense of server licenses may be greater than the enterprise software (for the same coverage).

Designing and Implementing a Backup Solution

Another effective security tool you can implement is a network backup plan. Network backups can ensure that users do not (intentionally or otherwise) permanently delete or modify critical information. However, network backups are only an effective tool if information is saved regularly.

When you are formulating your backup plan you will need to decide what computers you will include. You will also need to discuss how many backup devices you will have on the network. One factor that will play heavily in these decisions is the combination of operating systems and backup software you are using. For example (depending on the backup software in use), some Windows 95 clients cannot be backed up by a Windows NT server, while Windows NT workstations can. Also, a Windows 2000 server may not be backed up by anything but another Windows 2000 server.

Deciding to back up the client machines keeps the user from having to store every piece of critical information on the server. The users do not need to worry about whether the latest copy of their work is on the server or not. However, backing up all of the information on every client can take up an enormous amount of tape space.

Another downside to running a backup on client PCs is network bandwidth. Backup software tends to fully utilize the amount of bandwidth available to it. Otherwise, with the amount of information being backed up on an average network, the process would never finish. Backing up client PCs only adds to the bandwidth (and thus the amount of time) needed to complete a backup.

When you back up client systems you are also at the mercy of users leaving their PCs on. If the users turn off their machines before a scheduled backup, you run the risk of losing their latest information if anything were to happen.

A better solution is to instate a policy instructing users to store all critical information on a particular server, and then back up that machine. This process will save you time, money, and bandwidth.

Because backup licenses tend to be expensive, the fewer licenses you need the better. Eliminating the client machines from the scenario cuts out a large number of software licenses. Also, because you are not backing up the clients you save some bandwidth that can be devoted to the server.

However, the best reason I can offer for only backing up the servers is that you only save the information you need. When you back up a client machine you can tend to back up a lot of information that you really don't want to save. To ensure that you back up all of the data you need, require the clients to store their critical information on the server. This saves you from backing up any extraneous data.

To design your network to allow for the best possible backup situation, try to provide the strongest (fastest) links between servers that are backed up. For example, if your network is utilizing a mix of 100Mbit hubs and switches, utilize the switches for communication between the servers. This will ensure that the backup software can utilize the most possible bandwidth. However, in some cases you may need to establish dedicated links between servers for the purpose of backing up information.

Some clients may have 24-hour operations. In these situations backups are usually critical; however, the network may not be able to withstand the bandwidth drain during the process. In these cases it is best to establish a dedicated connection between servers for the purpose of backups.

These dedicated connections can be established in a few ways, depending on the number of servers involved. If you are only dealing with two servers (or pairs of servers) you can use permanent circuits to carry dedicated information between the two servers involved. For this scenario to work each server would need a second NIC. The server's interface (consult your operating system's documentation) can then be configured to contact the second server only through that interface.

If you are dealing with more than one server backing up multiple machines you may want a separate switch connecting all servers involved. Each server would need a second NIC. This NIC would be connected to the dedicated switch. Each server would then be able to communicate with the others without any drain on the rest of the network.

Keep in mind, these scenarios are not optimal, nor are they easy to implement. Use them only in cases where they are required.

Summary

- Network standards define an ideal operating environment for both hardware and software.
- Network policies outline a "code of conduct" for the users to adhere to.
- When drawing up your policies, try to avoid harsh implicative language.
- Routers can be used to restrict access on internal network segments.
- Static routing tables and access lists help the administrator control the flow of traffic across the network.
- Firewalls are used to control access to and from certain areas external to the local network.
- Be careful not to block out IP ports needed for certain pieces of software.
- Choose the antivirus protection that best suits the size and budget of your client's network.
- Network and client-only virus scanning tools generally do not include e-mail support.
- Avoid backing up information on a user's PC if possible.
- Backup software takes up massive amounts of network bandwidth.

Assembling the Components

PART

III

IN THIS PART

The Final Proposal

IN THIS CHAPTER

Your final proposal represents the culmination of two to four weeks of meetings and planning. These meetings were the base on which you built your network designs. Now that your designs are completed (on paper), it is time to wrap everything up and prepare for implementation.

The majority of time spent on a project is spent in implementation. Your final proposal needs to be solid to ensure a smooth implementation. The plans and designs you create and use going into the final proposal must reflect your expertise and confidence in your field. You do not want to find out during implementation that you miscalculated some part of the design. Having to go back to the drawing board during these final stages can be disastrous.

The final proposal can be viewed as the formal starting point for the implementation portion of the project. The client uses the documents handed in to make sure their needs have been fully covered. You use the final proposal as a form of checks and balances.

All work performed during the implementation of the network is done from the final proposal. If it is not in the documentation, it is not done. This gives you leverage if the client approaches you after the project is complete and questions some of the work. Conversely, the client can hold you to doing everything stated in the final proposal.

The final proposal will include your designs for the project, the names of any vendors being used, the names and roles of any consultants being used, and an accurate timeline for the completion of the project. This chapter walks you through each of these elements and prepares you for assembling your documents.

The first step toward completing your final proposal is to assemble a satisfactory list of vendors for your client to choose from. After your client chooses the vendors that suit their needs, you can move on the consultants.

By the end of this chapter, you will have enough data and documentation to begin implementation.

Choosing Your Hardware Vendor

For the remainder of this section, you will need to assume one thing: The client has decided to use a hardware vendor rather than build PCs from scratch. If the client wanted PCs built from scratch, the hardware ordering process would be a little longer. The process would also require more research on your part.

> **NOTE**
>
> If you are faced with a situation in which your client wants you to build PCs from scratch, read this section carefully. Even though I do not specifically cover the ordering process for component-level products, you will get an idea of what needs to be done.
>
> In essence, you will be following the same processes outlined here for every piece of hardware (or groups of hardware products) that you need to purchase.

We are now getting into the real core of network design and architecture. Designing a functional environment on paper is one thing; bringing that network to life is another thing entirely. Now that you have a working blueprint, you can begin to flesh it out.

You should begin looking at potential hardware vendors while you are drawing your plans. The client needs to have a list of potential vendors to choose from as soon as a clear picture of the finished network is available. The client can then make the most informed decision possible based on the information provided. Your goal here is not to force or lead the client toward a particular vendor. Giving your client as many vendors to choose from as you can (and showing the research behind it) is going to make a much better impression, and leave the client feeling as comfortable as possible.

I generally supply information on four to eight vendors, depending on the product. You will typically have fewer vendors for servers than you will for PCs. If you give the client too few choices, they may feel like they are making an uninformed decision. Conversely, if you supply the client with too many choices, they may find it confusing and not be able to come to a definite conclusion.

There are literally hundreds of potential vendors out there to choose from; deciding which are best for your particular project can be a daunting task. One of the best tools you can rely on in narrowing down the list of potential vendors is experience. Do not be afraid to include vendors you have worked with successfully in the past. This information can be beneficial to the client. Even though I would not state on the proposal which vendors I prefer, I would verbally inform the client as to any vendors with which I have had good experiences. Then if the client requested it, I would create a form showing my personal experience with any of the supplied vendors.

For example, over the years I have built a very good relationship with an online hardware vendor. Because I have used them on multiple occasions, (and even given them preference over other vendors) they can pass to me benefits that other vendors might not. I might be able to get critical equipment faster or an extra cable for nothing. These relationships can make a big difference in choosing your vendors. Many clients will respect your decision if you have a proven, long-term relationship with a particular vendor. However, even if you have a very sturdy contact at a particular vendor, you should still offer your client more choices (if for no other reason than to let them know you are willing to use whichever vendor they think is best for their needs).

NOTE

I mentioned that I have (on occasion) given a certain vendor preference over other vendors. Many clients will suggest (or insist) that you use more than one vendor for hardware. This is good for the client because it gives them something to fall back on if supply lines become jammed. Larger clients will especially benefit from using multiple vendors because of the sheer volume with which they tend to order equipment.

Having a client who wants to use multiple vendors also gives you the chance to build a solid relationship with a particular vendor. You can quickly become a vendor's best friend by offering them a big chunk of business over another vendor (letting them know that you gave them the business over someone else will get you pretty far).

The information that you should provide to your client about potential vendors includes pricing, product specifications, and availability.

NOTE

You need to include the same information for all vendors you suggest. If you price out one server with 512MB of RAM and an 18GB hard drive, you need to price out the remaining servers the same way. If (for some reason) one out of five vendors cannot provide you pricing on RAM upgrades, find out why and note it.

Doing this allows your client to compare apples to apples. It also shows that you can do adequate research and can handle dealing with vendors.

The information given to your client should be provided in table comparison form. Using a simple one-page table to convey and compare this information will help the client tremendously.

The table should be clear, concise, and easy to read. (You can give the client all of the best information in the world, but it will not help them if they cannot read it.) This is where you can run into the problem of providing too much data. Pictures of devices, brochures, and links to Web pages should be avoided. The client will generally not be concerned with the appearance of a device, only its functionality. (In some cases, if physical space is an issue, the client will need to know the dimensions of a machine. However, if you provide the dimensions for one server you need to provide the dimensions for all of them.) Do not give your client product brochures or links to Web sites—if there is pertinent information you want the client to see, copy that information into the table. Do not overload the client with data they do not need.

Table 12.1 is a sample of the table you should provide to your client showing hardware comparisons between vendors. I usually separate the information into two tables: one for PCs (clients) and one for servers.

TABLE 12.1 Sample Server Vendor Table

Vendor	Model	Hard Drive(s)	RAM	Dimensions	Availability	Pricing
ABC Servers	5000N	(3) 18GB RAID 5	512MB	12"x 23"x15"	Overnight	$2,300
Server Giant	2564	(3) 18GB RAID 5	512MB	15"x 18"x20"	2-3 weeks	$1,500
Custom Servers	1000CS	1 18GB drive (RAID 5 available as $1,200 third-party upgrade per Dave in sales)	512MB	23"x 20"x24"	Overnight	$3,600 ($2,400 without RAID)

Notice the table entry for Custom Servers. This company did not have a RAID 5 standard configuration available. I noted in the Hard Drive column the fact that RAID 5 was a third-party add-on and listed the price quoted by their rep. I then reflected that price in the Pricing column.

In some cases (or for some clients), this may not be enough data to make a decision. If the client is not very technical (or at least not technical enough to interpret just the information provided in Table 12.1) I will include a Notes column. This column will provide additional data about the product in lay terms.

A format such as this is ideal for presentations before upper managers and board members. Many times the decision makers in the corporations will not be as technically knowledgeable as you are. The longer it takes for a group of clients to figure out exactly what you are proposing, the longer it will take for them to come to a decision.

Table 12.2 is the same sample table with an added Notes column.

TABLE 12.2 Sample Server Table with Notes Column

Vendor	Model	Hard Drive(s)	RAM	Dimensions	Availability	Pricing	Notes
ABC Servers	5000N	(3) 18GB RAID 5	512MB	12"x 23"x15"	Overnight	$2,300	Popular server vendor
Server Giant	2564	(3) 18GB RAID 5	512MB	15"x 18"x20"	2-3 weeks	$1,500	Reliable 'low-end' server

TABLE 12.2 Continued

Vendor	Model	Hard Drive(s)	RAM	Dimensions	Availability	Pricing	Notes
Custom Servers	1000CS	1 18GB Drive (RAID 5, which includes 2 additional drives available as $1,200 third-party upgrade)	512MB	23"x 20"x24"	Overnight	$3,600 ($2,400 without separate RAID)	Will require support contract for RAID controller

The information provided in the Notes column should be as objective as possible. You do not want to come right out and say. "I think you should use the Server Giant server because it is the best" unless the client specifically asks for your opinion. It is not uncommon for a client to solicit your opinion about certain products; they should have hired you because they trust your judgment and ability.

In cases where the client asks me to provide my opinion of a particular product, I reformat the tables as shown in Table 12.3.

TABLE 12.3 Sample Server Table with Personal Opinion

Vendor	Model	Hard drive(s)	RAM	Dimensions	Availability	Pricing	Personal Experience
ABC Servers	5000N	(3) 18GB RAID 5	512MB	12"x 23"x15"	Overnight	$2,300	Easy to maintain server, very few problems
Server Giant	2564	(3) 18GB RAID 5	512MB	15"x 18"x20"	2-3 weeks	$1,500	Poor customer service response times
Custom Servers	1000CS	1 18GB Drive (RAID 5 available as $1,200 third-party upgrade)	512MB	23"x 20"x24"	Overnight	$3,600 ($2,400 without RAID)	Never used product in a production environment

In the Personal Experience column you want to offer your honest opinion of a product without praising or bashing a vendor too much. You want to try to stay as objective as possible, but if you are asked for your thoughts, be clear.

Does this mean you could potentially be modifying the same table three times? No. You do not want to redo any of your documentation after handing it to the client. After spending upwards of four weeks in meetings with your client, you will know which of the three table formats will suit them best.

The table showing client hardware comparisons (although on a separate sheet) should be formatted the same way. Try to include as much pertinent information as possible about the PCs without going overboard.

However, servers and clients are not the only pieces of hardware you need to buy. You should prepare a form for all hardware devices you will need to purchase. This includes routers, switches, hubs, firewalls, and other peripherals. I tend to put all of these remaining items in one table entitled Network Peripherals.

In many cases (especially when dealing with peripherals), you may be purchasing the hardware from someone other than the manufacturer. In other words, the manufacturer and the vendor will be two different entities. For these instances, you will want to include both a Vendor (the entity you will purchase the equipment from) and a Manufacturer heading in the table.

NOTE

Do as much research as possible before including Vendor information in a table where the vendor and the manufacturer are two different entities. Your goal should be to have only one vendor entry per item. Therefore, this vendor should be the one that best fits the client's needs. This could mean that they are economical or (depending on the client) they may have the equipment more readily available.

You are trying to avoid providing three vendors from which your client can purchase the same piece of hardware. Provide them only with the vendor you feel is best for that product and move on.

The client may not necessarily pick a vendor from your list. In some instances, the client may further narrow the field of possibilities and leave the final decision to you. This is not uncommon and you should choose the vendor you are most comfortable with. In any event, you should always approve your final decision with the client before ordering any equipment.

Once you have the client's approval, you can begin to order your hardware. Timing is everything when you are ordering your network devices. You generally want your equipment onsite in the following order: your server equipment followed by your connectivity devices followed by the PCs.

There is a simple logic behind having the equipment onsite in this particular order. This is the order in which it will be built and implemented. First, you need to install your servers, followed by your connectivity devices. The last piece of hardware to be implemented should be the PCs.

However, hardware is only half of the final process. You cannot fully implement hardware without software.

Choosing Your Software Plan

Your choices when dealing with software vendors are going to be a little different than those for hardware. Prices for software are not going to vary as greatly from vendor to vendor as those for hardware. However, you do still have some decisions to make.

To License or Not To License, That Is The Question

You should always be as accurate as possible when ordering your software products and licenses. Buying one copy of Windows 2000 Server does not license you to install it on every server you have. Unfortunately, that is exactly how many people order their software.

I can really find no instance or reason where full licensing is not an option. Therefore, when you are proposing particular software packages you should include the "per-license" cost for the product. This will help the client better understand exactly how much it will cost to be fully licensed for the product.

Licensing also applies to new hardware. Many server vendors (such as Acer) will sell you hardware without preloaded software. (I have found that an average server can be $100 to $200 cheaper without any preloaded software. Most vendors only preinstall Microsoft operating systems, therefore anyone looking to install Unix or NetWare needs to purchase their equipment "clean." I now order all of my equipment without operating systems and volume license any software I will not to install on the machine (including the operating system). You may have a harder time ordering PCs without operating systems than servers. (In fact, I have not had any luck, unless I built the machine myself.)

If licensing is an issue (for instance, in larger corporations), consider a volume licensing solution.

Volume Licensing

Many vendors will provide volume-licensing packages to help larger companies become compliant at a discounted rate. Volume licensing can work well for large companies where keeping track of used or active licenses can be extremely difficult. For these larger corporations, purchasing large blocks of "per-seat" licenses would be economically unfeasible.

The Microsoft Select Subscription

If your client is large enough and uses a majority of Microsoft products, you may want to consider a Select subscription. Microsoft Select offers enterprisewide licensing for most Microsoft products. At the time this book was written, Microsoft defined an enterprise (for purchasing Select) as having at least 500 seats.

There are downsides to purchasing volume licenses. Because many manufacturers have separate media for volume-licensed products, there can be a long wait time to receive your product. Many software vendors will be authorized to sell paper licenses but the physical media must be ordered from the manufacturer. This can cause delays in receiving software.

Another downside to volume licensing is license minimums. Many manufacturers have a minimum number of licenses you need to purchase under their volume license agreement. While this may not seem like a big deal in a large corporation, consider this: If the client needs a certain package for one department of 10 people, but the manufacturer has a minimum number of licenses you need to buy (say 20), the client may be paying for licenses they do not need.

Per-Seat Licensing

For manufacturers that do not offer volume licenses, your only choice is per-seat licensing. If you find yourself purchasing products that can only be licensed individually, you need to plan very carefully. Make sure you order enough copies of a product to meet the needs of the users, but do not order software for every user in the company (if not every user has a need for it). In other words, if the HR department will be using a particular product (which is expensive to license), order only enough copies to install on the HR machines.

Try to avoid including unlicensed software packages in a "standard image." By including unlicensed software in these images (see the following sidebar), you risk allowing the use of software that is not licensed.

Many consultants responsible for rolling out large numbers of PCs will use a "standard image." This is a hard-drive image that is used to clone multiple machines (making them identical to the original image). In creating an image, a consultant will include any software that could be needed by anybody in the company. This can cause licensing issues if you are not careful.

Before purchasing any software that is licensed per seat, inquire within the company as to who will need the software now, and how many people could potentially need it in the future. After purchasing and installing the software requested by the client, you need to supply them with a contact name and phone number (along with a reminder of how many licenses they own) for the vendor. This information will allow the client to purchase more licenses as needed.

Creating the Software Table

Table 12.4 is an example of a software table using the information just discussed. (It is arranged similarly to the hardware tables from the last section.)

TABLE 12.4   Sample Software Table

Vendor	Manufacturer	Package	Lic. Type	Lic. Needed	Per Lic. Cost	Cost
Jack's Software	JoeSoft	JoeSoft PIM	Volume	200	$10	$2,000
WackyWare	WackyWare	Wacky's Accounting	Per seat	25	$200	$5,000
Numbers R' US	Account Pro's	Accounting Master	Volume	25	$125 (minimum of 100 lics.)	$12,500

This should be enough to let the client choose what software is right for their environment. The table lists all of the pertinent information about each package.

Both the Hardware and Software tables will be given to the client at the same time. You can then begin to work on your timeline. You will need to do some estimating because you still do not have all of your solid information yet (that is, the client has not specifically decided what hardware and software they will use, but you should have a very good idea of what your timeline looks like).

The final item that you will need before assembling your proposal is the project plan. The project plan is going to map out your actions for the construction phase of the project.

Working with Timelines and Contract Help

The project plan is the most important document you will include in the final proposal. The project plan sets the parameters for the remainder of the job. Essentially, once the project plan has been approved (by both sides) it must be adhered to.

The base of your project plan will be a detailed timeline showing the breakdown of how the network will be assembled. (The more detailed you can be, the better organized your project will end up.) I tend to include (on the timeline) order dates, shipping dates, anticipated receiving date, implementation times, documentation time, testing, and roll out.

However, accurate times are not the only keystone in a good project plan. One of the main purposes of using a project plan (to create a timeline) is to budget cost and man-hours. Both you and the client will use the project plan to determine the amount of money and people needed to complete a job efficiently.

Before you start on the actual project plan, you should have a good idea of the anticipated completion date for the job. Generally, this is one of the first things discussed by the client. If the client has not yet mentioned to you an optimal finish date for the project, this is the time to ask.

Producing a Project Plan

To begin your project plan, you need to know exactly how many man-hours each portion of your network will take to implement. After you have a figure representing the total number of man-hours needed to complete your project, you can then determine the number of contractors needed.

Determining the number of contractors you need to complete a project is going to rely heavily on the amount of time allotted to the project as a whole. The first 11 chapters of this book represent two to four weeks of prep time. The implementation of the network can take anywhere from two to eight months (larger projects can take up to a year to fully implement).

In this section, I have included some typical implementation tasks with man-hours to give you a better idea of what you need to base your projections on. These timelines should give you a good rule of thumb to build your project plan. However, keep in mind that different people work at different rates and speeds. (I went back through four completed projects to create the averages shown in my sample timelines. Feel free to modify them using your own experiences.)

NOTE
Even though I have included these projections in table format, you should use a professional time project management tool. There are many tools on the market and most are competitively priced. I have found that Microsoft Project fits my needs the best. Whatever product you choose, it needs to be neat, concise, and easy to read.

Table 12.5 lists a sampling of network equipment and its related (average) implementation times.

TABLE 12.5   Network Equipment

Device	Man-Hours
Server (File) (RAID 5) w/operating system	8–10
Server (e-mail) (RAID 5) w/operating system	10–12
Server (Dial-in) (RAID 5) w/operating system	8–10

TABLE 12.5 Continued

Device	Man-Hours
Server (no RAID) w/operating system	5–7
Rack Mount kit	1
Router (internal routing)	4–6
Router (external routing)	6–8
Firewall (software based)	10–12
Firewall (hardware device, i.e. router)	14–16
VPN device	10–12
CAT5 cabling	.25 (per drop)
Storage rack	2
Hub (fully populated)	2–3
Switch (fully populated)	4–6
Bridge	4–6
Network printer	1–2
MAU (fully populated)	1–2

Table 12.6 lists a sampling of client (PC) equipment and its related (average) implementation times.

TABLE 12.6 Client Equipment

Device	Man-Hours
PC (fully configured and functional) (manual configuration)	6–8
PC (automated configuration)	1–2
Local printer	.5

Table 12.7 lists a sampling of operating systems and their related (average) implementation times.

TABLE 12.7 Operating Systems (Installed on Existing Hardware)

Product	Man-Hours
Windows NT 4 (server)	4–6
Windows NT 4 (client)	3–5
Windows 2000 (server)	3–5
Windows 2000 (client)	2–4
Windows 95	2–3

TABLE 12.7 Continued

Product	Man-Hours
Windows 98	2–3
Windows ME	2–3
Novell NetWare 3.12	6–8
Novell NetWare 4.1	4–6
Novell NetWare 5	4–6
BSD Unix	2–4
HP Unix	2–4
SCO	3–5
Linux	3–5

Table 12.8 lists a sampling of miscellaneous software packages and their related (average) implementation times.

TABLE 12.8 Additional Software (Times Include Installation and Configuration)

Product	Man-Hours
Standard server database (relational)	8–10
Antivirus (enterprise)	6–8
Antivirus (client only)	.25
Backup software	6–8
VPN client (including configuration)	1–2
Office (productivity) Suite	1–2

This information is going to help you do more than calculate the total amount of time needed on a project. The data here also represents the skill sets you will need to look for when you are considering consultants. For example, assume your project calls for the implementation tasks outlined in Table 12.9.

TABLE 12.9 Sample Project Table

Task	Man-Hours	Total
7 servers (Windows 2000)	10	70
1 Unix box (existing hardware)	2	2
50 clients	6 for first, 2 for each after	104

TABLE 12.9   Continued

Task	Man-Hours	Total
3 routers	8	24
6 hubs	3	18
		218 total man-hours

You determine that you have 218 man-hours in your project, and from that you can calculate the number of consultants needed to complete the job (see the formula in the next section). However, this table tells you more than that.

For example, say you determine five consultants are required to implement this network (just based on man-hours). You would not want to contract five consultants who are strong in desktops but know nothing about routers (you have almost three days of router work that needs to be done). Planning out your man-hours first lets you see what skill sets you need to be looking for in your consultants to efficiently complete a project.

The following sections provide a clear formula for determining the number of consultants you may need for your job. First you will determine how many people are needed for the project and then you will determine what their skill sets should be.

Determining How Much Help You Need

The formula I use to determine the number of contractors I need to complete a project is as follows:

Total Number of Contractors = [(Man-hours + (Man-hours * .20)) / number of weeks in project] / 40

I take the total number of projected man-hours and add twenty percent for padding. (Nothing looks worse for a project leader than to finish a project behind schedule; therefore, I always pad my times by twenty percent for safety. If I do not need the extra time, then I look good for finishing ahead of schedule.) I then take the padded total and divide it by the number of weeks allotted to complete the project. That will give me the total number of hours per week needed to finish the project. That number is divided by 40 to arrive at the total number of people needed for the project.

Let's take a look at this same example with some real numbers to illustrate how it works. I have a project that I have determined will take 560 man-hours to complete. I have two months before we go live. How many people will be needed to finish on time?

[(560 + (560 * .20)) / 8] / 40 = 2.1 contract employees (rounded down to 2)

This formula will tell you how many people you need, but it will not tell you where you need them. Now you need to determine the skill sets of the people you need.

Determining What Skill Sets You Need

You should now have an idea of how many consultants you need on your project. It is now time to determine where you need them. The first step to figuring out what skills sets you need is to consolidate the areas in which you need help. You can then group those areas by skill set.

Using the information in Table 12.9 you decide that you need five consultants to complete this job (this is an arbitrary value, I did not use any formula to arrive at it). Your first step is to combine tasks based on skills.

You can easily combine the router and hub implementation tasks (the logic is in assuming that a router expert will know something about setting up hubs). You can then combine the two server tasks (the Windows and the Unix). This one needs a little explanation.

There are only two man-hours of Unix time needed. This hardly justifies the cost of contracting a Unix expert (presumably at a longer minimum time than two hours). Therefore, you can hopefully find at least one Windows expert who knows enough about Unix to install it.

Finally, you can use two desktop consultants. Obviously there is more work to be done on the desktop portion of the project than can be efficiently done by two people. However, you can conceivably use the Windows Server consultants on the desktops after they finish the servers (giving you four people on the desktops).

> **NOTE**
>
> Do not forget to include yourself in the project plan. Not only can you help add to the expertise of the consultants working the project, clients will be very impressed by a leader who is willing to get into the trenches and work.

One important thing to keep in mind is that even though you should include yourself in the project plan, you must know how to delegate responsibility. I know these may sound like contradictory statements, but there is a fine line (as with most of the final proposal) between giving the appearance of not doing any work and not knowing how to staff your project.

Do not overwork yourself (in the project plan); you will have other duties to attend to during the construction phase of the network. Going back to the (man-hour) example, I would assign myself the Unix task and one of the Desktop tasks. (That does not mean that I would not help out anyplace else, but I will still have documentation to do during the network implementation.)

After you have finally determined how many consultants (and which skill sets) you need, you can begin the task of hiring.

Interviewing and Hiring Your Contractors

Your project plan is finished and you have an idea of how many contractors you will need to hire. Your first course of action is to have that number approved by the client, and then you can begin interviewing potential contractors.

Allow yourself two weeks from when you begin interviewing contractors to when you should expect them to start. Not every agency is going to have a candidate with your skill set requirements just waiting to start. (You may find that two weeks is rather short notice for some agencies. However, I do not feel it is too much to expect.)

> **NOTE**
>
> Some consulting firms may have good candidates waiting in the wings, but the majority will not. Most firms begin looking to place candidates one to two weeks before the conclusion of their current project. Therefore, you may need to be flexible when scheduling interviews.

You should begin your search for contract employees with your client. They obviously had to do some searching before they got to you. Find out whom they were impressed with and if they have any relationships established with other agencies. More importantly, you want to know whom they were not impressed with. Determining whom your client liked, disliked, or has used in the past will help you narrow your field of agencies to contact.

After you have compiled a list of four or five potential agencies to contact, you are ready to start calling. A list of five potential agencies to hire from will not always produce five potential consultants. If you come out of a list of five potentials with two agencies that are sending people over (that fit your needs exactly) to be interviewed, you are doing well.

After you begin calling agencies you will find that some of them may not fit your project's needs. Many agencies have a minimum amount of time you can contract a consultant for. These times can range from one week to six months (the average being three months). Other agencies may not have anybody available fitting your skill set requirements for the project timeline.

You have found a few agencies that have candidates ready, so you at the very least want to screen the candidates by phone.

On every project I have worked on there has been one agency that is willing to send candidates to start on a project without an interview. Insist on at least a phone screening (if for no other reason than to make sure the candidate realizes the scope of the project). Even if you are getting close to the start date of the project (and no one has been contracted to work), take the time to talk to each candidate.

I am not going to tell you who to hire and who not to hire. In some cases (mainly for security reasons), the client is going to want to interview your candidates as well. Your goal here is to assemble a staff that will be able to implement the network you have designed. Their actions and behaviors are going to reflect on you. If you contract a bunch on consultants who slack off all the time, they will make you look bad.

What it comes down to is this: Choose candidates who will make you look good and make the client happy.

Creating the Final Proposal

It is finally time to assemble your final proposal. This is the last document you hand to the client until the project is complete (you will hand over the remainder of you documentation during the final walk-through of the network in Chapter 13, "The Construction Begins"). Both you and the client need to agree upon the terms in the final proposal before construction can begin.

The final proposal consists of two main documents: the final diagram and the timeline.

These two documents will eventually be approved by both parties. They will represent what the client expects of you and when the project is slated to be complete.

The Final Diagram

The final diagram depicts the network as you envision the final product. Like the other network diagrams you have produced to this point, it should be completed with a professional diagram tool. (A trial version of Microsoft Visio 2000 has been included in this book.)

The final diagram, depending on the size of the network, can be quite large. Therefore, you need to lay out the diagram logically onto separate pages. I separate my diagrams as follows:

- High-level Overview
- Geographic Region 1

  Subnet A

  - Server Side
  - Client Side

  Subnet B

  - Server Side
  - Client Side
- Geographic Region 2

I find that this format is the most logical and the easiest to read, especially on larger networks. For networks with more than one geographic region, I will separate the networks onto pages based on location. However, the first page will always represent a high-level view on the network as a whole. Even though the diagram itself will be drawn rather small (to fit the entire network on one page), I like to provide the client with a bird's-eye view of their environment.

The remaining diagrams in the packet will be much easier for the client to read and interpret. The geographic regions are broken down further by subnet, then by server environment and client environment.

All of the designs in the final diagram will include the following information (as applicable to the design):

- Subnet information
- Address information (per device)
- Line speed
- Network type information
- Defining server characteristics (that is, e-mail server, database server, DNS server)
- Department labels
- WAN links and types
- Model information (if you are using multiple models of a certain device. For instance, in Chicago, we have a Cisco 2923 Switch; in Boston, we have a Cisco 5505 switch.)

Remember that if it is not on these diagrams, it is not part of your contract to complete. Therefore, these diagrams need to represent everything that will be put in this environment. Obviously there are some tasks that cannot be represented in the diagram (like preparing documentation and registering domain names). These tasks are put into the timeline.

The Timeline

The timeline is the second of the two documents in your final proposal. Your timeline should be prepared in a professional project management tool to create a neat and easy-to-read document.

The timeline will represent (man-hour by man-hour) when certain tasks on the network will be accomplished and who will be accomplishing them. You want to assign consultants (or yourself) to every task on your timeline. Everything that is to be done to complete the project needs to be accounted for on the timeline.

You need to have tasks on your timeline representing documentation preparatory time, testing, clean up, and the final walk-through.

The final diagram and timeline are then bound and presented to the client. (To see a completed final proposal, see Appendix B, "Sample Documentation.") You will typically give the client the final proposal during a presentation where you will be able to explain step by step what will be expected of you during implementation. By the end of the presentation (or shortly thereafter), you should have an approved course of action to begin the implementation stage of the project.

> **NOTE**
>
> During the presentation of the final proposal, you may be faced with a question that is not represented in the documentation. For example, "What is the performance difference if we use X router instead of Y router?" or "What is the cost difference to go with Token Ring instead of Ethernet?"
>
> In these cases I have to go back and prepare a cost/function analysis. This document simply compares and contrasts the question by the client to what I have in the final proposal.
>
> If I think a certain question will come up I will prepare the cost/function analysis ahead of time and bring it to the presentation.

Summary

- Give your client a list of potential hardware and software vendors to choose from.
- Compare all of the offerings by the potential vendors in table form.
- Try to provide as much pertinent information about each vendor as possible.
- Before you start looking for consultants, calculate the number of man-hours you will need to complete your project.
- You want to suggest/hire consultants that will help you finish the project efficiently and professionally.
- Your final proposal will consist of two documents: the final diagram and the timeline.
- The final diagram should be your best representation of the network as a finished environment.
- The timeline will represent (hour by hour) what will be needed to complete the project.

Building the Network

IN THIS PART

The Construction Begins

IN THIS CHAPTER

Both you and the client have agreed to the parameters of the final proposal; now it is time to begin construction. The construction of a network can be the longest part of a project and therefore must be approached very methodically. If you do not have an organized project plan going into the construction phase, you will have a very hard time completing the job successfully.

There are two main scenarios you can face going into the construction phase of the project. The first is having to build a complete network from the ground up (no existing equipment at all). The second (and more common) is a project involving an existing network. The projects involving existing networks can range from total network upgrades to small integrations of servers. You will need to approach each of these projects in slightly different ways.

As the project winds down you will start preparing your final documentation packet. This packet will contain everything the client will need to research, re-create, or modify anything you have done. The final documentation packet will be the last document to change hands between you and your client.

Finally, you will accompany your client on a walk-through of the new environment. This walk-through will give the client a last chance to point out anything that they see as being questionable. After you address any issues raised during the walk-through, the project can be considered complete and you can pass ownership of the environment to the client.

This chapter guides you through the two types of construction, preparing your final documentation, and conducting the walk-through. By the end of this chapter, you will be able to successfully bring a design project to completion.

The last chapter of this book will help you implement a monitoring solution on the new network. This will help the client keep their environment functioning as well as the day it was rolled out.

However, right now the major portion of the project is still ahead of you. You need to order, receive, build, and install the equipment (not to mention document, document, and document).

Building a Network from the Ground Up

This section walks you through the construction process for a new network. In particular, it focuses on the network implementation as it applies to a clean environment. We will cover all of the major events and tasks that you will need to accomplish to complete your project.

Your first construction task (which we touched upon lightly in the last chapter) is to order all of your equipment. This task is not as easy as it sounds and must be done in a specific, organized way. Your goal here is to have certain tasks accomplished in a certain order (we will cover each of these tasks later in the chapter). Your first step is to have the cabling completed (this also includes the ordering of any WAN links). After the cabling is complete, you want your (server) consultants and your server equipment to arrive. If there is an overwhelming number of clients (PCs) you can begin building them simultaneously to the server equipment, otherwise both the equipment and the consultants should arrive next. Finally, you want to implement your connectivity devices and roll out the network.

Before you begin assembling your network there is one thing you should have. Because this is an empty environment (there is no existing network), you should have a notebook computer or other small (networkable) computing device. You will need to troubleshoot your network as you build it; therefore, a small portable device is going to be invaluable to you.

A notebook computer will also be very useful as you prepare your documentation. You should consider loading your notebook with all of the essential tools for network design, maintenance, documentation, and monitoring. I try to keep the following programs loaded on my notebook:

- Windows 2000 Server
- Microsoft Office 2000 (I use Word, Excel, Project, and Visio for documentation)
- SQL Server 7.0 (to troubleshoot database issues)
- SMS 2.0 (to use Network Monitor)
- LapLink (for the emergency transferal of files or systems)
- Norton Antivirus (for virus protection)
- LAN Sniffer (I use this when I am working on Token-Ring networks—it helps to identify the active monitor)
- Symantec Ghost (to create standard images)
- I also have WINS, DNS, and DHCP services installed to aid with and issues that may arise

A Note About Organization

I cannot give you an exact formula to follow here because it is going to vary for every project you encounter. Your overall goal is to organize your equipment orders, your consultants, your Telco (WAN) orders, and your software orders in such a way that the network can be assembled in a logical fashion.

If everything flows smoothly, you want to implement the network in the following order:

1. Server equipment
2. WAN links
3. Connectivity devices
4. Client equipment

Will your plan always work out this way? No. However, in a perfect world, your network should be assembled in this order.

Most networks revolve around the servers. Therefore, the servers should be assembled first. This will give the architects and administrators a chance to work out any bugs or connection issues before any other devices are introduced to the environment.

Next, if your environment includes multiple sites, your WAN links should be installed. After your WAN circuits are dropped, you can start on the remaining connectivity devices. Keep in mind that in a WAN situation, most of your connectivity devices will rely on the WAN link for full functionality. Therefore, it makes sense to have the WAN circuits installed before you begin working on the routers.

NOTE

When you place your order with the WAN vendor, you should discuss the topic of IP addresses. Typically, the vendor needs to know what IP addresses will reside at either end of the WAN circuit to process the order. Therefore, you can use this opportunity to discuss IP schemes with the vendor. This is when you need to obtain all of the private (routable) addresses you need (or at least as many as the vendor will assign you) to implement your IP scheme.

After you have your private addresses, you can use the imminent delay between when you place your WAN order and when the order is fulfilled to work on IP issues. Tasks such as domain registration and DNS establishment can be completed before the WAN circuit is implemented. Keep in mind that domain registration can be a lengthy process as well, especially if the client has a fairly common name to register. However, because you need both your domain registered and your IP addresses to implement DNS, the timing of these tasks is crucial.

After the WAN circuit is ordered and you have your private IP addresses, you should create the public (non-routable) IP address scheme for the remaining devices. This process could include any of the following tasks:

- Implementing NAT on external interface routers
- Reconfiguring IP addresses on installed servers
- Implementing a DHCP server
- Implementing DNS

Once you have a functional server (WAN) environment, you should start introducing users (PCs). However, if you want to double-check your work (to this point), you should log in to the new network with your notebook. This is always a good way to ensure that the environment is functioning properly. Remember, it is easier to catch and resolve an issue now (before users are on the network) than having to interrupt someone's workflow later.

Ordering Your Equipment

After the final proposal is approved you can begin to order your equipment. Obviously the network cannot be implemented until the equipment arrives; therefore the timing of the equipment orders is crucial.

On one hand you don't want truckloads of equipment pulling up to the project site at the same time. The longer equipment sits unattended in boxes, the more susceptible it can be to tampering, theft, and damage. Equipment should be unpacked, assembled, and installed as soon as it arrives. (That does not mean every piece of equipment will be finished and operational the day it arrives. However, you should try to have servers and other rack or stationary hardware unpacked and in its place.) This process will also give you a better idea of the space utilization in certain areas of your environment and allow you to make small adjustments before too much work is finished.

On the other hand, you do not want any of your consultants sitting around with nothing to do while they wait for equipment to arrive. This can be costly and cause the project to run longer than expected. Remember, most of these consultants are getting paid by the hour. The longer you have them sit around and be unproductive (and pay them for it), the less happy your client will be.

Cabling the Workspace

The next order of business is to have the workspace cabled according to your designs. For most projects this will be contracted out to a cabling company. The cabling can be done while some of the first pieces of equipment are being assembled. On some small projects (one office, 20-person or smaller networks) I will consider doing the cabling myself. However, no matter the size of the project, if you do not have experience laying cable (which includes knowing and identifying other types of cable that could exist in the environment), leave it to a professional. Whether you tackle the job yourself or contract it out, there are certain things you want to have when the cabling is finished.

If you contract a cable vendor to wire your environment, I suggest you also have them certify that every port is functional. That is, have the vendor test the connectivity of every wall port as it runs back to the patch panel.

If you are cabling the environment yourself, test every port before you finish. (Complete port testing kits can be found for around $300.)

Whether you use a vendor or do the cabling yourself, you will want to purchase pre-assembled cabling. Creating 4-pair cables yourself (although very self-fulfilling) can be more troublesome and time-consuming than it is worth.

As with every aspect of the project thus far, the goal here is document, document, document. There are two main items of documentation that should be produced by the cabling contractors: a cabling map (or wiring diagram) and a fully labeled wiring closet (it's a stretch, but I consider this a document). These two documents are arguably the ones an administrator will reference the most when troubleshooting network problems.

A cabling map traces the physical mapping of every port in the workspace to its corresponding port in the wiring closet. This is extremely convenient when you are trying to troubleshoot a dead connection.

A well-labeled wiring closet will have every patch panel port labeled with its originating office and all T1s and analog lines labeled with their respective IDs. This will help the administrator of the new network tremendously with troubleshooting the environment.

One cabling job that you will most likely do yourself is extending the cables from the patch panel to the connectivity devices. Again, when you are doing this, neatness counts.

CAT5 (and sometimes fiber) cables come in a myriad of colors. When I extend cabling from a patch panel to a connectivity device, I always color-code the wires to make identification of the connected devices easier to trace. I will then create a legend and affix it to the rack holding the patch panel. A typical legend will look like this (the colors below are arbitrary; however, these are the colors I use in my wiring schemes. You should choose colors that you are comfortable with and can use consistently):

Blue = Windows Server

Red = Novell Server

Green = Unix

White = Upstream Connectivity Device

Yellow = Downstream Connectivity Device

Gray = Client (PC)

Color-coding the cables in your wiring closet will prove very useful for your client. A well-organized and easy-to-troubleshoot wiring closet will say a lot about you as a consultant and might earn you some very good references.

When you are extending the patch panel cables, use all of the wire management tools available to you. Nothing looks worse than a mess of cables hanging off a rack. Even if you do not have professional cable management tools, you can use items such as twist ties to organize a patch panel very well. Administrators will also find that troubleshooting and expanding are easier when the wiring closet is neat and organized.

Assembling the Servers

By this point, your workspace should be cabled and (in a perfect world) you should have your functional WAN links. (Don't worry too much if the WAN links are not in yet. As long as they are in before you begin adding connectivity devices, you should be okay.) Your goal now is to focus on implementing the first wave of servers.

The first thing you should do is document the following information about each server:

- Server hardware (processor, hard drive configuration, RAM, and any peripherals)
- Server name (domain name for NT)
- Protocol address, subnet mask, default gateway, Wins and DNS addresses
- Operating system (and rev or service pack)
- Installed applications
- Serial numbers for warrantee and technical support issues

This information will be compiled and given to the incoming network administrator at the end of the project.

Because your network on a whole is not functional yet, I would not worry about which servers you set up first. However, as a general rule of thumb, here is the order I usually follow:

1. Primary authentication server (If this server is a Windows Primary Domain Controller, it must be the first server you implement)
2. DNS
3. DHCP
4. Application servers
5. File servers
6. Remote connectivity servers
7. Backup authentication servers
8. E-mail server
9. Firewall servers

Because not every project will include all of these servers and because many of them may actually reside on the same physical machine, this rule of thumb may not apply in every case. Remember, you are building the environment from scratch. There are no users needing access to information or services. Right now, you can proceed however you see fit.

I try to implement my servers in this order (in an empty environment) for one main reason: It builds logically (one device utilizes services implemented on the previous device) and allows for testing before new devices are implemented.

The first server to be implemented, the primary authentication server, is the keystone of the network. When this server is set up and running, you can not only begin to install other servers, but you can also begin work on the user lists, groups, and security models. That is the main reason I start with this server.

On smaller networks, the next two services (DNS and DHCP) can both be installed on the primary authentication server (another reason to install that server first). However, in larger environments, you are going to separate them. Therefore, they should be the next servers (services) to be installed.

After these first three servers are installed, take some time out to troubleshoot. (You could possibly do some troubleshooting while the consultants proceed with building the next server.) Use your notebook to log in to the new environment and test DNS and DHCP, but be thorough. If everything works correctly, try changing settings on your notebook and see if the environment fails. Sometimes making sure a server does not work is almost as important as making sure it does.

The next servers to be installed are the application servers and the file servers. These servers may take a little extra time because you want to install all applications that need to be present on the servers. Therefore, if you are installing a database server, you will want to install and test the database. Testing for this phase of the server implementation is pretty straightforward: making sure the applications work.

The five servers installed to this point are prerequisites for the next devices. The next project is remote connectivity. When you are testing your remote connectivity server, you want to test logging in and application usage. These are very important issues and you should not continue until they are functional.

Implementing the next three servers may rely on one key element. If your WAN links are not in yet, you will not be able to fully implement the remote connectivity server, e-mail server, or firewalls. If installation of the WAN links has been unforeseeably delayed (which can happen), move your resources to setting up the client PCs. There is enough of the internal network built that you can successfully begin to implement and test PCs. This will also keep your consultants working while you wait for the WAN links.

NOTE

You want to be certain that each piece of your network is fully functional and working correctly before you move on to the next. Each device you implement is going to be based on settings in the previous ones. Therefore, if your first devices are not fully tested you may find that you need to go back and change settings that will now affect other devices.

Implementing the E-mail Solution

Implementing e-mail should be next on your list. During testing, you want to send and receive e-mails both internal and external to the network (this includes testing e-mail functionality through remote connections).

> Keep in mind that before you can implement your e-mail system you need to have your IP address scheme in place (and functioning correctly) and (if you will be sending and receiving Internet e-mail) you need to have your domain name registered.

Lastly, you should implement your firewall. Implementing the firewall last gives you one less avenue you need to troubleshoot if the e-mail and remote connectivity servers do not function correctly. If you install the firewall last and e-mail stops flowing, you know you have a firewall problem rather than an e-mail problem. This is another reason you should fully test each server before introducing another element to the network.

Once all of your servers are installed and functional, there are a few tasks you want to tackle before proceeding. The first is to install, configure, and test your network backup systems. If you will be using backup software of any kind, this is the place to implement it. The next task is to get your documentation in order. Try to take periodic breaks to keep up with your documentation (this will be easier to do if you have other consultants helping you). Documenting the particular part of the project you are working on will save you from having to remember every detail later.

Adding the Connectivity Devices

You most likely needed to install a few of these to implement the servers. However, any devices that did not need to be installed to get your servers up and running should be installed now. These devices will include routers that link your site to any smaller sites, any hubs or switches needed by client PCs, and any devices needed to subnet your environment.

Again, because there are no existing users on this network, you can dictate the order in which these three items are accomplished. However, I would try to tackle them in this order:

1. Subnetting devices
2. Office linking routers
3. Hubs and switches

Your subnetting devices will most likely be the hardest to implement. They will control access to and from areas of your new environment. That is the main reason you want to install them next. Like firewalls, you want to be sure that everything on the network is functional first. This will limit the amount of time spent troubleshooting any problems that may arise in the new subnets.

Finally, after all of your devices are installed and functional, it is time to install the new client PCs (see "Rolling Out Clients and Migrating Users" later in the chapter).

The following section outlines the construction process for replacing or integrating with an existing network.

Using Parallel Networks

If your project requires you to replace or integrate with an existing network, your course of action should include building a parallel network. A parallel network allows you to implement and troubleshoot a chunk of your new environment without causing too much disruption to the existing user community. There are two scenarios you can use to build a parallel network: replacing a network and integrating with an existing network. Each scenario follows a different order of implementation:

- **Scenario 1**—Replacing a Network
    1. Segregate parallel network
    2. Implement servers
    3. Upgrade/replace connectivity devices
    4. Migrate users
- **Scenario 2**—Integrating with an Existing Network
    1. Segregate parallel network
    2. Implement servers
    3. Upgrade/replace connectivity devices
    4. Phase new servers into existing network
    5. Upgrade existing client PCs

Notice how each project follows an identical path until the final stages. Because of this, we will address them both in this section.

Segregating a Parallel Environment

The purpose of separating the existing network from the new environment is clear: Until the new environment is fully tested you do not know what kind of issue it may cause with the existing network. Therefore, it is best to keep the two separated for a time. Depending on the size of the project, there are two ways to approach this.

The first is to install a few new connectivity devices and create a fully functional, separate networking environment. While this scenario may work well in large corporate environments, a more likely solution is to branch the new environment off some existing hardware.

The first scenario is going to begin much like the example from the previous section. You will be setting up the new network from scratch (this will change after the server implementation). If you are replacing a very large network using a parallel environment, follow the server implementation guidelines in the section "Building a Network from the Ground Up." Keep in mind that only the server implementation will be similar to what is explained in that section. The remainder of the project is outlined in the following text.

If your environment is not very large, you may opt for the second scenario. This scenario involves creating your new, parallel environment by branching it off existing equipment. If this is done correctly, network integrity can still be maintained and users will not be affected.

Branching a new environment off existing equipment is best done with switches. Switches (see Chapter 7, "Connectivity Devices") have to segregate traffic by port. To begin building your new environment, separate a couple of ports on the switch for your new environment. (That is, assuming you have available ports on a switch.)

This will allow you use the same IP scheme and at least one of the connectivity devices while you implement your servers. This is extremely important because you want to have your new environment configured as closely to the existing one as possible while still restricting access.

If you are running low on available ports or do not have a switch, you do still have an option (however, not a optimal one). You can purchase a small hub (just for use in the new environment) and chain it off the existing connectivity devices. You can then keep your traffic separated by using a completely different IP scheme on the new environment.

There are two downsides to segregating network traffic in this way. The first is that you will be testing your new environment with a phony IP scheme. This scheme will need to be changed to match the existing network before the two are merged. The other downside is that you will be adding more traffic to an existing network. This can cause unintentional issues in the existing environment.

Once the environment is established, you can begin installing your servers.

Installing the Servers

If you are replacing an existing network, you can follow the server installation steps outlined in the preceding section. However, if your project is to integrate with an existing network, you may need to follow a slightly different course of action.

The only servers you will need to implement are those that do not exist on the current network. In most cases, this includes application and file servers. However, you will most likely be implementing a new primary server.

When a project calls for the implementation of a new primary server, I try to stay away from upgrading the existing one. There are too many chances during an upgrade for things to go horribly wrong. Therefore, I will almost always replace the existing primary with a new one, store the old one until I am comfortable with the reliability of the new server, and then reuse the older server somewhere else on the network.

One major difference in implementing a network like this is that you will be integrating some new components into the existing ones as you go along. This will allow for a less disruptive migration between the two environments. One server that you will integrate with the existing network as soon as it is tested is the primary server.

To replace an existing primary server, you must first install and fully test the new server. If you can, attach an existing client (or two) to the segregated environment. Use these client PCs to test the functionality of the new primary server.

> **NOTE**
>
> Whenever possible you want to export and import data (among compatible systems) between the old and new servers. This can include user lists, application data, DNS tables, or other information critical to the operation of the new environments. This will ensure that the new environment is as close to the existing one as possible. You can then make whatever changes are needed to the imported data.
>
> You should also try to keep things such as IP addresses, shared folder names, and computer names identical between the two servers.

After you are satisfied with the performance of the new server, you can replace the existing one. You should always do this at night (or during the non-business hours of the company). If the client runs a 24-hour operation, you will need to schedule an outage with the client and perform the replacement.

Replace the existing server by physically moving it and putting the new server in its place. The new server can then be powered on and should function as normal. Physically replacing the server will rule out any subnetting or port trunking issues that you may not have located yet.

You should also keep the old server intact for a small amount of time. This will let you roll the old server back onto the network if an unforeseen disaster happens with the new one.

I would continue testing and replacing servers in this fashion. However, do not let the small amount of space devoted to this subject lead you to believe that it is a quick or easy job. In fact, performing network server integration in this way can be very time-consuming. The major reason for this is that you need to mock an environment that has been built, tested, and had time to settle. You need to match this environment flawlessly or the transition will not be seamless.

After the primary server has settled into place (depending on the amount of network activity, this could be one or two days), you can reincorporate the old primary server into the network. If your network makes provisions for reusing the hardware of the old primary server, you can feel safe to do so now. If not, you can proceed on to the remaining servers. I try to reuse as much as possible without compromising the integrity of the new environment. If the old server is antiquated equipment, it still may be usable as a network monitor or a test system. Either way, you should consider reusing equipment wherever possible.

> **NOTE**
>
> You may have noticed that I have not mentioned connectivity devices yet. In general, the connectivity devices on an existing network will not need to be replaced. However, in cases where the old network has reached the limit of a device (either port capacity or bandwidth), the device will need to be replaced. I will always replace these devices before implementing servers.
>
> By replacing the connectivity devices first, you can ensure their functionality in the environment. This will also give them a chance to settle in while you prepare the servers.

After your servers have been integrated into the existing environment, you can move on to the client PCs.

Rolling Out Clients and Migrating Users

Rolling out the PCs is going to take a couple of steps to complete (depending on the project). If you are working on a network integration, you will need to roll out clients. If you are working on a network replacement, you will be migrating users. Each method of bringing users to the new environment has its own steps and pitfalls, and each is covered in this section.

Test Groups

The best way to test both the clients and the servers' reaction to them is in test groups. If you are on an integration project, the test group may be only one or two client PCs put on the segregated network with the new servers. This test group should be introduced to the segregated network before the servers are integrated into the current environment.

> **NOTE**
>
> Before you bring up a test group, try to have as much server testing completed as possible. Your goal here is to test the configuration of the clients and anticipate how the existing clients will react when the new server is put in place. Therefore, you want to rule out as many server-side issues as possible by having the server fully tested.

13

THE CONSTRUCTION BEGINS

For an integration project, I typically try to arrange testing with one existing user (and his or her PC) and one new PC. This gives me the opportunity to test a couple of different configurations and scenarios. I will have a chance to tweak the configuration of the new PC and ensure the existing PCs can integrate with the new server. Whenever possible, have users from the existing network test the new client PCs. They would be best qualified to tell you what is or is not working correctly.

If the project is a replacement, there is a little more leeway when working with a PC test group. After all of the servers are functional on the new network segment, you can begin implementing a test group of users. This will need to be arranged with the client, but I will typically set up between five and ten new PCs in the new environment. These clients are encouraged to conduct their daily business on the new environment (with the knowledge that they are working with test data).

These clients will not only ensure that both the server and client configurations are correct, they will begin to check the integrity of the imported data. These users can also begin to populate data that could not be imported.

> **NOTE**
>
> Utilizing client PC test groups will also give you a chance to not only document new procedures, but also introduce the users to any significant changes in the environment.

After a successful phase of test groups, you can begin the actual roll out of client PCs. The method used to roll out the new clients will depend (again) on the type of network project you are working on. If you are on an integration job, you will want to follow the roll out of your client PCs either manually or by automation. However, if you are replacing an existing network you are going to migrate your users from one network to the other.

Automated and Manual Client Roll Outs

If you are on an integration project, you will want to either automate or manually roll out the client PCs into your new environment (as opposed to migrating users). Which method you choose will depend on the number of clients you need to roll out. However, you can determine the cutoff number between the two.

If you were dealing with only a handful of users (one to five), I would just manually roll out the clients into the network. Manual client roll out consists of the following tasks:

- Setting up the new hardware
- Installing the new software
- Migrating the user's data to the new platform (if applicable)
- Replacing the user's PC

The first step in manually deploying a new client PC is to configure the hardware. (In almost every case, the new hardware will be different from the old hardware.) After the hardware is ready, all of the software including the OS is installed. Finally, the user's data is migrated from the old PC.

Migrating the user's data may take some work. If the users have not been instructed to store all of their data on a file server, you will need to scour the PC for information. This can be the tedious difference between a manual and an automated roll out.

> **NOTE**
>
> In cases where you have to scour the user's PC for data, keep the old PC intact for as long as possible. This will let you revisit the PC to get any missed information.

Because migrating data from one platform to another can be a lengthy ordeal, I try to automate the process whenever possible.

To establish an automated client roll out, a few parameters must be met. First, the operating systems of the old and new clients must match. Second, the hardware configurations should be similar. After you have determined that these requirements are met, you can begin the process.

A few vendors produce PC cloning software, such as Symantec's Ghost. The theory behind the process is simple: Clone the users' existing PCs on their new ones, thus creating an exact replica of the old data. These cloning programs work great as long as you are moving between similar hardware platforms.

If you are using PC cloning software and you are not moving between similar hardware platforms, fear not, it may still work. If your client operating system is Windows 95, 98, or ME, you can generally boot the system (after cloning) and change the OS drivers to correspond to the new hardware. However, if you are using Windows NT you may not get so lucky. Because NT's kernel is hardware specific, you may have trouble even booting the systems if the hardware changes.

Your second option (other than PC cloning software) is application and data transferring software such as Aloha Bob's PC Relocator. These programs will transfer data and applications independent of the operating system. These packages are ideal if the new PCs you are rolling out will have a different operating system or hardware configuration.

If you are not integrating PCs, but rather migrating users from one network to another, your process will be a little different.

Migrating Existing Users

The process of "cutting over" from an existing environment to a parallel one is the major difference between an integration project and a replacement. To perform the cut over, you need to migrate users from the existing network to the new environment. This action can be performed one of two ways. The following sections will illustrate how to successfully migrate users from one network to another.

Connectivity Cut Over

The easiest way to perform a migration to a new network is to migrate the connectivity device to which the users are connected. This provides for a mass migration to the new environment. Figures 13.1 and 13.2 illustrate a connectivity device cut over.

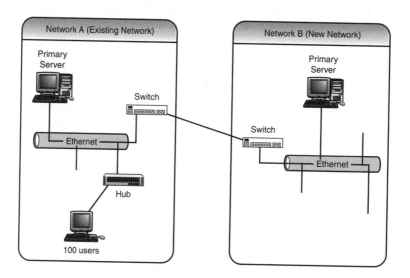

FIGURE 13.1

Networks before cut over.

The hub containing all of Network A's users was simply rerouted to Network B. Because Network B was running parallel to Network A, using the same addressing scheme and naming conventions, the users noticed little change or disruption.

> **NOTE**
>
> If both your old and new networks use DHCP, you will want to set the old network DHCP lease expirations to one day. You can then perform the cut over early in the morning while the PCs are powered off.

This step will ensure that the PCs release their old assigned IP address and query your new DHCP server for a new address. Even though the IP schemes may be the same, this step is critical. The new DHCP server will have no knowledge of what addresses have been assigned to the existing PCs. Therefore, if these addresses are not released, you end up with duplicate addresses on your network.

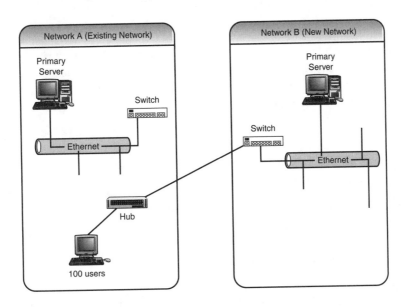

FIGURE 13.2

Networks after cut over.

If the majority of the equipment on the old network is being replaced, you will only need to migrate users from one platform to the other.

PC Migration

To perform a PC migration, the majority of the equipment in the old network should be marked for replacement. This will mean that the segregated environment will contain servers and connectivity devices, including hubs or switches.

If this is the case, the bulk of the migration can be performed at the patch panel. Begin your migration by moving groups of users (patch panel cables) from the old environment to the new environment. Stop for a period of time between each group of migrations to test the environment. Testing each group as you migrate them will provide for a smooth transfer to the new platform.

The Final Walk-through

Your project is complete (you think) and you want to show off your accomplishments to the client. The final task you will need to perform is the walk-through. The walk-through gives the client an opportunity to make a final inspection of the network and voice any opinions they may have regarding whether they feel it accurately represents the agreed-upon proposal.

However, before letting anyone inspect the network, you have to clean it up.

Clean Up

You want the network to be as neat and organized as possible. This means that every piece of equipment should be labeled and all cabling should be tied back. Equipment labels should be placed uniformly on the equipment and contain the equipment's describing features (that is, name, protocol address, and function).

Make sure that you have completely finished all testing that needed to be done on the network and patched any problems that arose from the testing. You do not want to conduct the walk-through and say, "This is your new e-mail server, it's still not working, but it will be." That just does not sound professional.

Finally, make sure you have every time sheet, bill, and packing slip in order for the client. The fewer questions they have to ask, the better.

Inspecting the Environment

This is what it all comes down to, the final inspection. Accompany the client on a tour of the new environment using the final proposal as a guide. You want to point out key points such as added functionality that did not exist before.

If you had to make any last-minute changes to the proposal to make the new network function properly, point those out as well. Above all, be clear and concise when answering any questions about the environment. You never want to answer with "I don't know."

If anything major is brought up during the walk-through, address it immediately.

Handling Issues

Handle any issues that are pointed out during the walk-through quickly and efficiently. Chances are your consultants will no longer be around, and you will be performing the work yourself. If it is a minor task, such as an addition to the DHCP scope, it can be handled during a break in the walk-through. However, if the issue is larger, such as a missing server, you may need to produce an amended project plan and work on it as if it were a new job.

There is a diplomatic way and a not-so-diplomatic way to handle these things. Try not to push the blame for major issues onto the consultants; chances are they were only doing what they were instructed to do. Simply listen attentively to the client, note all of the issues they have, and resolve them.

After all of the issues have been dealt with, it is time to hand off the network.

Handing Off the Network

The handing off of the network is more of a symbolic gesture than a physical one. The hand off represents the point in time at which you are no longer responsible for the functionality of the environment. This is generally when the client hires or appoints an administrator to oversee the network's operations.

During the passing of the network from you to the client, you want to hand in the completed documentation packet. There are documents in this packet that will eventually be given to different departments within the client's company (accounting, HR, and MIS); however, the package as a whole should be given to one person.

To uphold your sense of professionalism, the packet should be neat, well formatted, and bound. The cover of the packet should contain your name (or your company's name), the client, and the dates of the project. (It is always recommended that you make multiple copies of this packet, both for your records and in the event that the client requests another.)

At this point, you can consider the project finished—or can you?

What if the client cannot find an adequate administrator and contracts you for the interim? What should your first order of business be?

In many cases the client will not have a suitable administrator waiting to take over the new network. The client may approach you to administer the new network while they look for a permanent replacement.

If you are asked to serve as an interim network administrator you need to change hats; that is, you have to stop thinking in terms of designing the network and start acting like a system administrator. (Depending on the part of the country you live in, factors such as pay rate may differ between administrators and designers and you should adjust accordingly.)

A good service to offer to the client (if it is not asked of you) is to train the administrator hired by the client. The client will feel much better about hiring somebody if they know you will ensure they can perform the job well. Keep in mind that the more helpful you can be at this point, the better you will look in the eyes of the client. This will lead to bigger and better projects.

The next chapter will discuss some of the various tasks you may be asked to perform as an interim network administrator.

Summary

- Most projects will follow a set order of events. First, the equipment orders are placed. Next, the consultants are hired. Finally, the hardware is implemented.
- If the network is being built in a new office space, you must first have the area cabled.
- The cabling contractors should provide a cabling map and label the wiring closet and test/validate each connection.
- After the area is cabled you can begin assembling the hardware.
- When you have fully tested the new environment, you can migrate users.
- The final walk-through will happen after all network testing has been finished.
- If the client has any issues with the final inspection of the network, address them quickly and efficiently.
- Finally, you need to hand over your documentation packet to the client to symbolically end the project.

Network Monitoring

IN THIS PART

Post Project Activities

IN THIS CHAPTER

It is not uncommon for a client to ask you (as a designer) to stay onboard with their company until a suitable administrator is hired. When you think about it, who else would be better suited to administer a network than the person who designed it? Therefore, the final chapter of this book deals with any issues you may need to handle should you be asked to administer the environment.

Often, the first few weeks of a new network's existence can be a learning experience. This time period can be a good gauge by which to mark the accuracy of your design skills. Use the time that you are administering the network to your advantage to improve and hone your skills for future projects.

You can learn a lot about the success of your design by following a few simple guidelines:

- Take notes
- Observe the users
- Monitor the network's statistics
- Correct any issues you find

The first point is pretty self-explanatory. You can learn more by simply taking adequate notes about a subject than by sitting down and trying to memorize it.

Take notes on what you observe in the user community. Are the users generally satisfied with the network's performance, stability, speed, and configuration? Don't be afraid to ask users about the network and how it does or does not meet their expectations. At any time, you can go out into the user community and see how the environment is holding up.

This chapter discusses monitoring the network's status and correcting any issues you find. By successfully monitoring certain aspects of the network, you can not only see the underlying problems behind some issues, but you may be able to stop some problems before they happen. We will look into using Microsoft's SMS server and other tools to monitor network traffic.

However, network problems are not the only things your client may want you to monitor. The second half of this chapter focuses on monitoring for security purposes. We will discuss how to monitor Internet and e-mail traffic at the client's site.

Finally, at the back of this book you will find three appendixes. Appendix A includes a complete glossary for your future reference. Appendix B is a collection of sample documentation for you to refer to when you are working on projects. Appendix C is a comprehensive troubleshooting guide to help you through some common (and some not-so-common) network and design issues.

Using SMS for Network Traffic Monitoring

Microsoft's Systems Management Server is a multipurpose product for controlling and managing large environments. Although we won't be discussing all of the features of SMS, we will be focusing on a few that will make your life a little easier.

Microsoft SMS includes two tools that you will find invaluable when monitoring network activity. These tools are Network Monitor and Network Trace. Network Monitor is a packet-viewing tool and Network Trace allows you to create network maps and layouts.

> **NOTE**
>
> Network Monitor and Network Trace are not integrated parts of the SMS program itself; however, they are installed with SMS (Administrator's Console). I will not be covering how to install SMS, but there are some things you should know about it before you begin.
>
> Microsoft's Systems Management Server is a very involved program with a myriad of tools for network administration. If you do not plan on using (or are not familiar with) all of the tools included in the package, you may want to check out other SMS resources (such as the Microsoft knowledge base at technet.Microsoft.com).
>
> SMS requires at least Windows NT 4.0 with service pack 3. (If you do not have an SQL server installed, the SMS installation package will install a runtime version for you.)

If you plan on using the entire feature set of Microsoft SMS on your network, it would be best to install the product on its own server. Because SMS performs functions such as network inventory and software distribution, you would be best served by keeping this product off a primary server.

> **NOTE**
>
> A full-featured SMS should not be placed on networks where available bandwidth is already an issue. SMS can use a lot of bandwidth performing functions such as network inventory, PC remote control, and software distribution.
>
> SMS utilizes a Microsoft SQL server database to store data such as inventory information. This software coupled with the bandwidth used by the product makes SMS a program that is not meant for fragile or troublesome environments.

14

POST PROJECT ACTIVITIES

Luckily, if you do not have the need or capacity for a fully loaded SMS on your network, Network Monitor and Network Trace can be installed separately (although Network Trace can only be utilized with at least two SMS servers in the environment). Network Monitor and Network Trace are installed as part of the Microsoft SMS Administrator's Console.

The following sections explain how to successfully use both Network Monitor and Network Trace to catch and diagnose issues on your network.

There are many different packet analyzers on the market and any number of them may serve your needs; however, I have chosen to discuss Microsoft's SMS Network Trace. It is the product that I am most familiar with and I am very accustomed to its feature set.

Network Monitor

Network Monitor is a type of tool known as a packet viewer. Packet viewers are used to capture and examine data frames traveling from one PC to another. This can be very useful when you are trying to diagnose network problems such as network congestion.

Packet viewers in general (not just Network Monitor) function by placing your NIC into promiscuous mode. When the NIC of your device is in promiscuous mode it accepts, copies, and forwards every packet it can see. The key to this is "every packet it can see." Packet viewers will only be able to work with data that is either originating from or bound for its local subnet. Figure 14.1 illustrates why Network Monitor can only work with data on its local subnet. In the figure, data traveling from Subnet A to Subnet C never touches Subnet B. (I drew this as a separate line traveling around Subnet B to show the logical path of the data.) However, the information traveling from A to C would actually pass through Subnet B's routers; it would just be routed straight through. After reading the header information in the packets, the routers would send the data directly to Subnet C without stopping at Subnet B.

The Network Monitor on Network B will detect and read all packets that cross its path. That is, any packet bound for or originating from a device on Network B will be captured by the monitor. However, when a packet (frame of information) is forwarded from a device on Network A to a device on Network C, that packet has no need to travel through Network B. Therefore, the Network Monitor will not be able to view any of these frames.

Here is a description of what the packet monitor does to packets that are on its local subnet:

- For every packet (regardless of who sent it or where it is going) the packet monitor captures it.
- The monitor compares that packet to its set of packet filters.
- If the packet does not match any of the filters, the viewer ignores the packet.
- If the packet does match a filter, the viewer copies the packet to its internal buffer.

- The monitor continues to capture packets until it is told to stop (if the monitor is not told to stop before it fills its internal buffer, it begins to overwrite the oldest packets in the buffer).

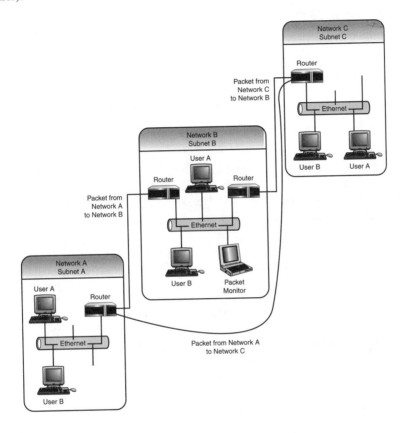

FIGURE 14.1

A Network Monitor in a three-subnet environment.

As you can well imagine, turning on Network Monitor and capturing every packet will not only fill your buffer very quickly (causing you to possibly lose vital information), but you will quickly tax your machine's resources.

> **NOTE**
>
> Because of the amount of resources used capturing and examining network packets, it is highly recommended that you do not run Network Monitor from a primary server. Running Network Monitor from a server that already has a high workload could cause it to become slow and unresponsive.

To minimize the number of packets you need to capture, set up capture filters within Network Monitor. Filters can be established to capture frames based on any of number of criteria that make up a packet. You can use filters to segregate on

- Protocol type
- Source address
- Destination address
- A specific bit pattern in the packet data

Then, to ensure you do not overwrite any of the frames (by overfilling the buffer) you can establish a trigger.

> A trigger in Network Monitor is used to perform an action when certain criteria are reached. Triggers can be used to call external programs, stop capturing data, and other actions based on anything from buffer sizes to source addresses.

A trigger can be set up to turn off the capturing of frames when the buffer hits its limit. This will let you examine the captured packets at your leisure without the risk of overwriting your capture buffer.

Now that you are capturing packets, what can you do with them (and what are you looking for)?

What Can Network Monitor Do?

Network Monitor will examine network packets and display the following information:

- Protocol type
- Source address
- Destination address
- Packet data
- Checksum

This information alone can tell you a great deal about a network. The first piece of data, the protocol type, can show you what protocol each device is using to send information across the network. For example, if you are running an IP network and a router stops working after being rebooted, you could examine the packets being sent from it. Then, looking at the protocol type, you may find that the router reverted back to a default protocol (something other than IP) during the reboot, causing the break in communication.

Examining data in the source address section of a packet will show you when information is being sent to your network from addresses (and presumably devices) outside your local environment. For example, your local addressing scheme for Network A is 192.168.75.x, Network B is 192.168.76.x, and Network C is 192.168.77.x. While capturing packets, you notice an inordinate amount of packets being sent to your primary file server from the source address 10.91.55.143. This address obviously should not be on your local network and you should investigate the issue further (by looking at your firewall and using other security measures). Receiving packets from addresses outside of your IP scheme could indicate that there has been an unauthorized presence on the local network.

The information contained in the destination address portion of a packet can tell you two important things about the purpose of that packet. The destination address can tell you whether the message is a broadcast message or a direct message.

> A broadcast message is an IP packet that is processed by every device on a particular network. These messages can be distinguished from other data because they are always sent to the address 255.255.255.255. A direct message, on the other hand, is an IP packet that is sent to one particular device. These messages are processed by the receiving device only and contain that device's IP address as the packet's destination address.

This information can be useful if you notice a large number of broadcasts emanating from a particular device (especially a connectivity device, which could indicate a potential problem). This information can be even more useful if you are trying to diagnose a specific network service problem such as slow DHCP server response time. In the case of a slow, overworked, or otherwise faulty DHCP server you would notice a large number of broadcast messages flooding the network.

14

NOTE

> When a PC is looking for a DHCP server to obtain an address, it sends a broadcast message. The closest server to the device responds with its address. If a DHCP server is not responding to requests in a timely manner, the device looking for an address may have to send more than one broadcast. Multiply this by the number of devices on your network and you could have a lot of traffic.

If the users are noticing long response times while obtaining IP addresses from a DHCP server, Network Monitor can help you diagnose the problem. Turn on the monitor shortly before the

POST PROJECT
ACTIVITIES

peak DHCP usage time (typically early in the morning). If you notice a large number of broadcasts (characterized by a message body of "IP request") but only a few responses, your server may be overworked.

There are several ways to troubleshoot this issue. For all of the broadcasts that go unanswered, look at the source address. Is the source address an address that has already been reassigned? Is the address not within your scope? Is the MAC address of the machine in the DHCP server list of reserved addresses? (The MAC address of every device transmitting can also be seen from Network Monitor.) These questions can point to issues other than an overworked DHCP server. (See Appendix C, "Resolution Guide for Common Network Conflicts," for a list of possible problems and solutions for this issue).

There are two pieces of information provided by Network Monitor that can be very valuable: packet data and checksum. For example, the packet data can tell you if a supposed static router is trying to broadcast its routing table (the packet data portion of the packet would appear as RIP data), while an invalid checksum on a particular frame may indicate a faulty NIC or a media problem.

Examining packets by hand can be a tedious process. For this reason Network Monitor provides a series of "experts" that monitor the environment for you (looking for issues). This is the main factor that draws me to use this product over others on the market.

Using Experts in Network Monitor

Microsoft provides a number of predefined Network Monitor jobs called experts. The experts automate the process of diagnosing common issues. The following experts are provided in Network Monitor:

- Property Distribution
- Protocol Distribution
- Average Server Response Time
- Top Users
- TCP Retransmit
- Protocol Coalesce

The Property Distribution expert displays the number of frames matching a certain filter property. The Protocol Distribution expert displays the number of frames sent using a given protocol. The Average Server Response Time expert calculates the amount of time a server takes to respond to a direct request. The Top Users expert displays (by number of frames) the devices that transmit the most packets. The TCP Retransmit expert displays the frame data for any TCP frames that need to be retransmitted across the network. Finally, the Protocol Coalesce expert displays an entire IP session reassembled from its frames.

There are three experts I find myself using more than any others: the Average Server Response Time expert, the Top Users expert, and the TCP Retransmit expert.

- The Average Server Response Time expert can be used to create a baseline of network activity for the client. This data can be given to the client in the documentation packet that you hand over at the conclusion of the project. The Average Server Response Time expert monitors the network for a specified amount of time and calculates the average amount of time a server takes to respond to a request. The client can then use this baseline activity document as a basis for comparison during future projects. Any administrators who take over the environment after you leave will also find the document valuable when diagnosing network response problems.

- The Top Users expert is used when diagnosing broadcast storms or faulty NICs. This expert lists the devices that send the most packets across the network. While this information by itself is not enough to fully diagnose a network problem, it may reveal the symptoms. A device that is transmitting an unusually high number of frames could be broadcasting (possibly looking for another device) or, in rare instances, it may have a faulty NIC.

  Use any information you receive from the Top Users expert as a starting point in diagnosing network problems, but don't rely on it as the only tool you will need.

- The TCP Retransmit expert is used to find devices that may be failing or congested. If PC A is sending data to PC B (using TCP) and PC A does not receive an acknowledgment back indicating the packets were delivered, it retransmits them. This expert lists for you the devices with the highest numbers of retransmitted packets. This information could be used to indicate a faulty NIC on the receiving device. However, if the problem appears on a server, it could be a sign of high network congestion.

When a device is receiving packets faster than it can process them, the packets are placed into a buffer. When this buffer is full, the oldest packets are dropped. Subsequently, when the receiving device does not acknowledge receipt of the old packets (because they were dropped from its buffer), they are retransmitted. On an overworked server, this could cause a lot of network traffic. If you notice that many of your retransmits are related to a server, you may want to look into splitting some services off the server onto another. (See Appendix C for more network troubleshooting tips.)

Network Trace

Network Trace is a utility that is bundled with Microsoft SMS. Unlike Network Monitor, Network Trace requires at least two SMS server installations in your environment to function properly. Network Trace is a tool that graphically maps a path between two or more SMS servers. These maps will include

- Servers
- Connectivity devices

- Server names
- Subnets
- IP addresses

This information can be useful in testing for IP communication between subnets. However, I use this tool more for creating (on-the-fly) network diagrams than for testing connectivity issues.

If you need to produce a snapshot of the network (including IP information and router and hub location) this is a great product. If a client indicates that they are interested in using SMS, I will use Network Trace to polish or reinforce my documentation.

For more information on the installation and uses of Network Monitor and Network Trace, you can visit www.microsoft.com/TechNet and search the knowledge base.

Tracking User Activity on the Internet

One concern for many business owners is the use (and possible abuse) of the Internet by their employees. In today's society, the Internet has become so ingrained in both our social and business lives that it can be hard for users to distinguish between appropriate content for either type of use. While many companies have policies stating that the Internet is to be used for "appropriate business uses," it can be very hard to define what that is. The line between what is deemed suitable for business use and what isn't is becoming more blurry every day.

One certain fact remains; most (if not all) businesses will want to restrict access to particular Web sites. Be they pornographic, violent, religious, or by the client's definition "offensive," some sites can be banned from the general user community.

For this reason you may be asked (after the implementation of the network) to establish a means by which the client can monitor or restrict access to any number of Web sites. There are two types of tools that can be used for these purposes; however, each works in a different way. These tools are proxies and firewalls.

Firewalls can be used to restrict access to certain sites based on content or URL parameters, whereas proxies can be used to restrict access to an individual user (or group of users) based on certain criteria. Both of these tools can be used together to create a very secure environment for both incoming and outgoing data.

Firewalls

One of the most common Internet security devices is a firewall (for more information on firewalls see Chapter 11, "Securing Your Network"). Firewalls are most commonly used to restrict access originating from the Internet bound for the local network. However, most firewalls can also be used to restrict access from the local network to the Internet.

Firewalls such as CheckPoint's Firewall-1 provide content security.

> **NOTE**
>
> I will be using CheckPoint's Firewall-1 as an example for this section, but most commercial firewall products provide similar services.

Content security lets an administrator block access to Web sites based on the URL or IP address. Firewall-based content security works by keeping an extensive table of Web addresses the network administrator wishes to deny access to. This table can usually contain full URLs such as `www.reallybadillegalstuffthatsoffensive.com`, or you can filter sites based on keywords. If your client does not want users to access any sites with pornographic content, you can try to use a URL filter. A filter on the word "sex" would block any URL containing that word. However, this is not an exacting method for blocking sites. You may block sites you do not mean to (such as a government site for Essex County Massachusetts) or conversely (since some pornographic Web sites have URLs that do not contain the word sex), you may leave access to many sites open. A more precise way to restrict access to sites is by using the full URL. (However, it would be nearly impossible to manually enter every site you want to block.)

Therefore, if a client knows they want to block users from accessing `www.reallybadillegalstuffthatsoffensive.com`, they can do so by entering the URL into the firewall's content security interface and effectively block all access to the site from the local network.

As you can imagine, entering a full URL to block every site you can think of would be nearly impossible. There could be thousands to tens of thousands of addresses that any given client could find objectionable. For this reason, most firewalls that provide content security not only allow you to edit your own URL blocking table, but you can also purchase lists from a URL screening vendor.

URL screening vendors such as Symantec (I-Gear for Firewall-1) and SurfControl (SuperScout for Firewall-1) provide the ability for administrators to block access to Web sites based on URLs. However, these third-party products also come with their own precompiled lists of URLs with questionable content. The URL screen vendor will generally have a service you can subscribe to that will provide updates to the URL screening table on a periodic basis. This will keep your list up to date and allow for the least amount of administration (as compared to configuring every URL you want to block yourself).

Third-party URL screening vendors can be a very good solution for clients who want the control to choose what the user community can and cannot view online. However, URL screening at the firewall level does have its drawbacks. It most cases these policies must apply globally. That is, you cannot block one person from reaching a particular URL without blocking everybody.

Proxy servers, on the other hand, allow for greater flexibility when it comes to applying rules to individual users.

Proxies

A proxy server is more of a general tool; that is, a proxy is used to grant Internet access. In a standard proxy configuration such as the one shown in Figure 14.2, a proxy server is used as a central gateway through which all users access the Internet.

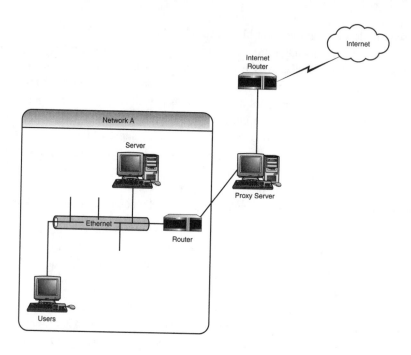

FIGURE 14.2

A standard proxy server configuration.

Because all users must pass through a proxy server before reaching the Internet, several operations can be performed on them both before and during an Internet session. Rather than restrict where the users can go online, some clients may want to restrict who can use the Internet.

A proxy server can be configured to allow or deny access to the Internet based on individual or group settings. You can configure a group of users (for example, Executives) and allow only people in that group to access the Internet. This would give the client control over who in the company could use the resources of the World Wide Web. For many clients this may be a more desirable course of action. Rather than worry about blocking out the right (or wrong) sites, access is granted to trusted users. If the privilege is abused, the user can easily be denied access to the Internet altogether.

For some clients, putting users into groups to determine Internet access may be administrative overhead. It is one more server interface to maintain and a completely different user list to update. Clients worried about the amount of administrative time needed to maintain group permissions on a proxy server do have another option. Many proxy servers can also maintain an individual user list.

In the case of Microsoft Proxy Server or Novell's Border Manager, the proxy server draws its user list from the operating system. Therefore, you can indicate in an individual's network user preferences whether they should have access to the Internet. This seems to be the most common setup for proxy servers, and it allows for the easiest administration.

> **NOTE**
>
> If you are already using a firewall, such as CheckPoint's Firewall-1, and you want to implement a per-user means of Internet authentication, read your firewall documentation before purchasing a proxy server.
>
> Some newer, full-featured firewalls also provide an authentication mechanism. This allows them to maintain individual user lists for allowing access to the Internet.

Because proxy servers work on an individual user basis, the server needs to maintain a table listing all of the users and their related permissions. This table provides the groundwork for the most useful function of a proxy server: tracking online usage.

Since all Internet requests pass through the proxy server, and the proxy server maintains a table with an entry for every user, one thing can be deduced. The proxy server can also be used to track where each user visits online. Depending on the server, this table can hold information from the URL the user visited (or tried to visit) to the time of day they went there. Information about a user's online habits can be useful for clients worried about tracking Internet usage. For example, a particular client may be accessing the Internet through a leased line, which they pay for according to how much they use it. They may want to ensure their users are only accessing business-related sites to justify the cost of the leased line. By implementing a proxy server, the client could not only specify who had access to the Internet, but also find out if the users were accessing sites they shouldn't be.

However, some clients may want even more control over the online actions of their employees. For these clients I would suggest a combination of firewall and proxy server.

Using Proxies and Firewalls Together

The great thing about using firewalls and proxies together is that it is not an either/or situation. Because the two products work at different stages of the user's access, they can be implemented on the same network (see Figure 14.3).

14

POST PROJECT
ACTIVITIES

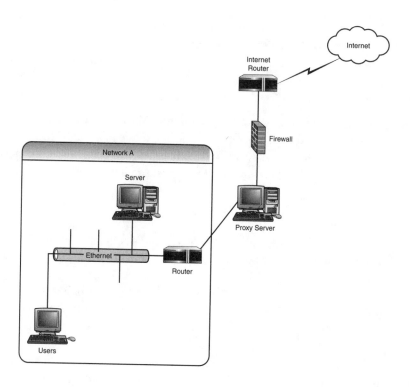

FIGURE 14.3

A firewall and proxy server network.

By using a firewall and a proxy server, the client can have control over who has access to the Internet and what they can do once they get there. This tends to be the most comfortable level of internal Internet security a client can have. The proxy keeps unwanted users from gaining access to Internet resources, while the firewall keeps them from using the Web for anything other than approved uses.

Monitoring E-mail

At some point after the implementation of a new network, you may be asked to provide a solution allowing the client to track user e-mail. In most cases, it is not the executive at a company wanting to peer through users' personal e-mail who requests this ability. Rather, it is an administrator concerned about users from outside the local environment spamming through his server.

NOTE

While I'm not going to discuss ridding your e-mail server of spammers (by turning off e-mail routing), I will be discussing how to detect them through e-mail monitoring.

This brings us back to the Swiss army knife of network devices, the firewall.

Using a Firewall to Monitor E-mail

Some firewalls (and some proxy servers) allow for monitoring e-mail activity through the protocol on which e-mail travels. E-mail uses SMTP (Simple Mail Transfer Protocol) to travel from server to server. An advanced firewall can monitor SMTP traffic flowing through it. When an SMTP packet comes across the network, the firewall can examine the sender and recipient addresses and compare them to a preconfigured list of filters. The messages can then be turned away based on whether they matched a filter property.

Therefore, administrators can filter for messages being sent through their e-mail server from an address outside the local environment and turn the message away. Administrators can also create a filter to turn away messages based on the number of recipients. (One popular way to filter spam is to filter out messages that are addressed to more than 200 users.)

Even though firewalls provide one form of e-mail monitoring, (protocol-based e-mail filtering), many e-mail servers provide yet another.

Monitoring Messages from the E-mail Server

Most e-mail servers have within them the ability to store and monitor user e-mail. Clients concerned about illegal activity or corporate espionage may have policies concerning the right of the employer to monitor users' e-mail. You may be approached to design such a solution.

Unencrypted e-mails are basically flat text files that are sent from server to server. Given that fact, it is very easy for a server to keep copies of messages both sent and received through the network.

E-mail servers such as Microsoft Exchange allow for the creation of a special mailbox (Message Journaling). This mailbox will store a copy of every e-mail that passes through the server. The administrator can then log in to the mailbox Message Journaling to read or search through all of the e-mails.

After a process is in place to obtain a copy of the e-mail on a particular network, filters can be created to search through those e-mails for specific keywords. Clients can look for patterns such as "I have secrets to sell about my company's latest product."

Message Journaling does have one obvious drawback. On larger networks, the amount of e-mail processed by a single server in a single day can reach the thousands. Keeping a copy of every one of those messages can consume a lot of disk space. However, for clients who have secrets to protect, there may be no alternative to the security of having a searchable copy of all e-mails.

Summary

- Microsoft Systems Management Server comes bundled with tools for helping to monitor networks: Network Monitor and Network Trace.
- Network Monitor is a packet analyzer.
- By analyzing individual packets, you can tell if a NIC is failing, a server is not responding, or a network segment is too congested.
- Network Trace can create a graphic map of a network between two SMS servers.
- Firewalls can be used to block access (globally) to certain Web sites.
- Proxy servers can be used to restrict access to the Internet based on user properties (individual or group).
- Some clients may want to monitor users' e-mail activities.
- Message Journaling saves a copy of every e-mail sent or received through the local server.

Appendixes

PART

VI

IN THIS PART

Appendix A

Glossary

10BASE-2   Also known as thinnet, 10BASE-2 cabling is an approved IEEE transition media for carrying 10Mbps of data for 185 meters. Thinnet is most often found on older networks. Slightly more flexible than thicknet.

10BASE-5   Also known as thicknet, 10BASE-5 cabling is an approved IEEE transition media for carrying 10Mbps for 300 meters. Thicknet is most often found on older networks. Being a thicker, rigid cable, 10BASE-5 was often used as a backbone cable.

access lists   Access lists are configurable tables (stored on a router) that contain a list of IP addresses and related permissions. These addresses will either be granted or denied access to resources behind the router based on the access list. Access lists can be used as a form of network security.

Active Directory   According to Microsoft, "Active Directory is the directory service used in Windows 2000 Server and is the foundation of Windows 2000 distributed networks." An Active Directory stores information about the users, permissions, and other pertinent information for Windows 2000 domains.

Active Monitor   An integral part of a Token-Ring network, the Active Monitor is a PC designated (by random selection) to create tokens and monitor the ring for problems. If the Active Monitor detects an issue on a Token-Ring network, it generates a beacon. This token alerts the other devices on the ring to the problem and, if a redundant ring exists, the devices are told to use it.

Aloha Net   Aloha Net was the first production network created using Ethernet. Aloha Net was developed at the University of Hawaii in conjunction with Xerox PARC.

ALPHA   Found in some high-capacity servers, the ALPHA chip is a 64-bit microprocessor.

AppleTalk   Apple's default networking protocol. Some connectivity devices do support AppleTalk; however, the protocol is mostly found in the mixed network.

Application layer   The Application layer is the seventh layer of the OSI model. The main function of the Application layer is to synchronize data flowing between clients and servers.

ARPAnet   ARPAnet (Advanced Research Projects Agency Network) was the first prototype network built in the United States. The technology used to create ARPAnet would later become Ethernet.

bandwidth   Bandwidth is the amount of data a particular device or segment of media can transfer. Bandwidth is normally measured in bits-per-second. Factors such as hardware and physical media play a part in how a device uses bandwidth.

BDC (backup domain controller)   A backup domain controller is a Windows NT server whose function is to accept replication of the SAM and user databases. The BDC uses these databases to authenticate users to the network environment. If the PDC (primary domain controller) falls offline, the BDC will take over the functions of the PDC.

beacon   A beacon is a broadcast message sent over a Token-Ring network by the Active Monitor. If the Active Monitor detects that a device on the ring is not functioning (making the ring unstable), it sends a beacon to alert the remaining devices.

bindery   A bindery is the user database used by Novell NetWare servers prior to version 4.1. After version 4.1, Novell employed a tree directory structure, also known as NDS (Novell Directory Structure).

bridge   A bridge is a connectivity device used to connect two network segments. These segments will generally use dissimilar media access methods (for example, Ethernet and Token Ring).

broadcast   A broadcast message is sent by an IP client to get a response from an unknown host.

CAT 3   Category 3 cabling was the first cable designed for use with the 10BASE-T Ethernet standard.

CAT 5   Category 5 cabling was introduced to replace CAT 3 on 100BASE-T-X networks.

CAT 5e   The latest cabling standard to be approved, CAT 5e is the cabling used on 1000BASE-T networks.

CIR The CIR (Committed Information Rate) is the amount of bandwidth (negotiated by you and your vendor) for your Frame Relay link. Often there is a nominal charge for exceeding the CIR.

client This term refers to the employer, or the people you are reporting to for a particular project. This term more commonly refers to the PC in a client-server relationship.

Client32 Released by Novell, Client32 was the preferred client for connecting to a NetWare server.

Client Concerns (document) The Client Concerns document is a list that you should create during your meeting with the client. This document will be used to determine the preliminary look and feel of the project.

Client Needs (document) During your preliminary meetings with the client you will be formatting your notes into four sections: Client Concerns, Hardware Specifications, Software Specifications, and Client Needs.

CO The CO is the central office for a Telco Company. WAN services are often dependent on location as compared to the vendor's CO.

connectivity devices The term connectivity devices refers to a class of machines used to route or distribute information from one area to another. These devices include routers, hubs, and switches.

Cost/Function Analysis During your final presentation, the client may request from you a Cost/Function Analysis. This document compares different classes of devices based on cost; for example, the cost difference in using a hub over a switch on a particular network.

CPE The CPE (Customer Premise Equipment) is any equipment or devices located at or on the client's site (usually used in descriptions of a WAN link).

cracker This term is commonly used to refer to someone who attempts to gain access to resources without the consent of the owner.

CSMA/CD CSMA/CD (Carrier Sense Multiple Access/Collision Detect) is the media access method employed by Ethernet devices.

CSU/DSU The CSU/DSU (Channel Service Unit/Data Service Unit) encrypts and decrypts WAN data between routers.

D.O.S A D.O.S (Denial of Service) attack is aimed at online businesses, usually overloading their Web sites and cutting off their only source of revenue.

Data Link layer The second layer of the OSI model is the Data Link layer. The Data Link layer is responsible for the proper addressing of packets on the network. To accomplish this the Data Link layer is divided into two sub-layers: the MAC and the LLC.

dedicated servers A dedicated server is a server utilized for one purpose or application.

demarc The demarc, or demarcation point, is the point at which control over a network and its traffic reverts from the client to the vendor.

DHCP   A DHCP (Dynamic Host Configuration Protocol) server is used to assign IP addressing information to clients as they request it. This information can include IP address, default gateway, WINS, and DNS locations.

dial-in access   Referring to a remote network connection, dial-in access is achieved via a telephone or other non-dedicated line.

DMZ   A DMZ (Demilitarized Zone) is a network segment designated for access from users on the local network and users from other environments. Users from other environments are restricted access to the local network by connectivity devices.

DNS   DNS (domain name service) associates IP addresses with easier-to-understand names. These names can be registered through an approved institution for routing over the Internet.

domain name   A domain name is a name associated with a particular IP address. Publicly registered domain names are necessary for the routing of e-mail.

DSL   A DSL (Digital Subscriber Line) is a high-bandwidth digital connection that utilizes existing telephone lines.

duplexing (Ethernet)   In an Ethernet environment, devices can communicate with each other in one of two ways: half duplex, in which each device can either send or receive; and full duplex, in which each device can send and receive.

dynamic routing   In a dynamic routing environment, each router on the network broadcasts its routing table. Each router can then have an up-to-date picture of what the network looks like. This allows the routers to make changes to their tables, accommodating changes in the environment.

Enterprise Virus scanning   An antivirus solution that scans and protects an entire network environment is known as an Enterprise Virus scanning solution.

Ethernet   Developed by Xerox PARC in 1972, Ethernet was arguably the first standard for allowing communication between computers. The first Ethernet network was installed at the University of Hawaii in 1973.

fiber   Fiber optic cabling has a glass core. This glass core allows the media to transmit without the threat of electromagnetic interference. However, due to its glass core, it is less flexible and more fragile than its copper counterparts.

Final Diagram   The Final Diagram is the last version of your proposed network you will submit to the client. After both you and the client have approved the parameters proposed in the Final Diagram, the construction phase of the project will begin.

firewall   A firewall is a device used to grant or deny access to network resources (from the Internet) based on rules established by the network administrator.

FQDN   The FQDN (fully qualified domain name) of a computer is a combination of the computer's name and the network's domain name. For example, the FQDN of the PC "speedy" on the domain "drivingonthehighway.com" is "speedy.drivingonthehighway.com."

Frame Relay   A Frame Relay WAN link is a dedicated, high-speed circuit provided by a WAN or Telecom vendor connecting two or more sites.

Gateway Services For Netware   A Windows NT service that allows users authenticated through a Windows NT server to access shares on a Novell NetWare server.

global economy   A term referring to the interconnection all businesses have with each other by virtue of the ease with which data and products can flow between them. With the emergence of the Internet it has become easier for businesses (regardless of size) to trade goods and information with any other entity across the globe. This ease of trade has created the global economy.

Hardware Specifications (document) One of the four sections your notes (from the initial client meetings) will be divided into, Hardware Specifications list all of the hardware found at the client's site.

hop count   The term hop count refers to the number of routers a routing protocol must pass through before reaching its destination. This is an important number to keep track of because most protocols have a maximum number of hops they cannot exceed.

Hosts.sam   The Hosts.sam file is a sample file provided with Windows operating systems. The file outlines the procedure for creating a hosts file. A local hosts file provides local DNS translations for a PC.

hub   A hub is connectivity device that is used to connect multiple devices. A hub (considered to be an unintelligent device) provides no routing or anti-broadcast capabilities.

ICMP   The ICMP (Internet Control Message Protocol) is used to test network communication between devices.

IEEE   The IEEE (Institute of Electrical and Electronics Engineers) creates the standards used in networking technologies (and other electronics fields). For example, IEEE standard 802.3 defines the CSMA/CD access method (otherwise known as Ethernet).

IGRP   A routing protocol developed by Cisco for use on larger networks.

Initial Design   The initial design is produced just before you start working on the project. This is what the client will initially agree to as the "scope" of the project. This document may be subject to many revisions as the project continues.

Initial Proposal   This may not be just one document but a series of documents. Using a professional tool such as Visio will save you a lot of work here. The content of the proposal will range from a high-level topology to a diagram of a wiring closet. Chances are the document will change many times, so you will want to keep all versions for your documentation.

IP classes   IP addressing has been broken into five classes. An institution is granted the right to purchase a particular class of licenses depending on their addressing needs.

IPX/SPX   Developed by Novell, IPX/SPX is the default protocol found on most Novell networks.

A

GLOSSARY

ISDN   An ISDN (Integrated Services Digital Network) line can provide up to 144Kps of bandwidth over a standard telephone wire (although some additional equipment will be required at both ends).

ISO   The ISO (International Organization for Standardization) sets standards for such things as manufacturing and documentation. (The ISO also created the OSI model for networking.)

LLC sub-layer   One of the sub-layers of the Data Link layer in the OSI model, the LLC (Logical Link Control) is responsible for establishing and maintaining communications between two Data Link layers.

local loop   The term used to define the path of a circuit between your local network and the public switch.

MAC sub-layer   The MAC (Media Access Control) is a sub-layer of the Data Link layer in the OSI model. The MAC serves two functions: It uniquely addresses the device (the MAC address of the NIC) and it negotiates media control between two devices.

Master Domain Model   The Master Domain Model is a design specification set forth by Microsoft whereby one domain (consisting of one PDC and at least one BDC) acts as the primary source of network authentication for several subdomains.

MAU   A MAU (Multiple Access Unit) is used to connect Token-Ring devices. By using MAUs, the devices are connected in a logical ring.

Member Server   A Member Server is a Windows NT–based server with no authority over the SAMS database. This prevents the Member Server from authenticating users to the network.

mixed network   A network combining two or more different technologies into one cohesive environment (for example, Token Ring and Ethernet).

Multiple Master Domain Model   The Multiple Master Domain Model is a design specification set forth by Microsoft whereby more than one master domain (see Master Domain Model) acts as the primary source of network authentication for several subdomains.

multiplexer   Used by devices such as CSD/DSUs to separate the channels of a T1.

MX record   An MX (mail exchange) record is a DNS entry used to define an e-mail server.

NAT   NAT (Natural Address Translation) allows multiple devices on a local network (using non-routable IP addresses) to be defined by one routable address for the purpose of Internet access.

NetBEUI   A fast (non-routable) protocol developed by Microsoft for use on small networks.

network latency   A term used to describe the amount of delay experienced on slower networks.

Network layer   Layer three of the OSI model, the Network layer is responsible for network routing.

network topology A network topology defines the physical architecture or layout of a network. (That is, star, bus, or ring.)

network type Network type is the term used to define the media access method of a network (that is, Ethernet or Token Ring).

NWLink NWLink is a protocol used on Microsoft-based devices that are required to communicate with Novell devices running IPX/SPX.

OSI The OSI (Open Systems Interconnection) model was created by ISO to define network data transfer between two or more devices. The model contains seven layers. Each of these layers defines one particular aspect of intercomputer communication.

PDC (Primary Domain Controller) Referring to Microsoft Windows NT–based servers, the PDC is the server all devices will attempt to be authenticated through first.

petabyte 1,000 terabytes.

Physical layer The first layer of the OSI model, the physical layer defines the media used to connect devices.

plenum grade Plenum grade cables will not emit toxic gases when burned. Plenum grade cables are generally used in the spaces between ceilings and floors.

Presentation layer The Presentation layer of the OSI model (layer six) is used to encrypt and decrypt data from the application layer.

PVC (Permanent Virtual Circuits) A statically mapped path between two devices over a public network (vendor-side). PVCs are specific to Frame Relay links.

RAID RAID (Redundant Array of Inexpensive Disks) defines different levels of fault tolerance in hard drive configurations.

RFC An RFC (Request for Comment) is a written policy developed by the IEEE.

RIP RIP (Routing Information Protocol) is most commonly used by routers to send routing updates to neighboring routers.

routed protocol A routed protocol is a communication protocol that is carried by a router (such as IP or IPX). Routed protocols are used by PCs and other devices to communicate with each other in networked environments.

routing protocol A routing protocol is a protocol used by routers (such as RIP, OSPF, or IGRP) to carry routed protocols. Routers use routing protocols to communicate with each other.

Session layer The purpose of the Session layer of the OSI model (layer five) is to establish connections between applications over a network.

Single Domain Model The Single Domain Model is a design specification set forth by Microsoft whereby one PDC acts as the primary source of network authentication for an entire domain.

SNMP The SNMP (Simple Network Management Protocol) is used by devices and administrators to test and manage devices.

A

GLOSSARY

Software Specifications (document) One of the four sections your notes (from the initial client meetings) will be divided into, Software Specifications list all of the software (as pertaining to each individual device) found at the client's site.

static routing The term static routing refers to the act of routing information through routers that have their tables hard-coded. In other words, the routers do not advertise their tables with other routers.

TCP/IP Originally developed by DARPA (Defense Advance Research Projects Agency), TCP/IP (Transmission Control Protocol/Internet Protocol) is a suite of protocols designed to efficiently transport data between clients and hosts.

token passing Token passing is the access method employed by devices on Token-Ring networks. A device on a ring cannot transmit any information until it has control of the token. After a device has transmitted its data, the token is passed to the next device.

Token Ring Token Ring is a network type developed by IBM. In a Token-Ring environment, all devices are attached in a logical ring.

Transport layer The Transport layer of the OSI model (layer four) provides flow control and the reliable transport of data from one device to another.

trusts Trusts are utilized on Microsoft Windows NT–based networks to define the privileges one domain may have to another. Users of domains participating in trusts can only access data (on the other participating domains) as outlined by the trust's permissions.

VPN VPN (Virtual Private Networking) provides an Internet- or IP-based solution for connecting users to remote networks. Many of today's connectivity devices support VPN solutions.

WINS A WINS (Windows Internet Naming Service) is used by Windows NT–based systems to translate between IP addresses and Windows computer names. Many devices on Windows-based networks will use the information provided by WINS to locate the PDC (Primary Domain Controller).

Sample Documentation

IN THIS APPENDIX

Documentation Packet

The following section is a sample documentation packet based on the examples in this book. It contains most of the documents that you would be handing to the client.

Please note that not all of the documents included here are from the same project. I tried to select documents that either related to the scenarios in the book or that were "best examples" from my previous projects.

Site Survey

Hardware Specifications

Server A

Processor	RAM	NIC	OS	Hard Drive
Pentium III 500	128MB	10/100 Auto Sensing	Windows 2000 Server	18GB

Server B

Processor	RAM	NIC	OS	Hard Drive
Pentium III 400	256MB	10/100 Auto Sensing	Windows 2000 Sever	18GB

PCs

Processor	RAM	NIC	OS	Hard Drive
20 Pentium II 233s	32MB	10Mbit	Windows 95	1.2GB

Software Specifications

- Servers
    - Server A
        Windows 2000 Server
        Microsoft Exchange
        Microsoft SQL Server
    - Server B
        Windows 2000 Server
        Norton AntiVirus
        Seagate Backup Exec
- PCs
    - All
        Windows 95
        Office (Client)
        Norton AntiVirus (Desktop)

Client Needs

The client expresses the need for a new corporate infrastructure that should incorporate (any reusable) elements of their existing network. The new network will allow the client the ability to scale the environment as the company grows, yet retain a level of "ease of management."

The client has noticed some issues with latency and instability on the existing network. These issues will be clarified in the new environment.

The new environment should be built to handle the newly purchased Help Desk Tracking System, Clarify. This network should also allow VPN-based remote access for home employees.

Prepared 02/21/2001

J. F. DiMarzio

Preliminary Design

Figure B.1 illustrates the preliminary design. This should be handed to the client as a document.

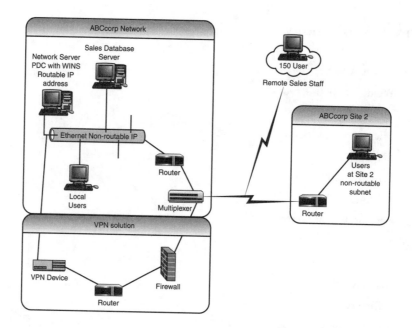

FIGURE B.1

Preliminary network design.

Server Equipment Vendor Study

Vendor	Model	Hard Drive(s)	RAM	Dimensions	Availability	Pricing
ABC Servers	5000N	(3) 18GB RAID 5	512MB	12"x 23"x15"	Overnight	$2,300
Server Giant	2564	(3) 18GB RAID 5	512MB	15"x 18"x20"	2-3 weeks	$1,500
Custom Servers	1000CS	1 18GB Drive (RAID 5 available as $1,200 third-party upgrade per Dave in sales)	512MB	23"x 20"x24"	Overnight	$3,600 ($2,400 without RAID)

Software Vendor Study

Vendor	Manufacturer	Package	Lic. Type	Lic. Needed	Per Lic. Cost	Cost
Jack's Software	JoeSoft	JoeSoft PIM	Volume	200	$10	$2,000
WackyWare Accounting	WackyWare	Wacky's	Per seat	25	$200	$5,000
Numbers R' US	Account	Accounting	Volume	25	$125 (minimum of 100 lics.)	$12,500

Project Timeline

This document is the projected timeline for the completion of the ABCcorp network implementation project.

Mesa Network

Server A		
Order Equipment	1 hr	
	Assigned to: DiMarzio	
Receive	1 hr	
	Assigned to: DiMarzio	
Implement	8 hr	
	Assigned to: Unnamed Consult.	

PCs		
Order Equipment	2 hr	
	Assigned to: Unnamed Consult.	
Receive	20 hr	
	Assigned to: All	
Implement (per PC)	2 hr	
	Assigned to: All	
Total (PC)	200 hr	

WAN Link

Order Link	6 hr
	Assigned to: DiMarzio
Test	2 hr
	Assigned to: DiMarzio
Implement	8 hr
	Assigned to: DiMarzio

Chicago Network

Server A

Order Equipment	2 hr
	Assigned to: DiMarzio
Receive	1 hr
	Assigned to: Brown
Implement	8 hr
	Assigned to: Adams

PCs

Order Equipment	2 hr
	Assigned to: DiMarzio
Receive	5 hr
	Assigned to: Brown
Implement (per PC)	2 hr
	Assigned to: Adams
Total (PC)	50 hr

WAN Link

Order Link	4 hr
	Assigned to: DiMarzio
Test	4 hr
	Assigned to: DiMarzio, Adams
Implement	8 hr
	Assigned to: Unnamed Consult.

Tampa Network

Server A

Order Equipment	2 hr
	Assigned to: DiMarzio
Receive	1 hr
	Assigned to: Cortez
Implement	8 hr
	Assigned to: Fulton

PCs

Order Equipment	2 hr
	Assigned to: DiMarzio
Receive	5 hr
	Assigned to: Cortez
Implement (per PC)	2 hr
	Assigned to: Fulton
Total (PC)	50 hr

WAN Link

Order Link	4 hr
	Assigned to: DiMarzio
Test	4 hr
	Assigned to: DiMarzio, Fulton
Implement	8 hr
	Assigned to: Unnamed Consult.
Total	422 hr

Final Diagram

Geographic Overview

Figure B.2 illustrates the Geographic Overview document.

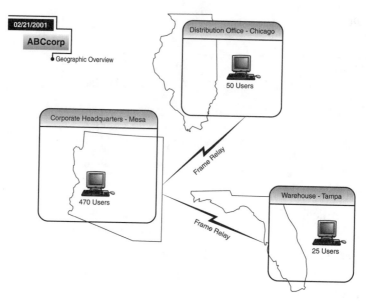

FIGURE B.2
Geographic Overview.

Network Diagram—Mesa

Figure B.3 illustrates the Network Diagram document for the network Mesa.

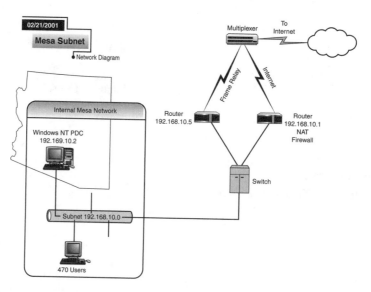

FIGURE B.3
Network Diagram—Mesa.

Network Diagram—Chicago

Figure B.4 illustrates the Network Diagram document for the network Chicago.

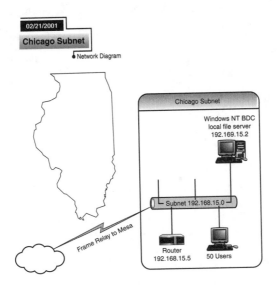

FIGURE B.4

Network Diagram—Chicago.

Network Diagram—Tampa

Figure B.5 illustrates the Network Diagram document for the network Tampa.

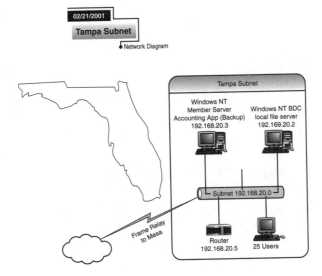

FIGURE B.5

Network Diagram—Tampa.

Cost/Function Analysis

The client has expressed a concern about the cost of using VPN over dial-in. The following analysis illustrates the comparison (in dollars) between the two connectivity methods. (Please note: For the purpose of the sample documentation, all dollar figures have been removed.)

VPN device for 200 users

> $XXXX

Internet Service (Monthly) per home user

> $XX
> * 200 users
> = $XXX

Dial-in Server

> $XXXX

(Option A)

Added Telephone Lines

> $XXX

(Option B)

Added Digital Line

> $XXX

Digital Line Connectivity Device

> $XXX

Server Roles

The following document illustrates a Server Roles sheet. This document would be created and given to the client near the end of the project.

Network Roles by Server

This document lists the current role of each server on the VERSYSS domain.

- **Server A**
  Windows NT
  PDC

Clarify

Backup Exec

MAS 90

SQL

- **Server B**

Windows NT

Exchange

IIS

- **Server C**

Windows 2000

DNS

WINS

DHCP

Source Safe

- **Server D**

Windows NT

BDC

SMS

RAS

SQL

- **Server E**

Windows NT

Proxy Server

IIS

- **Server F**

Windows Terminal Server

NetMeeting Server

RAS

Network Policies

The following document illustrates a corporate IT policy I wrote for a project I completed last year.

Corporate IT Policy

This document is the Corporate IT Policy as set forth by <Company Name> relating to computer use. Any deviation from this policy (implied or otherwise) could be grounds for termination.

1.1 PC Usage

Computers, as supplied by <Company Name>, are intended for approved business use only. No programs or files are to be installed, deleted, moved, or otherwise altered without the permission of the IT department. Only those applications approved for use at <Company Name> are to be installed (by a member of the IT department) on PCs. All computers and the contents thereof are subject to periodic search (with or without notification by a member of the IT department).

All PCs at <Company Name> are to be shut down nightly. For those whose job function requires the use of Windows NT or Windows 2000 you are responsible for "locking" your workstation when it is not in use. Users without Windows NT or 2000 should set their "screen saver" password to activate after 2 (two) minutes of inactivity.

At no time should any Laptop (or PC) owned by <Company Name> or in the possession of an employee of <Company Name> approved for business use be allowed to leave the borders of the United States or Canada without prior authorization.

PC users at <Company Name> will be responsible for the general upkeep of their computer.

1.2 Networked PCs

For computers attached to the VERSYSS Domain a password is required to gain access to many resources. Each user's password is unique. No passwords are to be supplied or divulged to any individual (employed by <Company Name> or otherwise) for any reason. If a password has been forgotten, compromised or otherwise rendered unusable, contact a member of the IT department immediately. All passwords will expire within 30 (thirty) days of their creation. All new passwords are to be at least 4 (four) characters in length and unique. A member of management or the IT department of <Company Name> will never ask for a specific user's password. If you are approached for your username, password, or any other information pertaining to the network and or systems at <Company Name>; by an employee of <Company Name> or otherwise, contact a member of the IT department immediately.

All user rights and privileges as pertaining to the access of network resources are subject to audit at any time by a member of the IT department. Such rights and privileges can be revoked, amended, or otherwise altered at any time.

1.3 E-MAIL Usage

E-MAIL is intended for approved, work related use only. The content of all e-mail (incoming and outgoing) are subject to monitoring at anytime. No personal e-mail is to be sent or received at any time. No e-mail with pornographic, racist, religious, sexist, or otherwise offensive content is to be sent or received by an employee of <Company Name>. All mail received at <Company Name> is to be scanned for viruses upon its receipt. If an e-mail is received from an unknown or unfamiliar sender it should be deleted immediately unless instructed otherwise by a member of the IT department. At no time should unapproved financial information, passwords, usernames, or other networked related information be exchanged via e-mail.

All user rights and privileges as pertaining to the uses of e-mail are subject to audit at any time by a member of the IT department. Such rights and privileges can be revoked, amended, or otherwise altered at any time.

1.4 Internet Usage

The Internet, as supplied by <Company Name>, is intended for work related use only. No sites with pornographic, racist, religious, sexist, or otherwise offensive content are to be viewed at any time. At no time should any information pertaining to <Company Name> (including but not limited to files, programs, passwords, and or usernames) be exchanged over the Internet to, unauthorized recipients, unless approved by the IT department. At no time should an employee of <Company Name> (in chat or on a bulletin board) state or otherwise imply affiliation with or approval by <Company Name> to discuss business (or other) related matters without permission from the IT department.

All user rights and privileges as pertaining to the Internet are subject to audit at any time by a member of the IT department. Such rights and privileges can be revoked, amended, or otherwise altered at any time.

Resolution Guide for Common Network Conflicts

IN THIS APPENDIX

This appendix illustrates four common problems faced by network designers. I will discuss some possible solutions for these issues and offer references to resources that will give you more information (where applicable).

The troubleshooting guide provided here is not meant to be a comprehensive troubleshooting tool. Rather, I have compiled some of the more common problems you might face as a result of performing many of the tasks outlined in the book.

Issue 1: Slow Network Response

One of the most common network issues is slow (mostly unexpected) network response. Unfortunately, with this particular problem, there can be as many solutions as there are networks. Following are a few possible scenarios and solutions.

Scenario 1

A client with an existing network mentions that the network has gradually become very slow. The client says that the network seems to be slowest from 8:00 a.m. to 10:00 a.m. and then again from 1:00 p.m. until the end of the day.

Network Diagram

Figure C.1 illustrates the client's network.

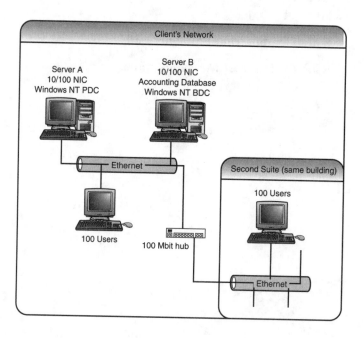

FIGURE C.1

A network experiencing slow response times.

Solution

The first thing that you should notice about the network in Figure C.1 is the use of the hub. This should be corrected. What is most likely happening is that when the users log in (in the morning), they are flooding the network with traffic. Then, after a few hours of being bombarded with traffic, the network is no longer able to handle the "normal" daily load.

I would replace the hub with a switch as illustrated in Figure C.2.

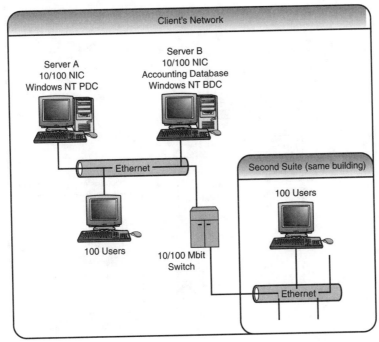

FIGURE C.2
Author's solution providing a switch.

In this solution a switch replaced the hub. This would allow for a quicker (non-broadcasting) transfer of data from one network to another. Even though this solution may have cleared up the latency issue, it may not have left the network in the best possible state.

The switch (in the solution) will be worked very hard. That is, because this is one large network (with one IP scheme) this switch will be responsible for moving data trough the entire network. I suggest not only replacing the hub with a switch, but I would also subnet the one larger network into two smaller ones.

After the network is subnetted I would do one more bit of housekeeping. The BDC (seen in Figure C.1) should be moved to the new (second) subnet. This would keep the users on the second subnet from having to be authenticated by a server on the first subnet. By moving the BDC to the second subnet, the authentication traffic on the first subnet is reduced by half. Figure C.3 shows my final solution for this issue.

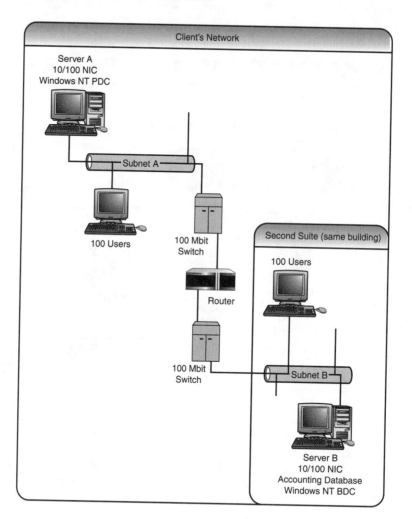

FIGURE C.3

Author's final solution.

This solution works by creating two separate (more manageable) networks. On the original network (Figure C.1) traffic was flowing everywhere, regardless of the intended recipient(s).

On the new, segmented networks, traffic only goes where it needs to. That is, traffic from one segment is going to stay there unless it is meant for a device on another segment. The switches help by limiting the broadcasts and keeping the data moving.

Scenario 2

A client is having latency issues early in the morning. Their network has recently been optimized during a network upgrade. The client notices the worst problems during the morning, then the network responds normally for the remainder of the workday. However, the client also notes that many users cannot access network resources during the time the network is not responding and usually need to reboot (sometimes repeatedly) before being able to gain access to resources.

Network Diagram

Figure C.4 illustrates the client's current network.

Solution

The client mentions that the issue only occurs in the morning. Given what we know about network operations, the majority of the network traffic generated in the morning can be attributed to the services required to authenticate. Your first task should be to troubleshoot the authentication process. The services needed for authentication are

1. DHCP (in a dynamic addressing environment)—A device authenticating to a network needs a valid IP address (for that network).
2. WINS—If the network uses Windows-based servers, a device seeking authentication will query the WINS server for the location of the closest domain controller.
3. Passing Of Credentials—The device will now try to match its credentials (for authentication) with those on the server.

Let's examine these processes one at a time. To participate in a network, a device needs a valid address for that network. To obtain one, the device must query the DHCP server. However, the device cannot communicate directly with the DHCP server if it does not have an IP address yet. Therefore, the device sends out a broadcast searching for the address of the DHCP server. The server will receive the broadcast and respond with its own IP address. When the device receives the address of the DHCP server, it can then query the server directly for addressing information.

After the device has the required IP information from the DHCP server, it then looks to authenticate to the network. The device will query the WINS server for the location of the closest domain controller. The WINS server will respond with the name and address of the controller that is closest to the device. The device will now attempt to pass credentials to that controller for authentication.

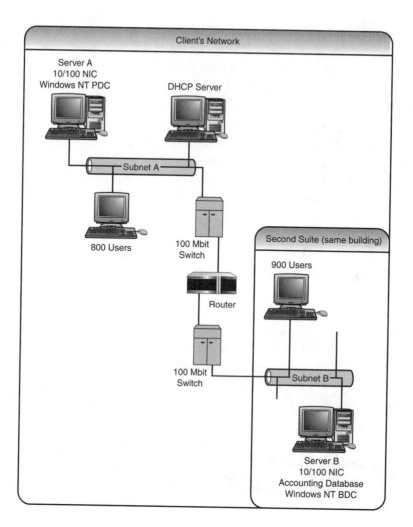

FIGURE C.4

A latent network.

One of the first methods I would employ to troubleshoot this problem is a packet analyzer. Remember that the client says they only have a problem in the morning (a possible authentication issue), some users cannot access network resources (possible lack of IP address), and if they reboot they tend to authenticate successfully (rebooting restarts the authentication process). My thoughts are that the DHCP server is overworked or malfunctioning.

With a packet analyzer you should look for a larger number of broadcasts (for a DHCP server) that have no responses. This would indicate the DHCP server is either receiving more requests than it can handle in a timely manner, or the network card on the server is failing. You could then replace the faulty equipment or add a DHCP server (as the situation warrants).

A malfunctioning or overworked DHCP server also explains the cause behind the other symptoms the client is experiencing. The fact that the network functions optimally during the rest of the day indicates there is no problem with the rest of the network. This would be consistent with a DHCP server issue. An issue with an overworked DHCP server would only affect users when they were looking for an address. Therefore, the pattern of latency (slow in the morning, fine in the afternoon) holds true.

The fact that the users gain access to the network after multiple tries (rebooting) can be explained by the lack of response from the DHCP server. (After the traffic settles down, machines that have rebooted can now access the network.) Most users (if they experience a problem with their PCs) try rebooting as a force of habit. In this case (an overworked DHCP server), the rebooting causes the computer to rebroadcast its request to the server. This causes more traffic, until the broadcasts start to ebb (either because users give up on retrying or the server starts to catch up on requests), at which point the users who are rebooting will experience no problems.

To test the theory that the DHCP server is the root of the problem, set the DHCP server lease expiration to one day. Then after a week (if the client can withstand the network issue for that long), set the expiration to three days.

NOTE

The reason for setting the expiration to one day first is to ensure that everyone has an expired lease when you set it to three days. That way, everyone's lease will expire on the same day. If you did not wait a week before switching from one day to three, you might not catch all of the leases. This would cause you to get inaccurate results during this test.

If after setting the DHCP lease expiration to three days you only see network problems every three days, this is a sure sign of a DHCP issue. However, a problem every three days is still a problem. I would suggest two possible solutions.

The first solution is to add a second DHCP server. This solution clears up the issue of an overworked server. Figure C.5 illustrates the client's network with a second DHCP server.

The placement of the second server is critical. Notice how (in Figure C.5) I placed the new server on the second network segment. This will keep the users on the second segment from having to cross through a switch looking for a DHCP server, thus reducing traffic.

My second solution is to simply test and replace any faulty equipment in the current server. While it might be easier to add RAM to a server to improve its performance, it may not improve it to the point that the network is usable during the time frame in issue.

C

RESOLUTION
GUIDE

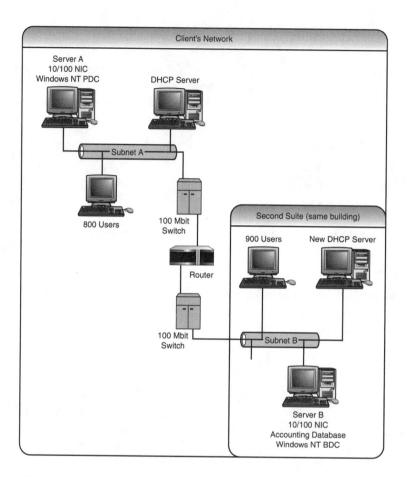

FIGURE C.5

Author's solution with second DHCP server.

Scenario 3

This scenario deals more with a specific user rather than an entire network. Your client states that on their existing network, a few users are experiencing network latency. The problem seems to have increased (for the affected users) over time. However, some users (accessing the same resources) experience no problems.

Network Diagram

Figure C.6 illustrates the client's network. The users experiencing the problem have been separated from the other users only for the purpose of the diagram. All of the users are configured identically and are all on the same subnet.

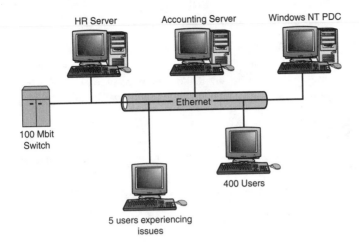

FIGURE C.6
A specific user experiencing latency.

Solution

In this situation I would start by examining the individual devices (the devices having the issues) rather than trying to diagnose the entire network. The first area to look at on a PC having this problem would be the routing cache. That is, using the NBTSTAT tool (on a Windows-based PC) to clear the PC's routing table. This will typically improve the PC's performance.

If the PC routing table looks fine, you can begin to look at the physical location of the devices. If all of the affected devices are within a close radius, there might be a geographic problem. Again, as in many cases with larger networks, you could look into subnetting the network to clear up any traffic issues.

Network latency is a big issue in today's environments. The issues I presented here are only a few of the possible problems and solutions you might encounter.

Another problem you could face, especially as a designer, is an interruption of e-mail services. If you have designed or implemented an e-mail solution, you know that e-mail servers are very rarely plug-and-play. There is a lot of configuration that needs to occur and, thus, a lot that can go wrong.

Issue 2: No E-mail Is Being Received from the Internet

This issue is quite common during the initial implementation of an e-mail solution. The new e-mail system may have some problems receiving mail from the Internet. Fortunately, because this is a fairly common issue, there is a fairly common solution.

Scenario

The client contracts you to implement an Internet and e-mail solution for an existing network. After implementing the design shown in Figure C.7, you realize that you are not receiving any e-mail from the Internet. E-mail sent from inside the company to employees inside the company seems to be working fine. Also, the users can access the Internet without any problems.

Network Diagram

Figure C.7 illustrates the client's network and the portion of the network that you designed.

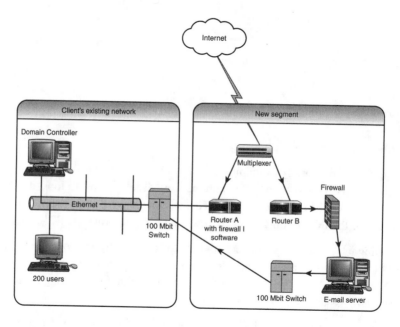

Figure C.7

A network not receiving Internet e-mail.

Solution

If e-mail is functioning fine internally, you are left with four devices that could be causing the issue: the e-mail server, the firewall, Router B, and the multiplexer. I would start troubleshooting the problem from the root, the Internet. Because the only messages that are not reaching you are originating from the Internet, you should begin your troubleshooting there. I will discuss each device in order from the Internet to the local network.

Multiplexer—The signal coming from the Internet could be getting interference from the multiplexer. However, in this scenario using the Internet is not a problem. Therefore, because the signal for the Internet and the signal for the e-mail system flow through the same multiplexer, it is unlikely that the multiplexer is at fault. If the multiplexer were the problem, Internet access would be interrupted as well.

Router B—The signal travels from the multiplexer to Router B. Because of the complexity involved in configuring routers, this is a prime location for problems to occur. One test would be to send ICMP packets through the router to the Internet. I would set up a notebook on the same network segment as the e-mail server. Then from the notebook, ping an Internet address (such as www.marzdesign.com).

If you receive a response, you can deduce two things. The first is that information can flow from your segment, through the router, to the Internet (you successfully sent an ICMP packet to an Internet address). The second thing this test shows is that Internet packets can flow through the router to the local segment (the ICMP packets were echoed back to you). Therefore if the ping test works, the router might not be the problem.

If the ping test fails, you need to look at reconfiguring the router. Try not to include any access lists that may interfere with the network and conflict with the firewall. I would leave the router configuration as simple as possible.

Firewall—If the router proves to be functioning fine but you still cannot receive e-mail, you should look at the firewall. Again, because of the complexity of this device, there is a greater chance that the problem may be here. The first place you should examine on the firewall is the rules. Remember, most firewalls implement an implicit deny policy. That means if you create a rule stating, "Allow TCP/IP traffic on port 80 (http)," the firewall will automatically block traffic on the remaining ports. This could prove to be an issue because you may (inadvertently) block traffic for Telnet port 25. SMTP traffic is transferred on Telnet port 25. Therefore, if you block data on Telnet port 25, you will not be able to receive e-mail from the Internet. (This problem might be hard to notice at first because the firewall can be set up to block data coming into the network and ignore data flowing out. When this is the case, you will be able to send e-mail to the Internet as well as the local network. You might not notice you are having a problem receiving e-mail for a couple of days.)

To test whether you have inadvertently blocked port 25, telnet to the e-mail server's IP address using port 25 from a computer that is not on the local network. If you cannot get into the server, check the firewall rules. However, if you cannot telnet to the server at all (regardless of the port) and the firewall rules are set up correctly, you should check the e-mail server itself.

E-mail Server—If you are not getting any response to your telnet requests, you should check your IP address. You could have an address configured into your server that works fine on your local network, but is invisible to the Internet. Keep in mind that your e-mail server needs to have a routable address assigned to it to receive e-mail from the Internet.

C

RESOLUTION
GUIDE

While e-mail problems can be common when a system is first implemented, problems that occur on an existing e-mail system are more rare, and can be harder to diagnose.

Most routers and firewalls should function properly after the initial configuration. Therefore, any problem that arises in an existing e-mail system would cause me to check the server first. Some simple tests to run on an e-mail server are

- Ping the standard list of troubleshooting addresses, one external (Internet) address, one internal (local) address, and the loopback (127.0.0.0) address.
- Stop and restart the service or program controlling the e-mail.
- Using a packet analyzer, monitor the SMTP traffic flowing into and out of the server.
- Check the network for conflicting IP addresses (a user might have mistakenly been assigned the same address as the e-mail server).

Another task that can be problematic for designers is network subnetting. The problems illustrated in the next section all pertain to the subnetting of a network. Keep in mind that most of these problems will only occur when a subnet is first implemented, which means you might not experience them on existing networks.

Issue 3: Subnetting Problems

Even the most experienced architects can be overcome by a large subnetting project. Subnetting an IP environment is one of the more complicated tasks that you will face on any project. The following scenario outlines a subnetting issue.

Scenario

A client has a network that needs to be subnetted (illustrated in Figure C.8). After one consultant tried to subnet the environment (illustrated in Figure C.9), the two segments are unable to communicate.

Network Diagram

Figure C.8 illustrates the client's original network, and Figure C.9 illustrates the first consultant's attempt to subnet the network.

Solution

The scenario I gave here is pretty specific, but it does illustrate a common subnetting problem. The networks illustrated in Figure C.9 cannot communicate for one simple reason: the subnet mask.

C

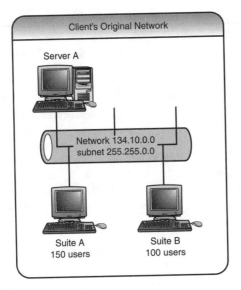

FIGURE C.8

The client's original network.

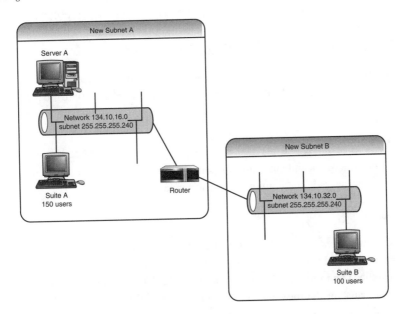

FIGURE C.9

The current (non-functional) subnet.

The first consultant took the client's current IP scheme of 134.10.0.0 (subnet 255.255.0.0), a valid class B IP network, and subnetted it into two pieces. The consultant created the networks 134.10.16.0 and 134.10.32.0 both using the subnet mask of 255.255.255.240.

The consultant actually subnetted the address correctly (producing the two subnets of 134.10.16.0 and 134.10.32.0), however he assigned the wrong mask to the networks. The subnet mask of 255.255.255.240 is a class C mask. The correct mask for these addresses should be 255.255.240.0. After implementing the new mask, the network should function properly.

This problem is one that you may not have noticed if you did not know exactly what you were looking for. When you are subnetting, try the new scheme on a test machine before you implement it; this will help you identify problems before they become larger issues. Also, if you are creating large amounts of subnets, map everything on paper first. Then if possible have a colleague double-check your work.

Subnetting an environment can be a difficult task, especially if you have never attempted to subnet before. I have found that any of the books written by Todd Lammle about TCP/IP contain very good information about subnetting. Please refer to these texts for more in-depth information on subnetting IP networks.

The final issue I will discuss is broadcast messages. Broadcasts can severely hinder a network's performance. The next scenario illustrates a broadcast message problem.

Issue 4: Broadcast Messages

An abundance of broadcast messages can grind even the beefiest network to a halt. The following scenario will help you identify the source of (and ultimately gain control over) such messages.

Scenario

A scan of a client's network indicates an inordinate amount of broadcast messages. These messages are starting to degrade the network's performance.

Solution

Some broadcast messages are normal, and some are even required by certain services (for example, DHCP clients must broadcast for the location of the server). However, masses of broadcast messages can indicate other network problems. The first task you should perform to troubleshoot the cause of the messages is to run a packet analyzer.

Try to determine where the packets are coming from. If the packets are all DHCP, or another services-related type of packet, refer to Issue 1, Scenario 2. However, if there is no consistency to the origin of the packets, you might have a faulty connectivity device.

Obviously, if your connectivity device is a hub, you should replace it with a switch to stop the broadcasts (hubs are designed to forward broadcasts; switches do not forward broadcasts). The first step I would take is to disconnect all of the devices from the switch (this requires a network outage). Then attach your packet analyzer, your laptop, and two other devices to the switch. After these devices are attached, telnet from your laptop to one of the other devices (by telnetting you are opening a direct connection, no broadcasts involved). Check the packet analyzer for any broadcasts.

If you detect broadcasts, you might have a faulty switch. If your analyzer did not detect any broadcasts, continue re-attaching devices until you find the source of the broadcasts.

This solution may seem like a very involved process to undertake; however, it is one sure way to identify the problem.

Closing

You may discover many other problems while you are designing your networks, but these are the four that I encounter the most. I hope the scenarios and solutions help you as you work with your projects.

Best of Luck,

J. F. DiMarzio

Resource Guide

IN THIS APPENDIX

With technology changing at an ever-quickening pace, network architects must stay abreast of the latest advances in their field to be truly marketable. However, especially if you are new to the fields of project management or network design, you may not know where to find the best information. Information, be it good or bad, can be found in abundance on the Internet, in print, and on television. It could take an entire day to just sift through the loads of material looking for one or two good pieces of data. The purpose of this appendix is to point you in the right direction for good resources.

This guide will be broken into two sections: general resources and product-specific resources. The general section will introduce you to resources that tend to deal with multiple topics. Such resources are good for a broad overview of the changes and advances in technology. However, what many of these references offer in unbiased opinion they lack in detail. That is to say, few general resource publications offer truly complete coverage of any one subject. Because they need to conserve space (and make the article readable), many details are left out. Product-specific resources tend to be, well, product specific—offering a lot of data on one or two subjects.

One major difference in the content of a general resource compared to that of a product-specific resource (even when dealing with the same subject) is that general resources lean more toward current or breaking news stories. A product-specific resource will offer more hands-on or on-the-job related data. Stories about how to implement a certain system will most likely be found in a product-specific resource, whereas a story about the latest product offering from a vendor will appear in a general resource.

IT consultants should subscribe to and use general resources as a weekly (or daily) recap of the latest and greatest in technology. A few headlines, a couple of diagrams, and maybe an equation might be all of the information you need to decide whether you want to research a subject area further. Also, as with a newspaper, you will have access to stories, guides, and other useful information about multiple fields of technology in one place. This can save you from having to spend a massive portion of your time looking for news or information that you may not even need.

General resources are also good for brushing up on old skills. For example, one general resource may cover command-line programming. Within this data there may be a few sections on "Batch Programming in DOS." This would give you a chance to refresh your knowledge of old DOS jobs.

NOTE

As some systems get older (like DOS), consultants who are fluent in those technologies become harder to find. Try to stay on top of the older systems as well as the newer ones. Being able to handle any system (regardless of age) is going to make you a stronger candidate for a job.

Keep in mind that many of the jobs you encounter will involve an existing (sometimes older) network. Therefore, it would help you tremendously to research some older systems and prepare yourself for whatever may happen.

I try to refer to a general resource at least two or three times a week. This gives me a good idea of the major headlines when it comes to new technology. I can easily flip through or browse a well-structured general resource before going to a project site or on a lunch break without having to read the entire story.

However, when you do find a piece of information (in a general resource) that piques your interest, you should then look into a product-specific resource. The general resource will give you a good outline of the story (and usually enough information to convey the major points of the story), but to get the big picture you may need to consult the story's source.

Product-specific resources offer network professionals and consultants the most in-depth knowledge of one particular subject or area of interest. Common product-specific resources exist for the larger fields of technology (such as telephony or Ethernet). Resources also exist for the more common vendors in a particular market, such as Microsoft, Cisco, and SCO. I find myself using references on one subject when I need an answer for a specific question. For example, if I am designing a network and need to know a certain configuration option for a Cisco router, I will turn to a Cisco resource.

The product-specific section of this appendix will introduce you to those resources that specialize in providing information about one particular product or area of knowledge. Product-specific publications tend to have more in-depth information about their subjects, but may lack the objectivity of a third-party, general publication.

General Resources

There are three places or mediums I have found for good, reliable general resources: the Internet, television, and printed magazines. This section lists what I feel are the best resources in those mediums, beginning with the Internet.

I like obtaining my general resources from the Internet. Internet-based resources are easier for me to receive; that is, I can access them at any time from multiple locations. This flexibility is something television lacks. Television programming is only available at a certain time in a certain place (wherever your TV is). Internet-based information is also more timely and up-to-date than magazines. In the case of a printed magazine, an author needs to write the story, and the entire product needs to be printed and shipped to your location. By the time you receive many printed magazines, the information in them can be two or more months old. I can get the same story within minutes on the Internet. (However, there are few things more portable than a magazine, if you don't mind the outdated data.)

One very good Internet-based general resource is www.slashdot.com. Figure D.1 shows Slashdot's home page.

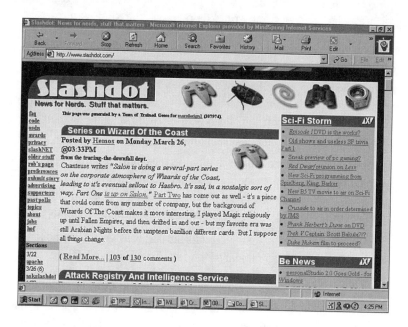

FIGURE D.1

Slashdot.com's home page.

One of the best features of Slashdot.com is the ability to customize the news to your personal interests. For instance, I pull in the news on Linux, BSD, and Quake 3.

Another good Internet-based resource for general information is www.techtv.com. Figure D.2 shows TechTV's home page.

I turn to TechTV's page as a supplement to their television programming. There are a few television stations offering programs that cater to the needs of IT professionals, and TechTV is one of them.

TechTV (available on most cable and satellite services) offers multiple programs geared for those who are, more or less, technically inclined.

The three most useful programs to catch on TechTV are *TechTV News*, *The Screen Savers*, and *Call for Help*. These programs offer very useful information about implementing and maintaining systems such as Linux, Windows, and Mac.

Keeping with the definition of a general resource, *TechTV News* is a headline-based news program focusing purely on topics of interest to IT professionals. The stories are not extremely in-depth, but they are followed up by more informative articles on the TechTV Web site.

FIGURE D.2

TechTV's home page.

The Screen Savers consists of intermediate to advanced troubleshooting topics presented by two knowledgeable hosts. The topics are presented in a question and answer format (the questions mostly emanating from live viewer calls and e-mails). The topics can range from configuring an Ethernet card on a Linux machine to which video cards work best under Windows 2000.

The final program that I try to watch on a regular basis is *Call for Help*. This program, following the same format as *The Screen Savers*, deals with basic beginner concepts. Even though this is a show that is geared for novices, it is a very good forum for listening to non-technical people present their computer-based problems.

Of the programs on TechTV, I find that I gain the most from this one. I not only get refreshers on technical tips and tricks (that I may have forgotten), but I get to listen to live people (most of whom are admittedly not very technical) present problems and issues in lay terms. Listening to these callers gives you a great perspective on how people perceive the problems they have. I find that I can better comprehend how to help clients understand their own needs (which is essential during the "gathering information" phase of any project).

The hosts for many of the shows on TechTV are very knowledgeable in their fields. When TechTV first went on the air, it was owned by Ziff Davis (a popular technical magazine publisher). Therefore, many of the hosts were (and still are) published authors with articles in multiple magazines.

I do not read as many printed general resources as I would like, but one that I do try to look at on a regular basis is *Network World*. If you have not looked into *Network World* I strongly suggest that you pick up a copy, especially if you are designing networks on a regular basis. *Network World* offers the best information on designing, implementing, and troubleshooting networks of any printed periodical I have seen.

Network World can be very thorough in its presentation of material for the reader and often follows up stories with additional Web-based information.

Product-Specific Resources

Again, I find the better product-specific resources on the Internet. Web sites such as Microsoft.com, Phoneboy.com, and Microsoft's TechNet offer unparalleled information on their specific subjects.

Microsoft's knowledge base (see Figure D.3) is one of the best places for Microsoft-specific resolutions. If you have a question about a Microsoft product, this is the place you should turn.

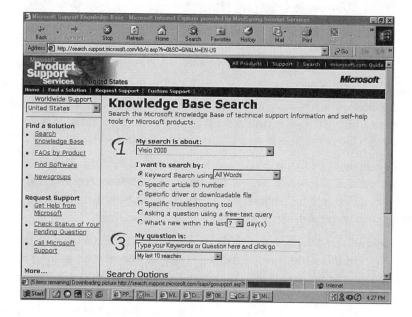

FIGURE D.3
Microsoft's knowledge base at Microsoft.com.

I use PhoneBoy.com during many of my projects (see Figure D.4). This is an independent Web site about CheckPoint's FireWall-1 firewall and VPN product. CheckPoint's products are fairly hard to get support for and it took me a while to find this site. However, to this day I have not had a Firewall-1 problem that this site did not answer.

NOTE

Under normal circumstances, you should always try to get technical support from the vendor of the product in question; and as far as I know, Phoneboy.com is not related to or endorsed by CheckPoint. However, there are circumstances in which you may not be able to obtain support information from the actual product vendor, in this case CheckPoint.

For example, many of CheckPoint's products are sold through sales partners (meaning vendors other than CheckPoint, such as Internet solution providers offering full/managed Internet packages). Not all of these outside vendors have the capacity to offer technical support for CheckPoint's products, and CheckPoint will only offer you support if you purchase the product directly from them. It seems like a catch-22; hence the existence of Web sites like Phoneboy.com.

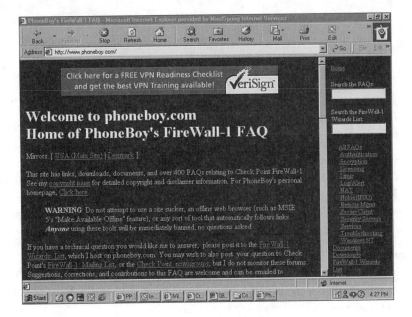

FIGURE D.4

Phoneboy.com's home page.

Another good Microsoft resource is the weekly TechNet subscription. (Not to be confused with the TechNet CD subscription.) The TechNet technical bulletin is an e-mail that covers the latest in Microsoft news, releases, and patches (see Figure D.5).

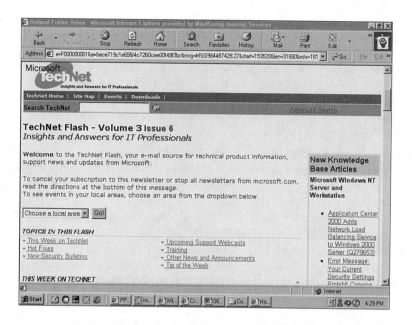

Figure D.5

Microsoft's TechNet technical bulletin.

Microsoft seems to dominate the market when it comes to product-specific literature; however, there are now more magazines focused on other technologies.

Linux Journal is a very well-organized magazine focusing on all topics related to Linux. I have found many informative articles pertaining to various Linux configurations and implementations that I have put to use in the field. Given that Linux is one of the more elusive products to obtain support for, *Linux Journal* is a must for anyone who encounters the operating system on a regular basis.

These resources are, I feel, the cream of the crop when it comes to providing timely, pertinent, and useful information about computers and computer networking. However, if you're looking for something a little more technical, you should look at the building blocks of technology as a whole: the RFCs. Appendix E covers some useful RFCs.

RFCs

IN THIS APPENDIX

The best information in our field (technological networking) comes in the form of RFCs or Requests For Comments. If you're like me and have a very strong urge to know how things work, this is the place to turn. When I started looking into computers as a career, I tried to read as many pertinent RFCs as possible to give myself a deeper understanding of the technology behind the technology.

Even today I try to keep up with RFCs as they are released.

Even if you do not care about the inner workings of sending an 802.2 packet over an IPX network (RFC 1042) you should still read these RFCs. Because you will write a lot of documentation over the course of your projects, reading these papers will familiarize you with the language used to convey technical information to a specific audience.

I have included several of the more pertinent RFCs (as far as this book is concerned) in this appendix; however, some of them have been edited for space. Feel free to browse through them and hopefully pick up some useful information.

RFC 1918   Address Allocation for Private Internets

Status of this Memo

This document specifies an Internet Best Current Practices for the Internet Community, and requests discussion and suggestions for improvements. Distribution of this memo is unlimited.

1. Introduction

   For the purposes of this document, an enterprise is an entity autonomously operating a network using TCP/IP and in particular determining the addressing plan and address assignments within that network.

   This document describes address allocation for private internets. The allocation permits full network layer connectivity among all hosts inside an enterprise as well as among all public hosts of different enterprises. The cost of using private internet address space is the potentially costly effort to renumber hosts and networks between public and private.

2. Motivation

   With the proliferation of TCP/IP technology worldwide, including outside the Internet itself, an increasing number of non-connected enterprises use this technology and its addressing capabilities for sole intra-enterprise communications, without any intention to ever directly connect to other enterprises or the Internet itself.

   The Internet has grown beyond anyone's expectations. Sustained exponential growth continues to introduce new challenges. One challenge is a concern within the community that globally unique address space will be exhausted. A separate and far more pressing concern is that the amount of routing overhead will grow beyond the capabilities of Internet Service Providers. Efforts are in progress within the community to find long term solutions to both of these problems. Meanwhile it is necessary to revisit address allocation procedures, and their impact on the Internet routing system.

To contain growth of routing overhead, an Internet Provider obtains a block of address space from an address registry, and then assigns to its customers addresses from within that block based on each customer requirement. The result of this process is that routes to many customers will be aggregated together, and will appear to other providers as a single route [RFC1518], [RFC1519]. In order for route aggregation to be effective, Internet providers encourage customers joining their network to use the provider's block, and thus renumber their computers. Such encouragement may become a requirement in the future.

It has been typical to assign globally unique addresses to all hosts that use TCP/IP. In order to extend the life of the IPv4 address space, address registries are requiring more justification than ever before, making it harder for organizations to acquire additional address space [RFC1466].

Hosts within enterprises that use IP can be partitioned into three categories:

Category 1: hosts that do not require access to hosts in other enterprises or the Internet at large; hosts within this category may use IP addresses that are unambiguous within an enterprise, but may be ambiguous between enterprises.

Category 2: hosts that need access to a limited set of outside services (e.g., E-mail, FTP, netnews, remote login) which can be handled by mediating gateways (e.g., application layer gateways). For many hosts in this category an unrestricted external access (provided via IP connectivity) may be unnecessary and even undesirable for privacy/security reasons. Just like hosts within the first category, such hosts may use IP addresses that are unambiguous within an enterprise, but may be ambiguous between enterprises.

Category 3: hosts that need network layer access outside the enterprise (provided via IP connectivity); hosts in the last category require IP addresses that are globally unambiguous.

We will refer to the hosts in the first and second categories as "private". We will refer to the hosts in the third category as "public".

Many applications require connectivity only within one enterprise and do not need external (outside the enterprise) connectivity for the majority of internal hosts. In larger enterprises it is often easy to identify a substantial number of hosts using TCP/IP that do not need network layer connectivity outside the enterprise.

Some examples, where external connectivity might not be required, are:

- A large airport which has its arrival/departure displays individually addressable via TCP/IP. It is very unlikely that these displays need to be directly accessible from other networks.
- Large organizations like banks and retail chains are switching to TCP/IP for their internal communication. Large numbers of local workstations like cash registers,

money machines, and equipment at clerical positions rarely need to have such connectivity.

- For security reasons, many enterprises use application layer gateways to connect their internal network to the Internet. The internal network usually does not have direct access to the Internet, thus only one or more gateways are visible from the Internet. In this case, the internal network can use non-unique IP network numbers.

- Interfaces of routers on an internal network usually do not need to be directly accessible from outside the enterprise.

3. Private Address Space

The Internet Assigned Numbers Authority (IANA) has reserved the following three blocks of the IP address space for private internets:

```
10.0.0.0       -   10.255.255.255  (10/8 prefix)
172.16.0.0     -   172.31.255.255  (172.16/12 prefix)
192.168.0.0    -   192.168.255.255 (192.168/16 prefix)
```

We will refer to the first block as "24-bit block", the second as "20-bit block", and to the third as "16-bit" block. Note that (in pre-CIDR notation) the first block is nothing but a single class A network number, while the second block is a set of 16 contiguous class B network numbers, and third block is a set of 256 contiguous class C network numbers.

An enterprise that decides to use IP addresses out of the address space defined in this document can do so without any coordination with IANA or an Internet registry. The address space can thus be used by many enterprises. Addresses within this private address space will only be unique within the enterprise, or the set of enterprises which choose to cooperate over this space so they may communicate with each other in their own private internet.

As before, any enterprise that needs globally unique address space is required to obtain such addresses from an Internet registry. An enterprise that requests IP addresses for its external connectivity will never be assigned addresses from the blocks defined above.

In order to use private address space, an enterprise needs to determine which hosts do not need to have network layer connectivity outside the enterprise in the foreseeable future and thus could be classified as private. Such hosts will use the private address space defined above. Private hosts can communicate with all other hosts inside the enterprise, both public and private. However, they cannot have IP connectivity to any host outside of the enterprise. While not having external (outside of the enterprise) IP connectivity private hosts can still have access to external services via mediating gateways (e.g., application layer gateways).

All other hosts will be public and will use globally unique address space assigned by an Internet Registry. Public hosts can communicate with other hosts inside the enterprise both public and private and can have IP connectivity to public hosts outside the enterprise. Public hosts do not have connectivity to private hosts of other enterprises.

Because private addresses have no global meaning, routing information about private networks shall not be propagated on inter-enterprise links, and packets with private source or destination addresses should not be forwarded across such links. Routers in networks not using private address space, especially those of Internet service providers, are expected to be configured to reject (filter out) routing information about private networks. If such a router receives such information the rejection shall not be treated as a routing protocol error.

Indirect references to such addresses should be contained within the enterprise. Prominent examples of such references are DNS Resource Records and other information referring to internal private addresses. In particular, Internet service providers should take measures to prevent such leakage.

4. Conclusion

With the described scheme many large enterprises will need only a relatively small block of addresses from the globally unique IP address space. The Internet at large benefits through conservation of globally unique address space which will effectively lengthen the lifetime of the IP address space. The enterprises benefit from the increased flexibility provided by a relatively large private address space. However, use of private addressing requires that an organization renumber part or all of its enterprise network, as its connectivity requirements change over time.

9. References

[RFC1466] Gerich, E., "Guidelines for Management of IP Address Space", RFC 1466, Merit Network, Inc., May 1993.

[RFC1518] Rekhter, Y., and T. Li, "An Architecture for IP Address Allocation with CIDR", RFC 1518, September 1993.

[RFC1519] Fuller, V., Li, T., Yu, J., and K. Varadhan, "Classless Inter-Domain Routing (CIDR): an Address Assignment and Aggregation Strategy", RFC 1519, September 1993.

RFC 1369   Ethernet MIB Implementations

Status of this Memo

This memo provides information for the Internet community. It does not specify an Internet standard. Distribution of this memo is unlimited.

Table of Contents

E

RFCs

1. Introduction

The Ethernet MIB Working group has been tasked with the following two work items:

1. Develop a document explaining the rationale for assigning MANDATORY status to MIB variables which are optional in the relevant IEEE 802.3 specification (the technical basis for the Internet Ethernet MIB). This shall not be a standards-track document.

2. Develop an implementation report on the Ethernet MIB. This report shall cover MIB variables which are implemented in both Ethernet interface chips, and in software (i.e., drivers), and discuss the issues pertaining to both. This report shall also summarize field experience with the MIB variables, especially concentrating on those variables which are in dispute. This document shall not be a standards-track document. While the Ethernet MIB is progressing through the standardization process, this document shall be periodically updated to reflect the latest implementation and operational experience.

This document reflects the currently known status of 11 different implementations of the MIB by 7 different vendors on 7 different Ethernet interface chips.

2. Observations

There are some interesting points to be noted from this information:

1. Only 4 variables are actually implemented in all implementations: AlignmentErrors, FCSErrors, ExcessiveCollisions and InternalMacTransmitErrors.

2. There were another five variables implemented in all but one of the reported implementations, SingleCollisionFrames, MultipleCollisionFrames, LateCollisions, FrameTooLongs, and CarrierSenseErrors.

Three of these variables exist in implementations that use the same chip as the implementation that does not contain the variable. Specifically:

A. SingleCollisionFrames is not implemented in implementation number 3, which uses the AMD LANCE. However, other AMD LANCE implementations (7, 8, and 10) do implement the variable, implying that it is available on the LANCE.

B. MultipleCollisionFrames is not implemented in implementation number 3, which uses the AMD LANCE. However, other AMD LANCE implementations (7, 8, and 10) do implement the variable, implying that it is available on the LANCE.

C. LateCollisions is not implemented in implementation number 1, which uses the Intel 82586. However, another Intel 82586 based implementation (11) does implement the variable, implying that it is available on the Intel 82586.

D. CarrierSenseErrors is not implemented on implementation number 2, which is based on the Fujitsu 86950 chip. However, there is only one implementation based on this chip and I have not been able to locate a data sheet on this part so no conclusion can be drawn at this time.

E. FrameTooLongs is not implemented on implementation number 5, which is based on the National NIC 8390 chip. However, there is only one implementation based on this chip and I have not been able to locate a data sheet on this part. It should also be noted that this variable is easily maintained by software as a "driver-level" function.

3. Of the 22 variables in the MIB, 11, or 1/2 of the variables, were implemented in about 1/2 or less of the implementations.

4. The number of variables implemented per implementation ranges from a low of 11 to a high of 16. The average number of variables truly implemented is 12.8.

5. The IEEE 802.3 encapsulation-specific variables (InRangeLengthErrors, and OutOfRangeLengthFields) are in 2 and 0 implementations respectively.

3. Conclusions

From this, the author concludes that:

The control variables (IntializeMAC, etc.) are not widely implemented, but this may be due to an aversion to implementing writable variables until security is in place.

One vendor has stated that the reason that these variables were not implemented was that the vendor did not believe the variables to be useful, and that they were hard to implement. Furthermore, this vendor has recommended dropping the variables entirely.

The two IEEE 802.3 encapsulation variables (InRangeLengthErrors and OutOfRangeLengthFields) are barely implemented. In Santa Fe, the Working group discussed moving them to an optional, 802.3 specific, group. The author believes that this is justified by this implementation data.

The collision histogram variables are also barely implemented. They should be in their own optional group—and they are.

Of the remaining 13 statistical variables, 9 of them are in 10 or 11 implementations. This is good.

Two of them (SQETestErrors and ExcessiveDeferrals) are in 3 and 1 implementations, respectively. This is bad.

The remaining variables (DeferredTransmissions and InternalMacReceiveErrors) are in 8 or 9 implementations.

E

It should be noted that one of the two systems that do not implement DeferredTransmissions is based on the AMD LANCE, and other AMD LANCE based systems do implement this counter, leading to the conclusion that DeferredTransmissions could easily be on all but one of the implementations.

The other such variable, InternalMacReceiveErrors, is a general catchall for all other errors. If no other errors are detected by the hardware or software then returning 0 for the counter is perfectly acceptable.

This all seems to imply either:

1. Splitting the statistics group into two groups, one of which is optional and contains SQETestErrors and ExcessiveDeferrals, or

2. Eliminating SQETestErrors and ExcessiveDeferrals from the MIB.

The variables with 8 or 9 implementations are a bit more problematic. They are implemented in more than 2/3s of the implementations, but it may not be appropriate to call this widespread implementation. However, it seems to be safe to conclude that the non-implementations of these variables is due to local implementation considerations rather than a fundamental lack of support for the variable.

4. Final Action

After consideration at the San Diego IETF Meeting on 17 March 1992, the Ethernet MIB Working Group made the following recommendations:

1. The dot3TestTdrValue object will be deprecated from the standard mib. There are effectively no implementations of this object, and some chips were reported to return an incorrect value for the TDR count.

2. The dot3StatsInRangeLengthErrors object and the dot3StatsOutOfRangeLengthFields object will be deprecated from the MIB. These objects were not widely implemented and their utility in diagnosing network problems was strongly questioned.

3. The dot3InitializeMac object, the dot3MacSubLayerStatus object, the dot3MulticastReceiveStatus object, and the dot3TxEnabled object will be deprecated from the MIB. These objects were not widely implemented and their utility in diagnosing network problems was strongly questioned.

4. The dot3StatsExcessiveDeferrals object will be deprecated from the MIB. Only one system implemented this object. Furthermore, its exact definition was called into question.

5. The dot3StatsSQETestErrors object received few implementations. However, the working group strongly supported its retention in the MIB on the basis that certain forms of transceiver and cable errors that are not uncommon can only be detected with this counter.

6. The collision histogram table (dot3CollTable) will be kept as an optional group, even though the objects are not widely implemented nor is there hardware support on all reported chips.

5. Implementation Data

The following raw data has been provided by vendors, each developing an implementation of the Ethernet MIB. Each reported implementation has a separate column in the following table. For each implementation/MIB Variable, a single character code has been entered indicating the rough implementation status of the variable. These codes are:

Y Fully implemented, reports a truthful count, or indication of state. All values may be written to the variable with the expected action occurring.

N Not implemented at all. Would return a noSuchName error if accessed.

C Implemented but returns a constant value for gets and returns a badValue error for any set attempt to set the variable to a value other than this constant (writable variables only).

MIB Variable	1	2	3	4	5	6	7	8	9	10	11	Yesses
InitializeMac	C	C	Y	Y	Y	Y	Y	C7	C7	N	Y	6
MacSubLayerStatus	C	C	Y	Y	Y	Y	Y	C7	C7	N	C	5
MulticastReceiveStatus	C	C	Y	C3	Y	C	C	C7	C7	N	C	2
TxEnabled	C	C	Y	Y	Y	Y	Y	C7	C7	N	C	5
TestTdrValue	C	1	C	C4	C	C	C	C4	C4	N	C	1
AlignmentErrors	Y	Y	Y	Y	Y	Y	Y	Y	Y	Y	Y	11
FCSErrors	Y	Y	Y	Y	Y	Y	Y	Y	Y	Y	Y	11
SingleCollisionFrames	Y	Y	Y	N	Y	Y	Y	Y	Y	Y	Y	10
MultipleCollisionFrames	Y	Y	Y	N	Y	Y	Y	Y	Y	Y	Y	10
SQETestErrors	Y	C	C	C	Y	C	C	C	C	Y	C	3
DeferredTransmissions	Y	C	Y	N	Y	Y	Y	Y	Y	Y	Y	9
LateCollisions	C	Y	Y	Y	Y	Y	Y	Y	Y	Y	Y	10
ExcessiveCollisions	Y	Y	Y	Y	Y	Y	Y	Y	Y	Y	Y	11
InternalMacTransmitErrors	Y	Y	Y	Y	Y	Y	Y	Y	Y	Y	Y	11
CarrierSenseErrors	Y	C	Y	Y	Y	Y	Y	Y	Y	Y	Y	10
ExcessiveDeferrals	C	C	Y	C	C	C	C	C	C	N	C	1
FrameTooLongs	Y	Y2	Y	Y	C	Y	Y	Y	Y	Y	Y	10
InRangeLengthErrors	C	C	C	N5	C	Y	Y	C	C	N	C	2
OutOfRangeLengthFields	C	C	C	C6	C	C	C	C	C	N	C	0
InternalMacReceiveErrors	Y	Y	Y	Y	Y	C	C	Y	Y	Y	C	8
CollCount	Y	Y	C	N	N	N	N	C	C	N	Y	3
CollFrequencies	Y	Y	C	N	N	N	N	C	C	N	Y	3
Yesses	13	11	16	11	15	14	14	11	11	12	13	

Notes:

1. does not implement TDR test, but reports TDR from last collision!
2. Not supported by the chip, detected solely in software.
3. But set to disabled(2) -> badValue
4. Underlying TDR function not implemented on this chip.
5. Only counts frames too short though.
6. Due to Ethernet encapsulation
7. Implementation does not support set operations but reports the correct value for these.

The implementations are:

Implementation	Vendor	Chip
1	1	Intel 82586
2	1	Fujitsu 86950
3	2	Sonic
4	3	AMD Lance
5	4	National NIC 8390C
6	4	Intel 82596
7	4	AMD Lance
8	5	AMD Lance
9	5	AMD ILACC
10	6	AMD Lance
11	7	Intel 82586

RFC 1231   IEEE 802.5 MIB

Status of this Memo

This memo defines a MIB for 805.5 networks for use with the SNMP protocol. This memo is a product of the Transmission Working Group of the Internet Engineering Task Force (IETF). This RFC specifies an IAB standards track protocol for the Internet community, and requests discussion and suggestions for improvements. Please refer to the current edition of the "IAB Official Protocol Standards" for the standardization state and status of this protocol. Distribution of this memo is unlimited.

1. The Network Management Framework

   The Internet-standard Network Management Framework consists of three components. They are:

RFC 1155 which defines the SMI, the mechanisms used for describing and naming objects for the purpose of management. RFC 1212 defines a more concise description mechanism, which is wholly consistent with the SMI.

RFC 1156 which defines MIB-I, the core set of managed objects for the Internet suite of protocols. RFC 1213, defines MIB-II, an evolution of MIB-I based on implementation experience and new operational requirements.

RFC 1157 which defines the SNMP, the protocol used for network access to managed objects.

The Framework permits new objects to be defined for the purpose of experimentation and evaluation.

2. Objects

Managed objects are accessed via a virtual information store, termed the Management Information Base or MIB. Objects in the MIB are defined using the subset of Abstract Syntax Notation One (ASN.1) [7] defined in the SMI. In particular, each object has a name, a syntax, and an encoding. The name is an object identifier, an administratively assigned name, which specifies an object type. The object type together with an object instance serves to uniquely identify a specific instantiation of the object. For human convenience, we often use a textual string, termed the OBJECT DESCRIPTOR, to also refer to the object type.

The syntax of an object type defines the abstract data structure corresponding to that object type. The ASN.1 language is used for this purpose. However, the SMI [3] purposely restricts the ASN.1 constructs which may be used. These restrictions are explicitly made for simplicity.

The encoding of an object type is simply how that object type is represented using the object type's syntax. Implicitly tied to the notion of an object type's syntax and encoding is how the object type is represented when being transmitted on the network.

The SMI specifies the use of the basic encoding rules of ASN.1 [8], subject to the additional requirements imposed by the SNMP.

2.1. Format of Definitions

Section 5 contains the specification of all object types contained in this MIB module. The object types are defined using the conventions defined in the SMI, as amended by the extensions specified in [9,10].

3. Overview

This memo defines three tables: the 802.5 Interface Table, which contains state and parameter information which is specific to 802.5 interfaces, the 802.5 Statistics Table, which contains 802.5 interface statistics, and the 802.5 Timer Table, which contains the values of 802.5-defined timers. A managed system will have one entry in the 802.5 Interface

E

Table and one entry in the 802.5 Statistics Table for each of its 802.5 interfaces. Implementation of the 802.5 Timer Table is optional.

This memo also defines OBJECT IDENTIFIERs, some to identify 802.5 tests, for use with the ifExtnsTestTable defined in [11], and some to identify Token Ring interface Chip Sets, for use with the ifExtnsChipSet object defined in [11].

4. Definitions

```
          RFC1231-MIB DEFINITIONS ::= BEGIN


          --                    IEEE 802.5 Token Ring MIB

          IMPORTS
                  experimental
                          FROM RFC1155-SMI
                  OBJECT-TYPE
                          FROM RFC-1212;
```

- This MIB Module uses the extended OBJECT-TYPE macro as defined in [9].

```
          dot5    OBJECT IDENTIFIER ::= { experimental 4 }
```

- All representations of MAC addresses in this MIB Module use, as a textual convention (i.e. this convention does not affect their encoding), the data type:

```
          MacAddress ::= OCTET STRING (SIZE (6))    -- a 6 octet
                                                    -- address in the
                                                    -- "canonical" order
```

- defined by IEEE 802.1a, i.e., as if it were transmitted least significant bit first, even though 802.5 (in contrast to other 802.x protocols) requires MAC addresses to be transmitted most significant bit first.

- 16-bit addresses, if needed, are represented by setting their upper 4 octets to all 0's, i.e., AAFF would be represented as 00000000AAFF.

- The Interface Table

- This table contains state and parameter information which is specific to 802.5 interfaces. It is mandatory that systems having 802.5 interfaces implement this table in addition to the generic interfaces table [4,6] and its generic extensions [11].

Transmission Working Group   [Page 4]

RFC 1231   IEEE 802.5 MIB   May 1991

```
          dot5Table  OBJECT-TYPE
                     SYNTAX  SEQUENCE OF Dot5Entry
                     ACCESS  not-accessible
                     STATUS  mandatory
                     DESCRIPTION
                             "This table contains Token Ring interface
                             parameters and state variables, one entry
```

```
                          per 802.5 interface."
              ::= { dot5 1 }


dot5Entry  OBJECT-TYPE
              SYNTAX  Dot5Entry
              ACCESS  not-accessible
              STATUS  mandatory
              DESCRIPTION
                      "A list of Token Ring status and parameter
                      values for an 802.5 interface."
              INDEX   { dot5IfIndex }
              ::= { dot5Table 1 }


Dot5Entry
    ::= SEQUENCE {
              dot5IfIndex
                  INTEGER,
              dot5Commands
                  INTEGER,
              dot5RingStatus
                  INTEGER,
              dot5RingState
                  INTEGER,
              dot5RingOpenStatus
                  INTEGER,
              dot5RingSpeed
                  INTEGER,
              dot5UpStream
                  MacAddress,
              dot5ActMonParticipate
                  INTEGER,
              dot5Functional
                  MacAddress
          }


dot5IfIndex  OBJECT-TYPE
              SYNTAX  INTEGER
              ACCESS  read-only
              STATUS  mandatory
              DESCRIPTION
                      "The value of this object identifies the
                      802.5 interface for which this entry
                      contains management information.  The
                      value of this object for a particular
                      interface has the same value as the
                      ifIndex object, defined in [4,6],
                      for the same interface."
              ::= { dot5Entry 1 }
```

E

RFCs

```
dot5Commands  OBJECT-TYPE
          SYNTAX  INTEGER {
                      no-op(1),
                      open(2),
                      reset(3),
                      close(4)
                  }
          ACCESS   read-write
          STATUS   mandatory
          DESCRIPTION
                  "When this object is set to the value of
                  open(2), the station should go into the
                  open state.  The progress and success of
                  the open is given by the values of the
                  objects dot5RingState and
                  dot5RingOpenStatus.
                      When this object is set to the value
                  of reset(3), then the station should do
                  a reset.  On a reset, all MIB counters
                  should retain their values, if possible.
                  Other side effects are dependent on the
                  hardware chip set.
                      When this object is set to the value
                  of close(4), the station should go into
                  the stopped state by removing itself
                  from the ring.
                      Setting this object to a value of
                  no-op(1) has no effect.
                      When read, this object always has a
                  value of no-op(1)."
          ::= { dot5Entry 2 }

dot5RingStatus OBJECT-TYPE
          SYNTAX  INTEGER
          ACCESS  read-only
          STATUS  mandatory
          DESCRIPTION
                  "The current interface status which can
                  be used to diagnose fluctuating problems
                  that can occur on token rings, after a
                  station has successfully been added to the
                  ring.
```

Before an open is completed, this object has the value for the 'no status' condition. The dot5RingState and dot5RingOpenStatus objects provide for debugging problems when the station cannot even enter the ring.

The object's value is a sum of values, one for each currently applicable condition. The following values are defined for various conditions:

```
             0 = No Problems detected
            32 = Ring Recovery
            64 = Single Station
           256 = Remove Received
           512 = reserved
          1024 = Auto-Removal Error
          2048 = Lobe Wire Fault
          4096 = Transmit Beacon
          8192 = Soft Error
         16384 = Hard Error
         32768 = Signal Loss
        131072 = no status, open not completed."
    ::= { dot5Entry 3 }


dot5RingState  OBJECT-TYPE
        SYNTAX  INTEGER {
                    opened(1),
                    closed(2),
                    opening(3),
                    closing(4),
                    openFailure(5),
                    ringFailure(6)
                }
        ACCESS  read-only
        STATUS  mandatory
        DESCRIPTION
                "The current interface state with respect
                to entering or leaving the ring."
        ::= { dot5Entry 4 }


dot5RingOpenStatus  OBJECT-TYPE
        SYNTAX  INTEGER {
                    noOpen(1),         -- no open attempted
                    badParam(2),
                    lobeFailed(3),
                    signalLoss(4),
                    insertionTimeout(5),
                    ringFailed(6),
                    beaconing(7),
                    duplicateMAC(8),
                    requestFailed(9),
                    removeReceived(10),
                    open(11)          -- last open successful
```

```
                                   }
                  ACCESS   read-only
                  STATUS   mandatory
                  DESCRIPTION
                          "This object indicates the success, or the
                          reason for failure, of the station's most
                          recent attempt to enter the ring."
                  ::= { dot5Entry 5 }


      dot5RingSpeed   OBJECT-TYPE
                  SYNTAX   INTEGER {
                                   unknown(1),
                                   oneMegabit(2),
                                   fourMegabit(3),
                                   sixteenMegabit(4)
                                   }
                  ACCESS   read-write
                  STATUS   mandatory
                  DESCRIPTION
                          "The ring's bandwidth."
                  ::= { dot5Entry 6 }


      dot5UpStream   OBJECT-TYPE
                  SYNTAX   MacAddress
                  ACCESS   read-only
                  STATUS   mandatory
                  DESCRIPTION
                          "The MAC-address of the up stream neighbor
                          station in the ring."
                  ::= { dot5Entry 7 }


      dot5ActMonParticipate OBJECT-TYPE
                  SYNTAX   INTEGER {
                                   true(1),
                                   false(2)
                                   }
                  ACCESS   read-write
                  STATUS   mandatory
                  DESCRIPTION
                          "If this object has a value of true(1) then
                          this interface will participate in the
                          active monitor selection process.  If the
                          value is false(2) then it will not.
                          Setting this object might not have an
                          effect until the next time the interface
                          is opened."
                  ::= { dot5Entry 8 }
```

```
dot5Functional OBJECT-TYPE
        SYNTAX  MacAddress
        ACCESS  read-write
        STATUS  mandatory
        DESCRIPTION
                "The bit mask of all Token Ring functional
                addresses for which this interface will
                accept frames."
        ::= { dot5Entry 9 }
```

- The Statistics Table
- This table contains statistics and error counter which are specific to 802.5 interfaces. It is mandatory that systems having 802.5 interfaces implement this table.

```
dot5StatsTable  OBJECT-TYPE
        SYNTAX  SEQUENCE OF Dot5StatsEntry
        ACCESS  not-accessible
        STATUS  mandatory
        DESCRIPTION
                "A table containing Token Ring statistics,
                one entry per 802.5 interface.
                    All the statistics are defined using
                the syntax Counter as 32-bit wrap around
                counters.  Thus, if an interface's
                hardware maintains these statistics in
                16-bit counters, then the agent must read
                the hardware's counters frequently enough
                to prevent loss of significance, in order
                to maintain 32-bit counters in software."
        ::= { dot5 2 }


dot5StatsEntry  OBJECT-TYPE
        SYNTAX  Dot5StatsEntry
        ACCESS  not-accessible
        STATUS  mandatory
        DESCRIPTION
                "An entry contains the 802.5 statistics
                 for a particular interface."
        INDEX   { dot5StatsIfIndex }
        ::= { dot5StatsTable 1 }


Dot5StatsEntry
    ::= SEQUENCE {
            dot5StatsIfIndex
                INTEGER,
            dot5StatsLineErrors
                Counter,
```

```
                          dot5StatsBurstErrors
                              Counter,
                          dot5StatsACErrors
                              Counter,
                          dot5StatsAbortTransErrors
                              Counter,
                          dot5StatsInternalErrors
                              Counter,
                          dot5StatsLostFrameErrors
                              Counter,
                          dot5StatsReceiveCongestions
                              Counter,
                          dot5StatsFrameCopiedErrors
                              Counter,
                          dot5StatsTokenErrors
                              Counter,
                          dot5StatsSoftErrors
                              Counter,
                          dot5StatsHardErrors
                              Counter,
                          dot5StatsSignalLoss
                              Counter,
                          dot5StatsTransmitBeacons
                              Counter,
                          dot5StatsRecoverys
                              Counter,
                          dot5StatsLobeWires
                              Counter,
                          dot5StatsRemoves
                              Counter,
                          dot5StatsSingles
                              Counter,
                          dot5StatsFreqErrors
                              Counter
                  }

        dot5StatsIfIndex  OBJECT-TYPE
                  SYNTAX   INTEGER
                  ACCESS   read-only
                  STATUS   mandatory
                  DESCRIPTION
                          "The value of this object identifies the
                          802.5 interface for which this entry
                          contains management information.  The
                          value of this object for a particular
                          interface has the same value as the
                          ifIndex object, defined in [4,6], for
                          the same interface."
                  ::= { dot5StatsEntry 1 }
```

```
dot5StatsLineErrors OBJECT-TYPE
        SYNTAX   Counter
        ACCESS   read-only
        STATUS   mandatory
        DESCRIPTION
                "This counter is incremented when a frame
                or token is copied or repeated by a
                station, the E bit is zero in the frame
                or token and one of the following
                conditions exists: 1) there is a
                non-data bit (J or K bit) between the SD
                and the ED of the frame or token, or
                2) there is an FCS error in the frame."
        ::= { dot5StatsEntry 2 }

dot5StatsBurstErrors OBJECT-TYPE
        SYNTAX   Counter
        ACCESS   read-only
        STATUS   mandatory
        DESCRIPTION
                "This counter is incremented when a station
                detects the absence of transitions for five
                half-bit timers (burst-five error)."
        ::= { dot5StatsEntry 3 }

dot5StatsACErrors OBJECT-TYPE
        SYNTAX   Counter
        ACCESS   read-only
        STATUS   mandatory
        DESCRIPTION
                "This counter is incremented when a station
                receives an AMP or SMP frame in which A is
                equal to C is equal to 0, and then receives
                another SMP frame with A is equal to C is
                equal to 0 without first receiving an AMP
                frame. It denotes a station that cannot set
                the AC bits properly."
        ::= { dot5StatsEntry 4 }

dot5StatsAbortTransErrors OBJECT-TYPE
        SYNTAX   Counter
        ACCESS   read-only
        STATUS   mandatory
        DESCRIPTION
                "This counter is incremented when a station
                transmits an abort delimiter while
                transmitting."
        ::= { dot5StatsEntry 5 }
```

E

RFCs

```
dot5StatsInternalErrors OBJECT-TYPE
        SYNTAX   Counter
        ACCESS   read-only
        STATUS   mandatory
        DESCRIPTION
                "This counter is incremented when a station
                recognizes an internal error."
        ::= { dot5StatsEntry 6 }

dot5StatsLostFrameErrors OBJECT-TYPE
        SYNTAX   Counter
        ACCESS   read-only
        STATUS   mandatory
        DESCRIPTION
                "This counter is incremented when a station
                is transmitting and its TRR timer expires.
                This condition denotes a condition where a
                transmitting station in strip mode does not
                receive the trailer of the frame before the
                TRR timer goes off."
        ::= { dot5StatsEntry 7 }

dot5StatsReceiveCongestions OBJECT-TYPE
        SYNTAX   Counter
        ACCESS   read-only
        STATUS   mandatory
        DESCRIPTION
                "This counter is incremented when a station
                recognizes a frame addressed to its specific
                address, but has no available buffer space
                indicating that the station is congested."
        ::= { dot5StatsEntry 8 }

dot5StatsFrameCopiedErrors OBJECT-TYPE
        SYNTAX   Counter
        ACCESS   read-only
        STATUS   mandatory
        DESCRIPTION
                "This counter is incremented when a station
                recognizes a frame addressed to its
                specific address and detects that the FS
                field A bits are set to 1 indicating a
                possible line hit or duplicate address."
        ::= { dot5StatsEntry 9 }

dot5StatsTokenErrors OBJECT-TYPE
        SYNTAX   Counter
        ACCESS   read-only
        STATUS   mandatory
```

DESCRIPTION
                    "This counter is incremented when a station
                    acting as the active monitor recognizes an
                    error condition that needs a token
                    transmitted."
            ::= { dot5StatsEntry 10 }

dot5StatsSoftErrors OBJECT-TYPE
            SYNTAX   Counter
            ACCESS   read-only
            STATUS   mandatory
            DESCRIPTION
                    "The number of Soft Errors the interface
                    has detected. It directly corresponds to
                    the number of Report Error MAC frames
                    that this interface has transmitted.
                    Soft Errors are those which are
                    recoverable by the MAC layer protocols."
            ::= { dot5StatsEntry 11 }

dot5StatsHardErrors OBJECT-TYPE
            SYNTAX   Counter
            ACCESS   read-only
            STATUS   mandatory
            DESCRIPTION
                    "The number of times this interface has
                    detected an immediately recoverable
                    fatal error. It denotes the number of
                    times this interface is either
                    transmitting or receiving beacon MAC
                    frames."
            ::= { dot5StatsEntry 12 }

dot5StatsSignalLoss OBJECT-TYPE
            SYNTAX   Counter
            ACCESS   read-only
            STATUS   mandatory
            DESCRIPTION
                    "The number of times this interface has
                    detected the loss of signal condition from
                    the ring."
            ::= { dot5StatsEntry 13 }

dot5StatsTransmitBeacons OBJECT-TYPE
            SYNTAX   Counter
            ACCESS   read-only
            STATUS   mandatory
            DESCRIPTION

```
                                "The number of times this interface has
                                transmitted a beacon frame."
                        ::= { dot5StatsEntry 14 }


        dot5StatsRecoverys OBJECT-TYPE
                    SYNTAX   Counter
                    ACCESS   read-only
                    STATUS   mandatory
                    DESCRIPTION
                                "The number of Claim Token MAC frames
                                received or transmitted after the interface
                                has received a Ring Purge MAC frame.  This
                                counter signifies the number of times the
                                ring has been purged and is being recovered
                                back into a normal operating state."
                        ::= { dot5StatsEntry 15 }


        dot5StatsLobeWires OBJECT-TYPE
                    SYNTAX   Counter
                    ACCESS   read-only
                    STATUS   mandatory
                    DESCRIPTION
                                "The number of times the interface has
                                detected an open or short circuit in the
                                lobe data path.  The adapter will be closed
                                and dot5RingState will signify this
                                condition."
                        ::= { dot5StatsEntry 16 }


        dot5StatsRemoves OBJECT-TYPE
                    SYNTAX   Counter
                    ACCESS   read-only
                    STATUS   mandatory
                    DESCRIPTION
                                "The number of times the interface has
                                received a Remove Ring Station MAC frame
                                request.  When this frame is received
                                the interface will enter the close state
                                and dot5RingState will signify this
                                condition."
                        ::= { dot5StatsEntry 17 }


        dot5StatsSingles OBJECT-TYPE
                    SYNTAX   Counter
                    ACCESS   read-only
                    STATUS   mandatory
```

```
          DESCRIPTION
                    "The number of times the interface has
                    sensed that it is the only station on the
                    ring.  This will happen if the interface
                    is the first one up on a ring, or if
                    there is a hardware problem."
          ::= { dot5StatsEntry 18 }


  dot5StatsFreqErrors OBJECT-TYPE
          SYNTAX  Counter
          ACCESS  read-only
          STATUS  optional
          DESCRIPTION
                    "The number of times the interface has
                    detected that the frequency of the
                    incoming signal differs from the expected
                    frequency by more than that specified by
                    the IEEE 802.5 standard, see chapter 7
                    in [10]."
          ::= { dot5StatsEntry 19 }
```

- The Timer Table
- This group contains the values of the timers defined in [10] for 802.5 interfaces. It is optional that systems having 802.5 interfaces implement this group.

```
      dot5TimerTable  OBJECT-TYPE
              SYNTAX  SEQUENCE OF Dot5TimerEntry
              ACCESS  not-accessible
              STATUS  mandatory
              DESCRIPTION
                        "This table contains Token Ring interface
                        timer values, one entry per 802.5
                        interface."
              ::= { dot5 5 }


  dot5TimerEntry  OBJECT-TYPE
          SYNTAX  Dot5TimerEntry
          ACCESS  not-accessible
          STATUS  mandatory
          DESCRIPTION
                    "A list of Token Ring timer values for an
                    802.5 interface."
          INDEX   { dot5TimerIfIndex }
          ::= { dot5TimerTable 1 }
```

E

```
Dot5TimerEntry
    ::= SEQUENCE {
            dot5TimerIfIndex
                INTEGER,
            dot5TimerReturnRepeat
                INTEGER,
            dot5TimerHolding
                INTEGER,
            dot5TimerQueuePDU
                INTEGER,
            dot5TimerValidTransmit
                INTEGER,
            dot5TimerNoToken
                INTEGER,
            dot5TimerActiveMon
                INTEGER,
            dot5TimerStandbyMon
                INTEGER,
            dot5TimerErrorReport
                INTEGER,
            dot5TimerBeaconTransmit
                INTEGER,
            dot5TimerBeaconReceive
                INTEGER
        }

dot5TimerIfIndex  OBJECT-TYPE
            SYNTAX   INTEGER
            ACCESS   read-only
            STATUS   mandatory
            DESCRIPTION
                "The value of this object identifies the
                802.5 interface for which this entry
                contains timer values.  The value of
                this object for a particular interface
                has the same value as the ifIndex
                object, defined in [4,6], for the same
                interface."
            ::= { dot5TimerEntry 1 }

dot5TimerReturnRepeat  OBJECT-TYPE
            SYNTAX   INTEGER
            ACCESS   read-only
            STATUS   mandatory
            DESCRIPTION
```

> "The time-out value used to ensure the
> interface will return to Repeat State, in
> units of 100 micro-seconds. The value
> should be greater than the maximum ring
> latency.
>> Implementors are encouraged to provide
> read-write access to this object if that is
> possible/useful in their system, but giving
> due consideration to the dangers of
> write-able timers."
    ::= { dot5TimerEntry 2 }

dot5TimerHolding OBJECT-TYPE
        SYNTAX INTEGER
        ACCESS read-only
        STATUS mandatory
        DESCRIPTION
> "Maximum period of time a station is
> permitted to transmit frames after capturing
> a token, in units of 100 micro-seconds.
>> Implementors are encouraged to provide
> read-write access to this object if that is
> possible/useful in their system, but giving
> due consideration to the dangers of
> write-able timers."
    ::= { dot5TimerEntry 3 }

dot5TimerQueuePDU OBJECT-TYPE
        SYNTAX INTEGER
        ACCESS read-only
        STATUS mandatory
        DESCRIPTION
> "The time-out value for enqueuing of an SMP
> PDU after reception of an AMP or SMP frame in
> which the A and C bits were equal to 0, in
> units of 100 micro-seconds.
>> Implementors are encouraged to provide
> read-write access to this object if that is
> possible/useful in their system, but giving
> due consideration to the dangers of
> write-able timers."
    ::= { dot5TimerEntry 4 }

dot5TimerValidTransmit OBJECT-TYPE
        SYNTAX INTEGER
        ACCESS read-only
        STATUS mandatory

DESCRIPTION
             "The time-out value used by the active
             monitor to detect the absence of valid
             transmissions, in units of 100
             micro-seconds.
                 Implementors are encouraged to provide
             read-write access to this object if that is
             possible/useful in their system, but giving
             due consideration to the dangers of
             write-able timers."
         ::= { dot5TimerEntry 5 }

dot5TimerNoToken   OBJECT-TYPE
         SYNTAX   INTEGER
         ACCESS   read-only
         STATUS   mandatory
         DESCRIPTION
             "The time-out value used to recover from
             various-related error situations [9].
             If N is the maximum number of stations on
             the ring, the value of this timer is
             normally:
             dot5TimerReturnRepeat + N*dot5TimerHolding.
                 Implementors are encouraged to provide
             read-write access to this object if that is
             possible/useful in their system, but giving
             due consideration to the dangers of write-able
             timers."
         ::= { dot5TimerEntry 6 }

dot5TimerActiveMon   OBJECT-TYPE
         SYNTAX   INTEGER
         ACCESS   read-only
         STATUS   mandatory
         DESCRIPTION
             "The time-out value used by the active
             monitor to stimulate the enqueuing of an
             AMP PDU for transmission, in units of
             100 micro-seconds.
                 Implementors are encouraged to provide
             read-write access to this object if that is
             possible/useful in their system, but giving
             due consideration to the dangers of
             write-able timers."
         ::= { dot5TimerEntry 7 }

dot5TimerStandbyMon OBJECT-TYPE
          SYNTAX   INTEGER
          ACCESS   read-only
          STATUS   mandatory
          DESCRIPTION
                    "The time-out value used by the stand-by
                    monitors to ensure that there is an active
                    monitor on the ring and to detect a
                    continuous stream of tokens, in units of
                    100 micro-seconds.
                         Implementors are encouraged to provide
                    read-write access to this object if that is
                    possible/useful in their system, but giving
                    due consideration to the dangers of write-
                    able timers."
          ::= { dot5TimerEntry 8 }

dot5TimerErrorReport OBJECT-TYPE
          SYNTAX   INTEGER
          ACCESS   read-only
          STATUS   mandatory
          DESCRIPTION
                    "The time-out value which determines how
                    often a station shall send a Report Error
                    MAC frame to report its error counters,
                    in units of 100 micro-seconds.
                         Implementors are encouraged to provide
                    read-write access to this object if that is
                    possible/useful in their system, but giving
                    due consideration to the dangers of
                    write-able timers."
          ::= { dot5TimerEntry 9 }

dot5TimerBeaconTransmit OBJECT-TYPE
          SYNTAX   INTEGER
          ACCESS   read-only
          STATUS   mandatory
          DESCRIPTION
                    "The time-out value which determines how
                    long a station shall remain in the state
                    of transmitting Beacon frames before
                    entering the Bypass state, in units of
                    100 micro-seconds.
                         Implementors are encouraged to provide
                    read-write access to this object if that is
                    possible/useful in their system, but giving

E

RFCs

```
                              due consideration to the dangers of
                              write-able timers."
                   ::= { dot5TimerEntry 10 }

          dot5TimerBeaconReceive  OBJECT-TYPE
                   SYNTAX  INTEGER
                   ACCESS  read-only
                   STATUS  mandatory
                   DESCRIPTION
                              "The time-out value which determines how
                              long a station shall receive Beacon
                              frames from its downstream neighbor
                              before entering the Bypass state, in
                              units of 100 micro-seconds.
                                 Implementors are encouraged to provide
                              read-write access to this object if that is
                              possible/useful in their system, but giving
                              due consideration to the dangers of
                              write-able timers."
                   ::= { dot5TimerEntry 11 }


          --                   802.5 Interface Tests

          dot5Tests           OBJECT IDENTIFIER ::= { dot5 3 }
```

- The extensions to the interfaces table proposed in [11] define a table object, ifExtnsTestTable, through which a network manager can instruct an agent to test an interface for various faults. A test to be performed is identified (as the value of ifExtnsTestType) via an OBJECT IDENTIFIER.

- The Full-Duplex Loop Back Test is a common test, defined in [11] as:

```
          --        testFullDuplexLoopBack
```

- Invoking this test on an 802.5 interface causes the interface to check the path from memory through the chip set's internal logic and back to memory, thus checking the proper functioning of the system's interface to the chip set.

Transmission Working Group   [Page 20]

RFC 1231   IEEE 802.5 MIB   May 1991

- The Insert Function test is defined by:

```
          testInsertFunc    OBJECT IDENTIFIER ::= { dot5Tests 1 }
```

- Invoking this test causes the station to test the insert ring logic of the hardware if the station's lobe media cable is connected to a wiring concentrator. Note that this command inserts the station into the network, and thus, could cause problems if the station is connected to an operational network.

```
                        802.5 Hardware Chip Sets
  ..

     dot5ChipSets   OBJECT IDENTIFIER ::= { dot5 4 }
```

- The extensions to the interfaces table proposed in [11] define an object, ifExtnsChipSet, with the syntax of OBJECT IDENTIFIER, to identify the hardware chip set in use by an interface. That definition specifies just one applicable object identifier:

```
  ..    unknownChipSet
```

- for use as the value of ifExtnsChipSet when the specific chip set is unknown.

- This MIB defines the following for use as values of ifExtnsChipSet:

```
     -- IBM 16/4 Mb/s
  chipSetIBM16      OBJECT IDENTIFIER ::= { dot5ChipSets 1 }


     -- TI 4Mb/s
  chipSetTItms380   OBJECT IDENTIFIER ::= { dot5ChipSets 2 }


     -- TI 16/4 Mb/s
  chipSetTItms380c16 OBJECT IDENTIFIER ::= { dot5ChipSets 3 }


  END
```

RFC 1042   IP and ARP on IEEE 802 Networks

Status of this Memo

This RFC specifies a standard method of encapsulating the Internet Protocol (IP) [1] datagrams and Address Resolution Protocol (ARP) [2] requests and replies on IEEE 802 Networks. This RFC specifies a protocol standard for the Internet community. Distribution of this memo is unlimited.

Introduction

The goal of this specification is to allow compatible and interoperable implementations for transmitting IP datagrams and ARP requests and replies. To achieve this it may be necessary in a few cases to limit the use that IP and ARP make of the capabilities of a particular IEEE 802 standard.

The IEEE 802 specifications define a family of standards for Local Area Networks (LANs) that deal with the Physical and Data Link Layers as defined by the ISO Open System Interconnection Reference Model (ISO/OSI). Several Physical Layer standards (802.3, 802.4, and 802.5) [3,4,5] and one Data Link Layer Standard (802.2) [6] have been defined. The IEEE

Physical Layer standards specify the ISO/OSI Physical Layer and the Media Access Control Sublayer of the ISO/OSI Data Link Layer. The 802.2 Data Link Layer standard specifies the Logical Link Control Sublayer of the ISO/OSI Data Link Layer.

This memo describes the use of IP and ARP on the three types of networks. At this time, it is not necessary that the use of IP and ARP be consistent across all three types of networks, only that it be consistent within each type. This may change in the future as new IEEE 802 standards are defined and the existing standards are revised allowing for interoperability at the Data Link Layer.

It is the goal of this memo to specify enough about the use of IP and ARP on each type of network to ensure that:

1. all equipment using IP or ARP on 802.3 networks will interoperate,
2. all equipment using IP or ARP on 802.4 networks will interoperate,
3. all equipment using IP or ARP on 802.5 networks will interoperate.

Of course, the goal of IP is interoperability between computers attached to different networks, when those networks are interconnected via an IP gateway [8]. The use of IEEE 802.1 compatible Transparent Bridges to allow interoperability across different networks is not fully described pending completion of that standard.

Description

IEEE 802 networks may be used as IP networks of any class (A, B, or C). These systems use two Link Service Access Point (LSAP) fields of the LLC header in much the same way the ARPANET uses the "link" field. Further, there is an extension of the LLC header called the Sub-Network Access Protocol (SNAP).

IP datagrams are sent on IEEE 802 networks encapsulated within the 802.2 LLC and SNAP data link layers, and the 802.3, 802.4, or 802.5 physical networks layers. The SNAP is used with an Organization Code indicating that the following 16 bits specify the EtherType code (as listed in Assigned Numbers [7]).

Normally, all communication is performed using 802.2 type 1 communication. Consenting systems on the same IEEE 802 network may use 802.2 type 2 communication after verifying that it is supported by both nodes. This is accomplished using the 802.2 XID mechanism. However, type 1 communication is the recommended method at this time and must be supported by all implementations. The rest of this specification assumes the use of type 1 communication.

The IEEE 802 networks may have 16-bit or 48-bit physical addresses. This specification allows the use of either size of address within a given IEEE 802 network.

Note that the 802.3 standard specifies a transmission rate of from 1 to 20 megabit/second, the 802.4 standard specifies 1, 5, and 10 megabit/second, and the 802.5 standard specifies 1 and 4 megabit/second. The typical transmission rates used are 10 megabit/second for 802.3, 10 megabit/second for 802.4, and 4 megabit/second for 802.5. However, this specification for the transmission of IP Datagrams does not depend on the transmission rate.

```
Header Format
                                                           Header

    ...--------+--------+--------+
                MAC Header      |                      802.{3/4/5} MAC
    ...--------+--------+--------+


    +--------+--------+--------+
    | DSAP=K1| SSAP=K1| Control|                        802.2 LLC
    +--------+--------+--------+


    +--------+--------+---------+--------+--------+
    |Protocol Id or Org Code =K2|     EtherType   |     802.2 SNAP
    +--------+--------+---------+--------+--------+
```

The total length of the LLC Header and the SNAP header is 8-octets, making the 802.2 protocol overhead come out on a nice boundary.

The K1 value is 170 (decimal).

The K2 value is 0 (zero).

The control value is 3 (Unnumbered Information).

The ARP Details

E

The ARP protocol has several fields that parameterize its use in any specific context [2]. These fields are:

Postel &
Reynolds

[Page 3]

RFCs

RFC 1042   IP and ARP on IEEE 802 Networks   February 1988

hrd	16 - bits	The Hardware Type Code
pro	16 - bits	The Protocol Type Code
hln	8 - bits	Octets in each hardware address
pln	8 - bits	Octets in each protocol address
op	16 - bits	Operation Code

The hardware type code assigned for the IEEE 802 networks (of all kinds) is 6 (see [7] page 16).

The protocol type code for IP is 2048 (see [7] page 14).

The hardware address length is 2 for 16-bit IEEE 802 addresses, or 6 for 48-bit IEEE 802 addresses.

The protocol address length (for IP) is 4.

The operation code is 1 for request and 2 for reply.

Broadcast Address

The broadcast Internet address (the address on that network with a host part of all binary ones) should be mapped to the broadcast IEEE 802 address (of all binary ones) (see [8] page 14).

Byte Order

As described in Appendix B of the Internet Protocol specification [1], the IP datagram is transmitted over IEEE 802 networks as a series of 8-bit bytes. This byte transmission order has been called "big-endian" [11].

Maximum Transmission Unit

The Maximum Transmission Unit (MTU) differs on the different types of IEEE 802 networks. In the following there are comments on the MTU for each type of IEEE 802 network. However, on any particular network all hosts must use the same MTU. In the following, the terms "maximum packet size" and "maximum transmission unit" are equivalent.

Frame Format and MAC Level Issues

For all hardware types

IP datagrams and ARP requests and replies are transmitted in standard 802.2 LLC Type 1 Unnumbered Information format, control code 3, with the DSAP and the SSAP fields of the 802.2 header set to 170, the assigned global SAP value for SNAP [6]. The 24-bit Organization Code in the SNAP is zero, and the remaining 16 bits are the EtherType from Assigned Numbers [7] (IP = 2048, ARP = 2054).

IEEE 802 packets may have a minimum size restriction. When necessary, the data field should be padded (with octets of zero) to meet the IEEE 802 minimum frame size requirements. This padding is not part of the IP datagram and is not included in the total length field of the IP header.

For compatibility (and common sense) the minimum packet size used with IP datagrams is 28 octets, which is 20 (minimum IP header) + 8 (LLC+SNAP header) = 28 octets (not including the MAC header).

The minimum packet size used with ARP is 24 octets, which is 20 (ARP with 2 octet hardware addresses and 4 octet protocol addresses) + 8 (LLC+SNAP header) = 24 octets (not including the MAC header).

In typical situations, the packet size used with ARP is 32 octets, which is 28 (ARP with 6 octet hardware addresses and 4 octet protocol addresses) + 8 (LLC+SNAP header) = 32 octets (not including the MAC header).

IEEE 802 packets may have a maximum size restriction. Implementations are encouraged to support full-length packets.

For compatibility purposes, the maximum packet size used with IP datagrams or ARP requests and replies must be consistent on a particular network.

Gateway implementations must be prepared to accept full-length packets and fragment them when necessary.

Host implementations should be prepared to accept full-length packets, however hosts must not send datagrams longer than 576 octets unless they have explicit knowledge that the destination is prepared to accept them. A host may communicate its size preference in TCP based applications via the TCP Maximum Segment Size option [10].

Datagrams on IEEE 802 networks may be longer than the general Internet default maximum packet size of 576 octets. Hosts connected to an IEEE 802 network should keep this in mind when sending datagrams to hosts not on the same IEEE 802 network. It may be appropriate to send smaller datagrams to avoid unnecessary fragmentation at intermediate gateways. Please see [10] for further information.

IEEE 802.2 Details

While not necessary for supporting IP and ARP, all implementations are required to support IEEE 802.2 standard Class I service. This requires supporting Unnumbered Information (UI) Commands, eXchange IDentification (XID) Commands and Responses, and TEST link (TEST) Commands and Responses.

When either an XID or a TEST command is received a response must be returned; with the Destination and Source addresses, and the DSAP and SSAP swapped.

When responding to an XID or a TEST command the sense of the poll/final bit must be preserved. That is, a command received with the poll/final bit reset must have the response returned with the poll/final bit reset and vice versa.

E

RFCs

The XID command or response has an LLC control field value of 175 (decimal) if poll is off or 191 (decimal) if poll is on. (See Appendix on Numbers.)

The TEST command or response has an LLC control field value of 227 (decimal) if poll is off or 243 (decimal) if poll is on. (See Appendix on Numbers.)

A command frame is identified with high order bit of the SSAP address reset. Response frames have high order bit of the SSAP address set to one.

XID response frames should include an 802.2 XID Information field of 129.1.0 indicating Class I (connectionless) service. (type 1).

TEST response frames should echo the information field received in the corresponding TEST command frame.

For IEEE 802.3

A particular implementation of an IEEE 802.3 Physical Layer is denoted using a three field notation. The three fields are data rate in megabit/second, medium type, and maximum segment length in hundreds of meters. One combination of 802.3 parameters is 10BASE5 which specifies a 10 megabit/second transmission rate, baseband medium, and 500 meter segments. This corresponds to the specifications of the familiar "Ethernet" network.

The MAC header contains 6 (2) octets of source address, 6 (2) octets of destination address, and 2 octets of length. The MAC trailer contains 4 octets of Frame Check Sequence (FCS), for a total of 18 (10) octets.

IEEE 802.3 networks have a minimum packet size that depends on the transmission rate. For type 10BASE5 802.3 networks the minimum packet size is 64 octets.

IEEE 802.3 networks have a maximum packet size which depends on the transmission rate. For type 10BASE5 802.3 networks the maximum packet size is 1518 octets including all octets between the destination address and the FCS inclusive.

This allows 1518 - 18 (MAC header+trailer) - 8 (LLC+SNAP header) = 1492 for the IP datagram (including the IP header). Note that 1492 is not equal to 1500 which is the MTU for Ethernet networks.

For IEEE 802.4

The MAC header contains 1 octet of frame control, 6 (2) octets of source address, and 6 (2) octets of destination address. The MAC trailer contains 4 octets of Frame Check Sequence (FCS), for a total of 17 (9) octets.

IEEE 802.4 networks have no minimum packet size.

IEEE 802.4 networks have a maximum packet size of 8191 octets including all octets between the frame control and the FCS inclusive.

This allows 8191 - 17 (MAC header+trailer) - 8 (LLC+SNAP header) = 8166 for the IP datagram (including the IP header).

For IEEE 802.5

The current standard for token rings, IEEE 802.5-1985, specifies the operation of single ring networks. However, most implementations of 802.5 have added extensions for multi-ring networks using source-routing of packets at the MAC layer. There is now a Draft Addendum to IEEE 802.5, "Enhancement for Multi-Ring Networks," which attempts to standardize these extensions. Unfortunately, the most recent draft (November 10, 1987) is still rapidly evolving. More importantly, it differs significantly from the existing implementations. Therefore, the existing implementations of 802.5 [13] are described but no attempt is made to specify any future standard.

The MAC header contains 1 octet of access control, 1 octet of frame control, 6 (2) octets of source address, 6 (2) octets of destination address, and (for multi-ring networks) 0 to 18 octets of Routing Information Field (RIF). The MAC trailer contains 4 octets of FCS, for a total of 18 (10) to 36 (28) octets. There is one additional octet of frame status after the FCS.

Multi-Ring Extension Details

The presence of a Routing Information Field is indicated by the Most Significant Bit (MSB) of the source address, called the Routing Information Indicator (RII). If the RII equals zero, a RIF is not present. If the RII equals 1, the RIF is present. Although the RII is indicated in the source address, it is not part of a station's MAC layer address. In particular, the MSB of a destination address is the individual/group address indicator, and if set will cause such frames to be interpreted as multicasts. Implementations should be careful to reset the RII to zero before passing source addresses to other protocol layers which may be confused by their presence.

The RIF consists of a two-octet Routing Control (RC) field followed by 0 to 8 two-octet Route-Designator (RD) fields. The RC for all-routes broadcast frames is formatted as follows:

```
 0                   1
 0 1 2 3 4 5 6 7 8 9 0 1 2 3 4 5
+-+-+-+-+-+-+-+-+-+-+-+-+-+-+-+-+
|  B  |   LTH   |D|  LF |   r   |
+-+-+-+-+-+-+-+-+-+-+-+-+-+-+-+-+
```

Note that each tick mark represents one bit position.

B - Broadcast Indicators: 3 bits

The Broadcast Indicators are used to indicate the routing desired for a particular frame. A frame may be routed through a single specified route, through every distinct non-repeating route in a multi-ring network, or through a single route determined by a spanning tree algorithm such that the frame appears on every ring exactly once. The values which may be used at this time are (in binary):

000 - Non-broadcast (specific route) 100 - All-routes broadcast (global broadcast) 110 - Single-route broadcast (limited broadcast)

All other values are reserved for future use.

LTH - Length: 5 bits

The Length bits are used to indicate the length of the RI field, including the RC and RD fields. Only even values between 2 and 30 inclusive are allowed.

D - Direction Bit: 1 bit

The D bit specifies the order of the RD fields. If D equals 1, the routing-designator fields are specified in reverse order.

LF - Largest Frame: 3 bits

The LF bits specify the maximum MTU supported by all bridges along a specific route. All multi-ring broadcast frames should be transmitted with a value at least as large as the supported MTU. The values used are:

LF (binary)	MAC MTU	IP MTU
000	552	508
001	1064	1020
010	2088	2044
011	4136	4092
100	8232	8188

All other values are reserved for future use.

The receiver should compare the LF received with the MTU. If the LF is greater than or equal to the MTU then no action is taken; however, if the LF is less than the MTU the frame is rejected.

There are actually three possible actions if LF < MTU. First is the one required for this specification (reject the frame). Second is to reduce the MTU for all hosts to equal the LF. And, third is to keep a separate MTU per communicating host based on the received LFs.

r - reserved: 4 bits

These bits are reserved for future use and must be set to 0 by the transmitter and ignored by the receiver.

It is not necessary for an implementation to interpret routing-designators. Their format is left unspecified. Routing-designators should be transmitted exactly as received.

IEEE 802.5 networks have no minimum packet size.

IEEE 802.5 networks have a maximum packet size based on the maximum time a node may hold the token. This time depends on many factors including the data signalling rate and the number of nodes on the ring. The determination of maximum packet size becomes even more complex when multi-ring networks with bridges are considered.

Given a token-holding time of 9 milliseconds and a 4 megabit/second ring, the maximum packet size possible is 4508 octets including all octets between the access control and the FCS inclusive.

This allows 4508 - 36 (MAC header+trailer with 18 octet RIF) - 8 (LLC+SNAP header) = 4464 for the IP datagram (including the IP header).

However, some current implementations are known to limit packets to 2046 octets (allowing 2002 octets for IP). It is recommended that all implementations support IP packets of at least 2002 octets.

By convention, source routing bridges used in multi-ring 802.5 networks will not support packets larger than 8232 octets. With a MAC header+trailer of 36 octets and the LLC+SNAP header of 8 octets, the IP datagram (including IP header) may not exceed 8188 octets. A source routing bridge linking two rings may be configured to limit the size of packets forwarded to 552 octets, with a MAC header+trailer of 36 octets and the LLC+SNAP of 8 octets, the IP datagram (including the IP header) may be limited to 508 octets. This is less than the default IP MTU of 576 octets, and may cause significant performance problems due to excessive datagram fragmentation. An implementation is not required to support an MTU of less than 576 octets, although it is suggest that the MTU be a user-configurable parameter to allow for it.

IEEE 802.5 networks support three different types of broadcasts. All-Stations broadcasts are sent with no RIF or with the Broadcast Indicators set to 0 and no Routing Designators, and are copied once by all stations on the local ring. All-Routes broadcasts are sent with the corresponding Broadcast Indicators and result in multiple copies equal to the number of distinct non-repeating routes a packet may follow to a particular ring. Single-Route broadcasts result in exactly one copy of a frame being received by all stations on the multi-ring network.

E

RFCs

The dynamic address discovery procedure is to broadcast an ARP request. To limit the number of all rings broadcasts to a minimum, it is desirable (though not required) that an ARP request first be sent as an all-stations broadcast, without a Routing Information Field (RIF). If the all-stations (local ring) broadcast is not supported or if the all-stations broadcast is unsuccessful after some reasonable time has elapsed, then send the ARP request as an all-routes or single-route broadcast with an empty RIF (no routing designators). An all-routes broadcast is preferable since it yields an amount of fault tolerance. In an environment with multiple redundant bridges, all-routes broadcast allows operation in spite of spanning-tree bridge failures. However, single-route broadcasts may be used if IP and ARP must use the same broadcast method.

When an ARP request or reply is received, all implementations are required to understand frames with no RIF (local ring) and frames with an empty RIF (also from the local ring). If the implementation supports multi-ring source routing, then a non- empty RIF is stored for future transmissions to the host originating the ARP request or reply. If source routing is not supported then all packets with non-empty RIFs should be gracefully ignored. This policy will allow all implementations in a single ring environment, to interoperate, whether or not they support the multi-ring extensions.

It is possible that when sending an ARP request via an all-routes broadcast that multiple copies of the request will arrive at the destination as a result of the request being forwarded by several bridges. However, these "copies" will have taken different routes so the contents of the RIF will differ. An implementation of ARP in this context must determine which of these "copies" to use and to ignore the others. There are three obvious and legal strategies: (1) take the first and ignore the rest (that is, once you have an entry in the ARP cache don't change it), (2) take the last, (that is, always update the ARP cache with the latest ARP message), or (3) take the one with the shortest path, (that is, replace the ARP cache information with the latest ARP message data if it is a shorter route). Since there is no problem of incompatibility for inter-working of different implementations if different strategies are chosen, the choice is up to each implementor. The recipient of the ARP request must send an ARP reply as a point to point message using the RIF information.

The RIF information should be kept distinct from the ARP table. That is, there is, in principle, the ARP table to map from IP addresses to 802 48-bit addresses, and the RIF table to map from those to 802.5 source routes, if necessary. In practical implementations it may be convenient to store the ARP and RIF information together.

Storing the information together may speed up access to the information when it is used. On the other hand, in a generalized implementation for all types of 802 networks a significant amount of memory might be wasted in an ARP cache if space for the RIF information were always reserved.

IP broadcasts (datagrams with an IP broadcast address) must be sent as 802.5 single-route broadcasts. Unlike ARP, all-routes broadcasts are not desirable for IP. Receiving multiple copies of IP broadcasts would have undesirable effects on many protocols using IP. As with ARP, when an IP packet is received, all implementations are required to understand frames with no RIF and frames with an empty RIF.

Since current interface hardware allows only one group address, and since the functional addresses are not globally unique, IP and ARP do not use either of these features. Further, in the IBM style 802.5 networks there are only 31 functional addresses available for user definition. IP precedence should not be mapped to 802.5 priority. All IP and ARP packets should be sent at the default 802.5 priority. The default priority is 3.

After packet transmission, 802.5 provides frame not copied and address not recognized indicators. Implementations may use these indicators to provide some amount of error detection and correction. If the frame not copied bit is set but the address not recognized bit is reset, receiver congestion has occurred. It is suggested, though not required, that hosts should retransmit the offending packet a small number of times (4) or until congestion no longer occurs. If the address not recognized bit is set, an implementation has 3 options: (1) ignore the error and throw the packet away, (2) return an ICMP destination unreachable message to the source, or (3) delete the ARP entry which was used to send this packet and send a new ARP request to the destination address. The latter option is the preferred approach since it will allow graceful recovery from first hop bridge and router failures and changed hardware addresses.

Interoperation with Ethernet

It is possible to use the Ethernet link level protocol [12] on the same physical cable with the IEEE 802.3 link level protocol. A computer interfaced to a physical cable used in this way could potentially read both Ethernet and 802.3 packets from the network. If a computer does read both types of packets, it must keep track of which link protocol was used with each other computer on the network and use the proper link protocol when sending packets.

One should note that in such an environment, link level broadcast packets will not reach all the computers attached to the network, but only those using the link level protocol used for the broadcast.

Since it must be assumed that most computers will read and send using only one type of link protocol, it is recommended that if such an environment (a network with both link protocols) is necessary, an IP gateway be used as if there were two distinct networks.

Note that the MTU for the Ethernet allows a 1500 octet IP datagram, while the MTU for the 802.3 network allows only a 1492 octet IP datagram.

E

RFCs

INDEX

SYMBOLS

A